When Leaving God is a Good Choice

# When Leaving God is a Good Choice

*Re-reading the Book of Job*

WILLIAM R. LONG, M Div, Ph D, J D

Sterling Reed Books

Copyright © 2020 by William R. Long

Cover and interior design by Masha Shubin | Inkwater.com
Cover Image: Let the Day perish Wherein I Was Born by William Blake from Blakes Illustrations of the Book of Job 1823

All rights reserved. No part of this book may be reproduced or transmitted in any form or by any means whatsoever, including photocopying, recording or by any information storage and retrieval system, without written permission from the publisher and/or author.

New Revised Standard Version Bible, copyright © 1989 National Council of the Churches of Christ in the United States of America. Used by permission. All rights reserved.

Publisher: Stirling Reed Books

ISBN 978-1-7350927-1-3

1 3 5 7 9 10 8 6 4 2

# Contents

Introduction............................................. xiii
   *Three Special Features of This Book* ...................... xv
   *Important Aspects of the Basic Argument* .................. xvi

## PART I
## Summary of This Book's Argument

*Introduction* ............................................. 1
*Contents of the Book of Job* ............................... 2
*Issues in the Book of Job* ................................. 4
*Why The Book of Job is About Leaving Rather than Reaffirming*
   *Faith in God* ......................................... 6

## PART II
## Four Preliminary Essays

Chapter 1: The Book of Job, Profound.................... 13
Chapter 2: The Book of Job, Provocative................. 15
Chapter 3: The Book of Job, An Outline of Contents ...... 17
Chapter 4: The Book of Job, Gaining a Perspective........ 21

## PART III
## A Detailed Exposition of the Book of Job

Chapter 5: Job 1-2, Getting Started . . . . . . . . . . . . . . . . . . . . . 31
   *Job 1:1-5, Job and His Family* . . . . . . . . . . . . . . . . . . . . . . . . . 31
   *Job 1:6-12, The Heavenly Conversation* . . . . . . . . . . . . . . . . . 33
   *Job 1:13-22, Job Loses Property and Children* . . . . . . . . . . . . . 34
   *Job 2:1-10, Attack on Job's Health* . . . . . . . . . . . . . . . . . . . . 35
   *Job 2:11-13, A Visit from the Friends* . . . . . . . . . . . . . . . . . . 36

Chapter 6: Job 3, The Dam Bursts . . . . . . . . . . . . . . . . . . . . . . 38
   *Job 3:1-12, Job's Torrent of Emotion* . . . . . . . . . . . . . . . . . . . 39
   *Job 3:13-19, A Reverie of Escape* . . . . . . . . . . . . . . . . . . . . . 41
   *Job 3:20-23, An Insistent Question* . . . . . . . . . . . . . . . . . . . . 42
   *Job 3:24-26, Uneasy Resolution* . . . . . . . . . . . . . . . . . . . . . . 43

Chapter 7: Job 4-5, Eliphaz's First Speech . . . . . . . . . . . . . . . 44
   *Job 4:1-6, Time to Listen, Job!* . . . . . . . . . . . . . . . . . . . . . . . 45
   *Job 4:7-11, The "Rule" of Life* . . . . . . . . . . . . . . . . . . . . . . . 46
   *Job 4:12-21, A Vision in the Night* . . . . . . . . . . . . . . . . . . . . 47
   *Job 5:1-7, Life's Pain* . . . . . . . . . . . . . . . . . . . . . . . . . . . . . . 48
   *Job 5:8-16, Commit Yourself to God—That is the Answer* . . . . . . . . 49
   *Job 5:17-27, Better Days are Coming!* . . . . . . . . . . . . . . . . . . 50

Chapter 8: Job 6-7, Job's Anger . . . . . . . . . . . . . . . . . . . . . . . 52
   *Job 6:1-7, What Did You Expect from Me? Silence?* . . . . . . . . . . 52
   *Job 6:8-13, Please Crush Me, God!* . . . . . . . . . . . . . . . . . . . 54
   *Job 6:14-23, The Treachery of "So-called" Friends* . . . . . . . . . . 55
   *Job 6:24-30, Show Me How I Have Sinned in This Instance* . . . . . . 56

Chapter 9: Job 7, Continuing the Barrage . . . . . . . . . . . . . . . 58
   *Job 7:1-6, A Window into Job's Desperate Life* . . . . . . . . . . . . . 59
   *Job 7:7-10, Life Is a Vanishing Breath* . . . . . . . . . . . . . . . . . . 60
   *Job 7:11-16, Nothing to Lose!* . . . . . . . . . . . . . . . . . . . . . . . 60
   *Job 7:17-21, Turning A Famous Scripture (Ps 8) on Its Head* . . . . . 62

Chapter 10: Job 8, Bildad Chimes In . . . . . . . . . . . . . . . . . . . 63
   *Job 8:1-7, Thrusting the Knife, Gently Retreating* . . . . . . . . . . . 64
   *Job 8:8-10, Learn from the Elders* . . . . . . . . . . . . . . . . . . . . 65
   *Job 8:11-19, The Reality of Judgment* . . . . . . . . . . . . . . . . . . 66

*Job 8:20-22, Hope for the Innocent*. . . . . . . . . . . . . . . . . . . . . . . 67
Chapter 11: Job 9-10, Job's Third Speech, Focusing on
    Job 9:1-12. . . . . . . . . . . . . . . . . . . . . . . . . . . . . . . . . . . . . . . . 68
    *Job 9:1-12, The Torment of God's Greatness* . . . . . . . . . . . . . . . 69
Chapter 12: Job 9:13-24, God's Anger and Moral Confusion. 73
Chapter 13: Job 9:25-35 , Longing for an Umpire . . . . . . . . . 77
    *Job 9:25-26, The Swiftness of Job's Days*. . . . . . . . . . . . . . . . . . 78
    *Job 9:27-31, Failed Strategies* . . . . . . . . . . . . . . . . . . . . . . . . . 79
    *Job 9:32, The Problem in a Nutshell*. . . . . . . . . . . . . . . . . . . . 79
    *Job 9:33-35, Longing for an Umpire* . . . . . . . . . . . . . . . . . . . . 80
Chapter 14: Job 10:1-13, The Sadness of God's Fury at Job . . 82
    *Job 10:1-7, Direct Address to God* . . . . . . . . . . . . . . . . . . . . . 83
    *Job 10:8-13, The Incredible Beauty of Creation* . . . . . . . . . . . . . 84
Chapter 15: Job 10:14-22, Defiance and Resignation. . . . . . . 86
    *Job 10:14-17, Job as God's Target*. . . . . . . . . . . . . . . . . . . . . . 86
    *Job 10:18-22, Let Me Have Some Peace* . . . . . . . . . . . . . . . . . . 88
Chapter 16: Job 11, Zophar Replies . . . . . . . . . . . . . . . . . . . . 90
    *Job 11:1-6, Less than You Deserve* . . . . . . . . . . . . . . . . . . . . . 91
    *Job 11:7-12, God is Smarter than You, Job*. . . . . . . . . . . . . . . . 92
    *Job 11:13-20, Hope for the Future* . . . . . . . . . . . . . . . . . . . . . 93
Chapter 17: Interlude. Job 12-14 and Beginning the
    Second Cycle of Speeches . . . . . . . . . . . . . . . . . . . . . . . . . 95
Chapter 18: Job 12, Gathering the Resources. . . . . . . . . . . . . 97
    *Job 12:1-6, A Laughingstock Indeed!* . . . . . . . . . . . . . . . . . . . 97
    *Job 12:7-12, God is Responsible for Everything, Including My*
        *Misfortune*. . . . . . . . . . . . . . . . . . . . . . . . . . . . . . . . . . . . 99
    *Job 12:13-25, Correct Theology, Miserable Life* . . . . . . . . . . . . 100
Chapter 19: Job 13, Preparing His Case. . . . . . . . . . . . . . . . 102
    *Job 13:1-12, Attacking the Friends* . . . . . . . . . . . . . . . . . . . . 103
    *Job 13:13-19, I Will Speak, Come What May*. . . . . . . . . . . . . 104
    *Job 13:20-28, Rules of Engagement* . . . . . . . . . . . . . . . . . . . 106
Chapter 20: Job 14, The Music of Job's Grief, Introduction. 108
Chapter 21: Job 14, The Music of Job's Grief, Analysis . . . . 110
    *Job 14:1-6, The Pain of Mortal Life* . . . . . . . . . . . . . . . . . . . 110

| | |
|---|---|
| Job 14:7-17, Hope for a Tree | 111 |
| Job 14:18-22, But Not for Me | 113 |
| **Chapter 22: Job 15, Eliphaz II, Back on the Offensive** | **115** |
| Job 15:1-6, Your Words Convict You, Job | 116 |
| Job 15:7-16, You Are Not So Smart, Job | 117 |
| Job 15:17-35, Let Me Teach You a Thing or Two | 119 |
| **Chapter 23: Job 16-17, Job Responds** | **121** |
| Job 16:1-5, You are the Ones Speaking Windy Words! | 122 |
| Job 16:6-17, A Description of God's Savage Attack on Job | 122 |
| **Chapter 24: Job 16:18-22, Job's Appeal to a Heavenly Witness** | **126** |
| **Chapter 25: Job 17, Exhausted!** | **129** |
| "My spirit is broken, my days are extinct, the grave is ready for me," (17:1) | 131 |
| "My eyes have grown dim from grief, and all my members are like a shadow," (17:7) | 132 |
| "My days are past, my plans are broken off, the desires of my heart," (17:11) | 133 |
| **Chapter 26: Job 18, Bildad Rides Again** | **134** |
| Job 18:1-4, Skillfully Slamming Job | 134 |
| Job 18:5-21, The Fate of the Wicked—Again | 135 |
| **Chapter 27: Job 19:1-12, The Redeemer, a Preparation** | **139** |
| Job 19:1-6, Repeated Humiliation by Friends | 139 |
| Job 19:7-12, God's Reproach | 141 |
| **Chapter 28: Job 19:13-22, Job the Repulsive** | **143** |
| Job 19:13-15, Repulsive to Those Far and Near | 143 |
| Job 19:16-20, Repulsive to Low and High | 144 |
| Job 19:21-22, Have Pity on Me, a Repulsive Person | 146 |
| **Chapter 29: Job 19:23-29, The Appeal to a Redeemer** | **147** |
| **Chapter 30: Job 20, Zophar Once More** | **152** |
| Job 20:1-11, The Fate of the Wicked, Part I | 153 |
| Job 20:12-18, The Poisonous Bite of Asps and Cobras | 155 |
| Job 20:19-29, The Fate of the Wicked, Part II | 156 |

Chapter 31: Job 21-27, Introduction to the Third Cycle of
  Speeches.................................................. 158
Chapter 32: Job 21, No Judgment on the Wicked ........ 160
  Job 21:1-16, Mock on, Friends! ........................ 160
  Job 21:17-26, The Wicked Suffer No Loss, Part I............. 163
  Job 21:27-34, The Wicked Suffer No Loss, Part II............ 164
Chapter 33: Job 22, Eliphaz's Allegations Against Job..... 166
  Job 22:1-11, Introduction and Job's Moral Lapses............. 167
  Job 22:12-20, God is Truly in Charge.................... 169
  Job 22:21-30, One Last Chance to Repent ............... 170
Chapter 34: Job 23, Job Is Back on the Offensive ........ 172
  Job 23:1-7, Laying Out the Case Before God............... 173
  Job 23:8-12, I am Innocent... But ...................... 174
  Job 23:13-17, ... Terrified ............................. 175
Chapter 35: Job 24, Continuing Job's Complaint......... 177
  Job 24:1, A Helpful Transition—On Holding Court........... 178
  Job 24:2-4, The Conduct of the Wicked.................. 178
  Job 24:5-12, The Life of the Poor and Vulnerable............. 179
  Job 24:13-17, Doing the Deeds in Darkness .............. 180
  Job 24:18-25, Judgment on the Wicked ................. 181
Chapter 36: Job 25, Bildad's Last Words ............... 183
Chapter 37: Job 26, Job's Third Speech in the Third Cycle . 186
  Job 26:1-4, Mocking the Friends ....................... 187
  Job 26:5-14, God's Unsearchable Majesty................. 188
Chapter 38: Job 27, Job and Zophar Talking Over Each
  Other ................................................. 191
  Job 27:1-6, Swearing on His Innocence .................. 193
  Job 27:7-12, Vengeance on the Friends................... 194
  Job 27:13-23, The Fate of the Wicked ................... 195
Chapter 39: Job 28, Searching for Wisdom ............. 197
  Job 28:1-11, The Diligent Search for Precious Metals .......... 198
  Job 28:12-19 But Where is Wisdom?..................... 200
  Job 28:20-28, God is the Source of Wisdom .............. 201
Chapter 40: Job 29, Job's Peroration ................... 203

    *Job 29:1-20, Longing for the Days of Old* . . . . . . . . . . . . . . . . . . 204
    *Job 29:21-25, The Reaction of Those Helped by Job* . . . . . . . . . . . 207
**Chapter 41: Job 30, Dramatic Reversal** . . . . . . . . . . . . . . . 209
    *Job 30:1-8, But Now They Make Fun of Me* . . . . . . . . . . . . . . . . . . 210
    *Job 30:9-15, The Mocking Never Ends* . . . . . . . . . . . . . . . . . . . 211
    *Job 30:16-23, Job's Physical and Psychic Pain* . . . . . . . . . . . . . . . 212
    *Job 30:24-31, Utter Desolation* . . . . . . . . . . . . . . . . . . . . . . . 213
**Chapter 42: Job 31, Job's Serial Denials** . . . . . . . . . . . . . . . . 215
    *Job 31:1-4, No Escape from God's Searching Eyes* . . . . . . . . . . . . 217
    *Job 31:5-34, A Series of Denials and an Oath* . . . . . . . . . . . . . 217
    *Job 31:35-37, Signing the Complaint* . . . . . . . . . . . . . . . . . . 220
    *Job 31:38-40, One Last Denial* . . . . . . . . . . . . . . . . . . . . . . 220
**Chapter 43: An Interlude at the End of Job's Words** . . . . . . 222
**Chapter 44: Job 32-37, Elihu's Speeches, An Introduction** . . 226
**Chapter 45: Job 32, Elihu Winds Up** . . . . . . . . . . . . . . . . . . 228
    *Job 32:1-5, Introducing Elihu* . . . . . . . . . . . . . . . . . . . . . . . 228
    *Job 32:6-10, Caution at First, then Throwing Off Restraints* . . . . . . 230
    *Job 32:11-15, The Hopelessness of the Friends* . . . . . . . . . . . . . 231
    *Job 32:16-22, Let Me Answer* . . . . . . . . . . . . . . . . . . . . . . . 232
**Chapter 46: Thinking About Elihu** . . . . . . . . . . . . . . . . . . . 234
**Chapter 47: Job 33, Elihu Continues** . . . . . . . . . . . . . . . . . 236
    *Job 33:1-7, Elihu's Passionate Prolixity* . . . . . . . . . . . . . . . . . . 236
    *Job 33:8-11, Job's Claims, According to Elihu* . . . . . . . . . . . . . . 237
    *Job 33:12-18, God Speaks Through Dreams* . . . . . . . . . . . . . . . . 239
    *Job 33:19-28, God Speaks Through Pain* . . . . . . . . . . . . . . . . . 240
    *Job 33:29-33, Listen Up, Job, I'm Just Getting Started!* . . . . . . . . 241
**Chapter 48: The Background to Job 34** . . . . . . . . . . . . . . . 243
**Chapter 49: Job 34, Elihu's Lack of Sympathy for Job** . . . . . 246
    *Job 34:1-9, Characterization and Condemnation of Job's Words* . . . . 246
    *Job 34:10-15, God Won't Act Wickedly* . . . . . . . . . . . . . . . . . . 248
    *Job 34:16-30, It's Inconceivable that God Could Be Unjust* . . . . . . 249
    *Job 34:31-37, Job Speaks without Knowledge* . . . . . . . . . . . . . . 251
**Chapter 50: Job 35, Elihu Continues Condemning Job** . . . . 253
    *Job 35:1-8, Job's Continuing Futility* . . . . . . . . . . . . . . . . . . . 254

*Job 35:9-16, Job's Empty Words and God's Strength in the Night* . . 255
Chapter 51: Job 36:1-21, Introduction . . . . . . . . . . . . . . . . . 258
Chapter 52: Job 36:1-21, Breakthrough! . . . . . . . . . . . . . . . 260
   *Job 36:1-4, Listen up, Job!* . . . . . . . . . . . . . . . . . . . . . . . . 260
   *Job 36:5-12, God and the Kings* . . . . . . . . . . . . . . . . . . . . 261
   *Job 36:13-14, A Brief Interlude on the Godless* . . . . . . . . . . . . . 262
   *Job 36:15-21, Interpreting Job's Distress* . . . . . . . . . . . . . . . . 263
Chapter 53: Job 36:22-37:24, Elihu's Peroration . . . . . . . . . . 266
   *Job 36:22-33, The Greatness of God* . . . . . . . . . . . . . . . . . . 267
   *Job 37:1-13, My Heart Trembles at God's Greatness* . . . . . . . . . . 268
   *Job 37:14-24, Job's Ignorance* . . . . . . . . . . . . . . . . . . . . . . 270
Chapter 54: With Job at the End of Job 37 . . . . . . . . . . . . . 272
Chapter 55: Prelude to the Divine Entry . . . . . . . . . . . . . . . 276
Chapter 56: A Personal Story to Understand the Divine
   Strategy of Job 38-41 . . . . . . . . . . . . . . . . . . . . . . . . . . 279
Chapter 57: Job 38:1-38, God Enters and Is not Pleased . . . 284
   *Job 38:1-3, God Appears and Beckons Job* . . . . . . . . . . . . . . . 285
   *Job 38:4-11, The Quiz Begins* . . . . . . . . . . . . . . . . . . . . . . 287
   *Job 38:12-38, Where Have You Been When I was Working So*
      *Hard, Job?* . . . . . . . . . . . . . . . . . . . . . . . . . . . . . . . 288
Chapter 58: Job 38:39-39:30, Prelude to a Biblical
   Natural History . . . . . . . . . . . . . . . . . . . . . . . . . . . . . 291
Chapter 59: Job 38:39-39:30, A Biblical Natural History . . . 295
   *Job 38:39-39:8, The Lion, Raven, Mountain Goats and Wild Ass* . . 295
   *Job 39:9-18, The Wild Ox and Ostrich* . . . . . . . . . . . . . . . . . 297
   *Job 39:19-25, The Majestic and Courageous Ways of the War Horse* 298
   *Job 39:26-30, The Hawk and the Vulture* . . . . . . . . . . . . . . . 299
Chapter 60: Job 40:1-5, A Brief Pause . . . . . . . . . . . . . . . . . 301
   *Job 40:1-5, Questioning Job* . . . . . . . . . . . . . . . . . . . . . . . 302
Chapter 61: Job 40:6-24, Ruling the World and
   Introducing Behemoth . . . . . . . . . . . . . . . . . . . . . . . . 305
   *Job 40:6-14, God's Invitation to Job to Take Over Management of*
      *the World* . . . . . . . . . . . . . . . . . . . . . . . . . . . . . . . 305
   *Job 40:15-24, Behold, Behemoth!* . . . . . . . . . . . . . . . . . . . . 307

Chapter 62: An Approach to Job 41.................. 310
Chapter 63: Job 41 Meet Leviathan................... 313
   *Job 41:1-11, Job's Inability to Control Leviathan* ............ 314
   *Job 41:12-25, Describing Leviathan* ..................... 316
   *Job 41:26-34, Leviathan the Terrifying* ................... 317
Chapter 64: Reading Job 42, Changing My Mind on the
   Meaning of The Book of Job ..................... 320
Chapter 65: Reading Job 42:1-6, A New Understanding ... 324
Chapter 66: Job 42:7-17, Essay One .................... 329
Chapter 67: Job 42:7-17, Essay Two ................... 332
   *Job 42:7-9, Commending Job*......................... 332
Chapter 68: Job 42:7-17, Essay Three.................. 335
Chapter 69: Job 42:7-17, Essay Four................... 338
   *Job 42:10-17, Job's Restoration* ....................... 338

# Introduction

THE BOOK OF JOB IS ONE OF THE MOST PROFOUND REFLECTIONS ON pain and its connection to religious faith in world literature. The profundity of the book arises in the first instance because of the complexity of its themes. Why does a good person suffer? How can one be a friend to one who suffers? Why is God silent so long when the suffering is so devastating and heart-rending? What strategies does one use to explain the pain to oneself or to the suffering friend? Are suffering and pain the last words in life?

But the Book of Job's complexity also emerges from the difficulty of the language. The argument of the book is often hard to follow. Specific verses often don't seem to make sense or don't fit the flow of the passage where they are found. In addition, we can't hear anyone's tone of voice and, as we know, tone of voice is crucial to catch the nuances of conversation and argument. At least 10% of the Book's 1068 verses either make little sense or are subject to multiple (and contradictory) interpretations.

Despite its complexity, many people who have some acquaintance with the Book of Job have a fairly straightforward explanation of what happens in it. Job, an honorable and faithful man, is tested

*When Leaving God is a Good Choice: Re-reading the Book of Job*

by divine permission, loses nearly everything, expresses his pain and anger at his resulting situation, gradually develops an understanding of a redeemer or witness who will help him (a redeemer who is none other than God), asks for an audience with God, finally gets it and is so overwhelmed by the words, presence and vision of God that he repents and gives up his complaint. God, in response, richly rewards him with double portions of the goods he lost and with ten children to replace the ten who had perished. It is thus a fairly simple and straightforward story. This picture is often buttressed by the brief mention of Job in the New Testament Book of James (5:11) as a person whose "patience" was rewarded. The purpose of the book in your hands is to take issue with that comfortable and straightforward picture of what happens in the Book of Job.

When friends heard that I was working on the Book of Job, several of them decided they would also start to read it. Perhaps they did it more out of sympathy with me than interest in Job, but before too long they all had abandoned the project. One man gave up somewhere in Chapter 6; another person reached Chapter 24. But, truth be told, he was brought up in the Midwest and had to endure Chicago winters, so he was steeled to the task. But still, he got mired in the nearly impenetrable thicket of the Third Cycle of speeches.

People give up on the Book of Job because they assume you can read the Book of Job like you might read a play of Shakespeare or even another book from the ancient world. Yet the Book of Job is no Homeric epic or even a story like the Babylonian Creation story. The difficulty of its language discourages all but the most determined reader. Yet there it is. It is a beacon that both attracts and repels; a book which diligent students of the Bible as well as those with other cultural interests *think* they ought to read but get bogged down in the process. As a result, people either adopt a rather simplistic view of the meaning of the Book of Job, as just described, or they abandon the project altogether. Or sometimes both.

## Three Special Features of This Book

The purpose of this book is to make the Book of Job accessible to the reasonably diligent reader as well as to advance an argument about the central message of the Book of Job. I present three unique features in this book which attempt to make the flow of the Book of Job clear to you, the reader.

First, I present a several-page introductory essay in which I lay out in detail the thesis and argument of my book, derived directly from the text of Job. I stress clear exposition instead of giving multiple ways that particular verses might be read. Second, I present the flow of this book in a series of 69 rather short mini-essays. Each tries to clarify one problem, one chapter or one segment of a chapter of the Book of Job. These essays attempt to follow the flow of the argument, pausing every once and a while to survey where we have been. Once you are familiar with the contents of the Book of Job, and the difficulty in trying to figure out exactly what that content is, you have a level of freedom in understanding the Book of Job that eludes most people.

Third, though literary features of the Book of Job are important to me, my focus here is more "legal," i.e., on the flow of the argument in the book. I take seriously that Job is presenting a legal case against God (Job 13:18), and I try to hear the nuances of the arguments that Job and others make throughout the book.

As I write I do so not only as a Biblical scholar but as a person trained in law. In addition to two decades in the study and teaching of religion, specializing in Biblical studies and allied fields, I spent an almost like amount of time studying, practicing, teaching and consulting on legal matters. Though I don't try to hypothesize about what might have been the nature of the ancient Hebrew legal system, I try to be sensitive throughout to the nature of arguments being made, what constitutes a persuasive argument, and how a knowledge of legal strategy might inform our reading of both Job's and God's speeches.

As I began writing this book, it dawned on me that even this book was just scratching the surface of this classic work. Thus, I have also written a detailed commentary on each verse of the Hebrew text of the Book of Job. That commentary, more than 450,000 words (about five times the length of this book), should be available sometime in 2020 for the most intrepid readers.

## Important Aspects of the Basic Argument

It should be acknowledged at the outset that the basic argument of this book—that the Book of Job is about leaving God rather than re-affirming faith in God--reflects a somewhat new direction in Joban studies. As you will see, I base my case on several factors: 1) Job's development of the ideas of a witness in heaven (16:19) and Redeemer of his life (19:25); 2) Elihu's suggestion of a way to interpret Job's pain in Job 36; 3) God's continual silence; 4) God's brusque treatment of Job when He finally speaks in Job 38-41 and 5) A fresh reading of Job 42:6 that takes the two significant verbs in that sentence as pointing to fading away from or disengaging from God and taking comfort in the ash heap rather than the traditional "despising" of the self and "repenting" in dust and ashes. My case is laid out in miniature in the introductory summary of the book and then, in more detail, in the essays on each theme just mentioned.

I am grateful to friends who not only decided to maintain their friendship with me despite my immersion in this project and my ignoring many of their pleas to spend more time with them but who were kind enough to listen to stages of these arguments and to make suggestions about the scope and presentation of the material here. At their encouragement, I have also included the English text of the Book of Job as I comment on it. The text

*Introduction*

is from the New Revised Standard Version. When giving my own translation of several verses, I sometimes give two verbs or nouns to capture the meaning of the underlying Hebrew. When I do that I separate the words by a "/". I use this device as a way to point out that the translation enterprise is as much art as science.

Salem Oregon<br>
October 2019

# PART I

## Summary of This Book's Argument

### Introduction

THE BOOK OF JOB OPENS AND CLOSES WITH A PROSE NARRATIVE, BUT then uses the form of dialogue and poetry to present an extended reflection on the issue of human pain. Its special focus is on the relationship of pain to a belief in a good God. Pain, like death and taxes, comes to all of us. It comes to us in all kinds of forms, physical and emotional. Sometimes we know the reason for it. For example, I may feel a pain in my foot because I got up from bed in the dark and inadvertently kicked the door. I nurse the hurt, sorrowfully rubbing the toes until the pain has subsided, and then vow not to do that again. Pain over.

Yet, often our pain doesn't leave us immediately. It persists. And persists. And, it can destabilize our life. Like an unwelcome guest who will not leave, or the din of unappreciated music that will not stop, pain can become not simply a throbbing reminder of our mortality but of our vulnerability to sources we cannot control. We try to do all we can to minimize it, but somehow it continues to find us, bind us, blind us.

The Book of Job explores pain attendant on great loss. It includes the loss of all Job's goods, his ten children and his health. The pain in the Book of Job is both emotional and physical, but those two sources of pain aren't easily disentangled in the book. The resultant anguish drives him to speak, fall silent, argue with the friends, demand to speak with God, and confidently assemble his legal case against God. As mentioned, the Book of Job explores the issue of how pain affects a reflective person of religious faith. Job not only seeks the source of his own pain, but also whether there is any meaning in it or convincing explanation for it.

## Contents of the Book of Job

The long poetic dialogue of the Book of Job (Chapters 3-41) is surrounded by a prologue (Chapters 1-2) and epilogue (Chapter 42). The prologue presents the problem of the Book of Job. God is in heaven along with various angelic figures when He strikes up a conversation with one whose name means "The Adversary" (the Satan in Hebrew). God is proud of His wealthy servant Job, who is described as "blameless and upright," but the Satan is wily enough to suggest that Job's fidelity to God is not disinterested—i.e., Job's faithfulness to God may be motivated by the blessings that have come his way. The Satan suggests that a way to test this hypothesis is to strip Job of all his earthly possessions, as well as his ten children, and then cause painful sores to break out on his body. Then, all will see if Job then worships God with the same kind of faithful devotion.

God goes along with the Satan's suggestion, allowing the Satan to wreak havoc in Job's life. In a series of devastating losses over a short period of time, Job loses his property and wealth, his children, and his health. He withdraws to the ash heap to scrape himself in his misery. Three friends come to visit him, but they don't say anything for a week because of the stunning transformation that has overcome Job. Perhaps, we think ruefully, they are at their best when they don't say a word.

There follows a profound and detailed dialogue between Job and three friends (Chapters 3-31), a monologue by a younger person who has been holding his tongue while listening to the debate (Elihu; Chapters 32-37), and a monologue by God which serves as a catalyst for resolving the problem of the book (Chapters 38-41).

More specifically, the dialogue between Job and the three friends consists of three cycles of alternating speeches (First Cycle is in Chapters 3-11; Second Cycle is Chapters 12-20; Third Cycle is Chapters 21-27). Each of the three cycles begins with a speech by Job, followed by one by the first friend, Eliphaz, then a speech by Job, followed by a speech by the second friend, Bildad, then a third speech by Job, and then one by the third friend, Zophar. After the three cycles are completed, the author inserts the searching and ruminative hymn to wisdom in Job 28 before Job concludes with his eloquent peroration in Job 29-31. Most scholars argue that the Third Cycle is incomplete—perhaps indicating that communication has fully broken down between Job and the friends.

Even though the Book of Job can be outlined fairly neatly, it is far from easy to read or understand. It consists of 1068 verses, and many more than 100 of these verses are either impossible to translate or seemingly relate not at all to what has preceded or follows. Though continuous meaning can sometimes be established, we often run into difficulty in making sense of what is going on. Almost every speech, in fact, presents some insuperable difficulties to translators and interpreters.

As a result, the Book of Job is almost impossible to read as one might read a play of Shakespeare or a few books of Homer's *Odyssey*. Almost no one is able to read it from beginning to end without the mind wandering and, before long, abandoning the task. Yet, there are enough signals throughout the Book of Job that the speakers not only understand the profound issues relating to faith and pain, but present them with an eloquence and understanding that is still breathtaking.

## Issues in the Book of Job

Job experiences the painful loss of almost everything of value to him in Job 1-2. Only his wife remains, but she speaks just one verse in the Book of Job (2:9), and she plays no role in the dialogue. One of the ways to try to capture the flow of the argument is to identify certain *emotions* of the heart and *issues* of the mind that arise in each successive cycle.

Though this is somewhat oversimplified, I would argue that Job's root or anchor emotion in the First Cycle (Job 3-11) is anger, and the most profound issue or idea that arises is one that he quickly squelches as not realistic—that there might be a mediator to stand between him and God in resolving Job's problem of pain (Job 9:33-34).

Job is angry because of the sudden, dramatic, inexplicably great reversal that he has experienced. As he will later say (12:9), he believes that the "hand of the Lord" has done this. His anger will be transmuted in the Second Cycle into a lawsuit against God, but in the First Cycle he just expresses the wild emotions of rage and cynicism. For a fleeting moment he expresses the hope for a mediator who would "lay his hand on both of us" (God and Job), giving Job a chance to speak and seek an explanation of his loss (Job 9:33-34). The friends, especially Eliphaz, begin

## Summary of This Book's Argument

with some sympathetic words to Job (Job 4), but they quickly retreat to comfortable theological categories that look for reasons to blame Job for his misfortune.

Job's anchor emotion in the Second Cycle (Job 12-20) is grief. Though several verses capture this emotion, one of the most memorable is Job 17:11, "My days are past; my plans are broken off, the desires of my heart." Rather than hoping for a brighter future, as his friends encourage him to do, Job will say about God, "So you destroy the hope of mortals" (14:19). His grief is numbing, overwhelming, and sometimes appears to be immobilizing.

Yet, he also begins to explore two issues of profound importance for the rest of the book in the Second Cycle. First is the idea of bringing a legal case against God. One of the things that I bring out in this book, and especially in my much longer commentary on Job, is the way that legal argument functions in the Book of Job. Job himself puts it succinctly, "I have indeed prepared my case; I know I shall be vindicated" (13:18). Most of Job's words in the Second Cycle can be understood as serving the greater purpose of assembling an air-tight case he will present to (and against) God. The case is based on the notion that Job has done nothing remotely deserving the losses he has experienced, and that God owes Job an explanation of why God has been complicit in bringing such huge distress into Job's life.

The second issue that emerges in the Second Cycle is the focusing of Job's hope. He doesn't remain in his anger of the First Cycle or even the grief of the early Second Cycle, but he gradually begins to express a hope for a heavenly figure who will help him in his lawsuit. The figure takes on more and more specificity as the Second Cycle develops. In Job 16:19 it is a "witness in heaven." In Job 19:25 it is the Redeemer of Job's life. One important point in my argument is that Job sees these figures as apart from or different from God. I make that argument because these figures appear in contexts where Job has just finished laying out how he feels God has mistreated him. The helper he desires will stand for him in making his case against God.

The Third Cycle (Job 21-27) presents some of the most difficult passages in the entire Book of Job. Many are the readers who enter into this Cycle but have an experience like Odysseus' men with the whirlpool Charybdis (*Odyssey,* Book XII)—they never come out. Suffice it to say that the major movement or issue of this cycle is to show communication breakdown on the one hand and Job's frustration and even despair on the other. He so much wants to bring a case against God to God, and is hopeful that he will be well-regarded by God. He is frustrated, however, because he can't find God; he can't find the place to deliver his complaint (Job 23).

All four participants have figuratively thrown up their hands by the end of Job 27. Just at that point the author inserts a beautiful and searching hymn to wisdom (Job 28), a hymn that speaks of the inaccessibility but value of wisdom. It serves as an intellectual and emotional break from the buildup of tension of the first 27 chapters. Finally, in Job 29-31, Job delivers his impassioned final speech in his defense. He is innocent of wrongdoing; he has been a model citizen and judge (Job 29); he has faced the most humiliating reversals in life (Job 30); now he wants his hearing. The dramatic words in 31:35, where Job says, "Here is my signature! Let the Almighty answer me!" are a fitting close to Job's words.

## Why The Book of Job is About Leaving Rather than Reaffirming Faith in God

The heart of my argument—that the Book of Job explores leaving rather than reaffirming faith in God—is based on several affirmations, derived from what has already been presented and then from Elihu's (Job 32-37) and God's (Job 38-41) speeches and, finally, from the Epilogue (Job 42). My case is based on the following twenty-one statements:

*Summary of This Book's Argument*

1. Job early suspects that the hand of God is behind his sufferings (12:9). He expresses his desire to be fully crushed by God (6:9), but his wish isn't granted.

2. Job interprets his pain as a result or manifestation of the divine anger, an anger that really has long has motivated God's actions (9:13).

3. Job knows that he is innocent and blameless (9:20), yet still he suffers unjustly.

4. He seeks an explanation from God for his suffering, but is afraid that God, acting out of irrationality, will continue to act in the divine anger and hurt him.

5. Job would like a mediator or umpire to help, to lay his hand on both parties (Job and God), but he knows that will not happen (9:33-34).

6. Job's anger matures into a case or lawsuit he would like to bring against God. He assembles his case—his innocence, his unwarranted suffering, God's culpability—and expresses confidence that he will be vindicated (13:18).

7. God is silent. The long silence of God, which may be literarily effective, is theologically problematic in Job. God is silent from Job 3-Job 38. That God's silence is theologically problematic is best illustrated from the relationship of parents and children. If children are left unattended too long, bad things not only may but probably will happen. In the case of Job, it might lead to his 'wandering' right away from God. God cannot fully be exculpated if this happens.

8. Without God's intervention, Job also has time to think. He not only puts together his case but he also imagines heavenly figures, different from God, who will rise and speak or

witness on his behalf. These are the witness in heaven (16:19) and the Redeemer of his life (19:25).

9. Job still affirms all the "right" or "traditional" beliefs about God, even until the end of his final speech, but he finally signs his complaint (31:35) and puts it in God's court.

10. Before God intervenes, another person, a young man Elihu, speaks (Job 32-37). After seemingly blustering his way ineffectively for a few chapters, Elihu gives Job a precious nugget to help him understand his distress.

11. That nugget is in Job 36:15-17, where Elihu says that God is using Job's distress to lure or entice him into a broader place of freedom. But Job would rather fight than be free, would rather have the justice and judgment a lawsuit provides rather than the broad spaces into which God is alluring him.

12. By the time Elihu finishes his speeches, Job has three things: his case, with witnesses lined up to support him; an alternative explanation from Elihu of what is happening through his pain; and a theological system that remains intact. Yet Job is skeptical by the time Elihu finishes regarding whether God really will 'show up' or 'fess up' or give Job an explanation for the pain that he suffers. Elihu has told Job that God is gently luring him into freedom.

13. When God appears, Job's worst nightmare is repeated. Not only does God not treat Job with any dignity, but God makes it seem that Job is the impertinent one by raising the questions that he has. Rather than dealing with any of Job's questions, God points out in four eloquent chapters how small Job is and how ignorant Job is about the world.

14. Scholars have long scratched their heads to try to understand what God is doing in so responding to Job. No one argues

that God directly answers Job's questions. I advance a thesis in the book, derived from my experience as an attorney and expert witness in a multiple-homicide case, that explains God's method of operation in Job 38-41.

15. In a word, God tries to divert the attention from Job's good questions by pointing out Job's insignificance and ignorance of the cosmos and the animal worlds. God hopes that by showing Job's ignorance, the 'jury' (i.e., the reader) would forget about Job's pertinent, but ignored, questions.

16. God's two speeches in Job 38-41 are somewhat beside the point. Though they contain some beautiful and stunning poetry, their main purpose is to cow Job into submission rather than to honor his questions.

17. Job's response to God in Job 42 is, at first glance, one of submission but in fact is one of defiance. The crucial verse to understand Job's defiance is Job 42:6, and the two crucial verbs are *masas/maas* and *nacham*. The scholarly world is gradually coming to the conclusion that rather than "despising" himself, Job just "fades away." There is no object after the verb *maas/masas*, which would be necessary for Job to "despise him/myself."

18. Job's "fading away" is a dramatic moment because it shows that Job was not overcome by the divine pyrotechnics of Job 38-41. Job will "fade away" and "take his comfort" (*nacham*) on the dust and ashes. Job has turned away from faith.

19. This explanation is the only satisfactory way to understand God's response in 42:7-17. God acts like guilty parents who have mistreated a child, come to themselves and want to make amends. By stating that Job had spoken of God what was right (42:7), a statement that rings a bit hollow if we look at what Job has actually said about God throughout the book, God demonstrates the parental behavior that says, 'Take the

car AND credit card and have fun and stay out all night...but PLEASE don't leave me!'

20. But it is too late. God has left Job alone too long. Job has developed an alternative explanation for his distress, has not been honored by God, and has developed the sense of independence to learn how to find joy in distress. He doesn't need God anymore.

21. God tries to make amends by giving him a substitute family and twice his possessions. But God doesn't give the principal thing that *might* have made Job willing to reconsider his decision. God gives no "rainbow." God gives no assurance that this will never happen again. In ten years a wily antagonist may approach God again and say, 'See that Job who serves you... ?' Job will have no more to do with a God who destroys his life, gives no explanation when reasonable questions are posed, and then pulls rank rather than honoring the reasonable queries of the creature. That is why leaving faith is a reasonable and even good choice for Job.

# PART II

## Four Preliminary Essays

This book presents 69 short essays that work through the contents and argument of the Book of Job. I begin with two introductory essays to get the 'feel' of the book, then provide an outline of its contents and finally try to locate Job historically.

# 1

## The Book of Job, Profound

THE BOOK OF JOB IS ONE OF THE MOST *PROFOUND* AND *PROVOCATIVE* reflections on human loss, and the relationship of loss to religious faith, in world literature. Older literature used the word 'theodicy' to describe the book—'theodicy' is, literally, an exposition that seeks to 'justify' or 'vindicate' God from charges of divine injustice. Yet it is perhaps more timely in our day to call the Book of Job an extended reflection on human loss or pain.

Pain and the human condition are inseparable. The Book of Job takes us through the labyrinthine maze of psychic and physical distress associated with extreme pain. That this pain is experienced in the context of a faith in the God of Israel makes it even more acute because it encourages the question: How is it possible, given the attributes of the God in whom we believe, that such unremitting pain seems not only to rack my body but also be stitched to my soul? In the midst of such pain, is religious faith an absurd proposition or is it a most comforting relationship? The Book of Job will help us explore this idea.

The Book of Job's *profundity* emerges both from its language and the ideas explored in the book. The vast sweep of the poetic language of Job is evident in the opening words of Job's first lament in Job 3 and continues through the resonant soliloquy of God in Job 41. Irony, sarcasm, legal argument, rhetorical flourishes and lonely declarations of forlorn abandonment are mingled with hopeful, defiant, searching, wistful and yearning desires for meaning in the midst of deep suffering.

But the ideas are also worthy of consideration. Ancient Israel, as every culture, had a world view that was both taught and assumed. For Ancient Israel that world view included the idea that faithful living, through upright ethical conduct and timely completion of religious ritual, would bring prosperity, peace, a large family and longevity in its wake. Because the God you served was both a God of grace and judgment, you could expect some of both in your lifetime. Yet, the way to assure that grace would come, as Israel was taught, was, in the words of the prophet Micah, "to do justice, love kindness and to walk humbly with your God" (Mic 6:8). Or, in the words of the Book of Proverbs: "Trust in the Lord with all your heart, and do not rely on your own understanding. In all your ways acknowledge him, and he will make your path straight" (Prov 3:5-6). Though the Hebrew tradition never would agree with the notion that humans could manipulate or force God's grace through dutiful completion of faithful service, they believed there was a correlation between fidelity to God and success or prosperity in life.

It is a powerful philosophy, one that continues to resonate thousands of years after the Book of Job was written.

# 2.

## The Book of Job, Provocative

THE BOOK'S *PROVOCATIVENESS* EMERGES FROM HOW THE IDEA, OR world view, just mentioned is handled both in the debate between Job and his friends in Job 3-37 and Job's restoration in Job 42. But even before we get to the debate, we need to examine the opening verses of the book, where the ideas of fidelity to God and prosperity seem to be affirmed. Job is a living exemplar of the tight, and right, relationship between obedient service to God and prosperity. He has everything going for him, from the number of his flocks, to the extent of his family and even to the harmony among his ten children. He is upright and just, taking care even to sacrifice for the unwitting sins of his children. We have an exemplary man, with an exemplary family and prosperity.

Yet that idyllic world of happy living comes crashing down in a series of ever-more-devastating disasters in Job 1 and Job 2. These disasters then provide the context for exploring the connection between faithful service to God and the prosperity and joy you thought were promised.

If all the Book of Job did was to explore the tensions between this idea and the experience of a wealthy man, it would be profound and even slightly provocative, but not especially significant. What brings the Book of Job to the pinnacle of world literature are the multiple approaches to this fidelity=prosperity idea suggested in its pages, approaches that sometimes seem incompatible with each other but are all grounded in the text.

One of the tasks of this book, both in the overview exposition of contents of Job as well as the detailed exposition of the text is to tease out the various ways that the Book of Job can be said to 'solve' or at least give helpful guidance on the problem of the relationship of religious fidelity and a good or prosperous life. While many possible approaches to this question might be suggested, I will argue below that Job's choice of living a life apart from God is both a clear and good choice in his situation.

# 3.

## The Book of Job, An Outline of Contents

THE PROFUNDITY AND COMPLEXITY OF THE BOOK OF JOB IS APPARently belied at first by the relative simplicity of its structure. But then, as we examine its structure more closely, we recognize several places where decisions on the reader's part have to be made for that structure to be clear.

In one sentence, one might say that the Book of Job begins with a presentation of the problem of the book (i.e., Is there a connection between religious fidelity and a happy, prosperous life? Job 1-2), progresses to a debate occasioned by that problem (Job 3-37), continues to the resolution of the debate by the divine appearance and soliloquies (Job 38-41), and then finishes by most of the characters doing one or more acts that seem to show their satisfaction or dissatisfaction with the resolution of the problem (Job 42). More specifically:

### Job 1-2 The Overview and Presentation of the Problem

Job is portrayed as an upright person who, in the height of his prosperity and family harmony, is struck down by the triad of devastating losses of property, children and health.

### Job 3-11 First Cycle of Speeches

The next large section of Job is Job 3-31, but it must be broken down into smaller units for easier understanding. Our story moves along through a debate format, where Job and his three friends engage in alternative monologues and consider various aspects of Job's experience and the relationship of that experience to the care and goodness of God. The format is presented through Three Cycles of speeches, where Job and each of the friends alternate in speaking. Thus, Job gets three times as much face time as any one of the friends, but the number of his speeches exceeds the sum of theirs by only one or two (depending on how you count).

An early question on the outline is whether the First Cycle of speeches goes from Job 3-11 or from Job 4-14, with Job 3 being a kind of "introduction" to the three cycles of speeches that follow. My approach is to see Job's first poetic speech in Job 3 as part of the First Cycle. In fact, it makes little sense to see the friends jumping into verbal action in Chapter 4 when they are silent for seven days and nights in Chapter 2. Using legal terminology, Job "opens the door" in Chapter 3 by his impressive cry of anguish, thereby inviting the first response of his friend Eliphaz in Job 4-5. The alternations continue. Job-Eliphaz, Job-Bildad, Job-Zophar is the pattern.

### Job 12-20 Second Cycle of Speeches

The order of speakers, as in the First Cycle, is Job-Eliphaz; Job-Bildad; Job-Zophar. One of the virtues of dividing the text as I have, looking at the first cycle beginning in Job 3, is that the first two cycles are identical in length—nine chapters each. Thus, even though some of Job's ideas may be wild wild or even rash (a term that Job uses about his own words in 6:3), the debate continues in a structured fashion. No parliamentarian necessary!

### Job 21-27 Third Cycle of Speeches

The nicely-presented structure of the previous two cycles seems at first to break down here. We have an Job-Eliphaz mini-cycle, as before, in Job 21-22, but then the next mini-cycle seems incomplete. Job speaks in Chapters 23-24, but Bildad's answer in Job 25 is only six verses. It appears truncated. Then, Job seems to speak the next two chapters (Job 26-27), with Zophar's name not appearing and his apparently not giving a third speech. Perhaps the author is trying to show us by an incomplete cycle (which is how most scholars characterize this section) that the discussion actually is breaking down among the friends. The cycle is shorter by two chapters than the others perhaps because they have run out of things to say. The friends may be talking past each other by this time.

Yet, I will present things differently in what follows. I see Job 26-27 as actually providing us a Job-Zophar speech to complete the Third Cycle just like the others. What I mean is that Job 26:1-27:12 is Job's speech, but then I see the continuation and completion of that chapter (Job 27:13-23) as the speech of *both* Job *and* Zophar. It represents the actual theology of Zophar, often noted by scholars, and Job's mocking this theology, which continues the mocking tone of Job in Job 26. Thus, I see Job 27:13-23 as Job and Zophar, as it were, talking over each other. They say the same words but with different intention: one mocking and one serious. The same words, though, can be used by both. Rather than looking at the absence of Zophar's name in Job 27 as an oversight of the author or a sign that the Third Cycle is incomplete, I see it as the author's brilliant way to say that the Third Cycle *is* complete, but they are now talking over each other. No one is listening to anyone anymore.

### Job 28 The Interlude on Wisdom

Everyone needs a break at this point, including the reader! The passage is intended to give us an eloquent statement on wisdom—so near and yet so inaccessible—that seems to sum up the debate well to this point.

### Job 29-31 Job's Peroration
After declaring his innocence, rebutting some charges brought against him by the friends, and expressing his sadness at the reversals that have entered his life, Job signs his complaint (31:35).

### Job 32-37 Elihu Speaks
The four discourses of Elihu here have confused scholars. I will argue below that they are integral to the book and do not simply provide 'background music' until God appears in Job 38-41.

### Job 38-41 God Enters and Is not Pleased!
These are among the most strikingly beautiful and expansive poetic expressions of the entire book. God speaks 125 verses, more than 10% of the entire book, and his words are interrupted only by a brief conversation with Job in Chapter 40.

### Job 42 Resolving the Issue
What the resolution of the dispute actually is, and how satisfactory we ultimately think it is, will be the focus of expositions both in the detailed consideration of contents as well as individual essays. I will argue that the crucial verse, Job 42:6 actually has Job not "despising himself" but rather "fading away" from God and then "finding comfort" on the ash heap.

# 4.

## The Book of Job, Gaining a Perspective

THIS ESSAY BRIEFLY DISCUSSES SOME IMPORTANT BACKGROUND ISSUES in the study of Job. There is perhaps no other book in the Bible whose study has occasioned more comment even before one gets to the study of the text. For example, Francis Anderson's useful but short (around 300 pages) commentary on Job devotes 75 pages of his book to discussing introductory issues. David Clines, whose masterful three volumes on Job are probably the contemporary high-water mark in Job studies, takes 115 pages to do the same. I promise I won't do that. But their focus on preliminary issues highlights the fact that Job has presented enormous challenges to interpreters from the perspective of literary form, time and place of composition, the nature of the book's language and a host of other things. Like the Gadarene demoniac, from whom Jesus cast out a "Legion" of demons, so the problems preliminary to understanding the flow of Job may be said to be legion.

Let me just indicate a handful of them in passing, with the

scholarly consensus summed up briefly in each case. *First* is the literary form of the book. Before reading any piece of literature, we ought to know what we are getting into. Is it an eyewitness account of an automobile accident? A deposition? A love poem? A satire on something? An obituary notice? As for Job, we don't know. There is narrative and there are laments and comedic and tragic elements, but its precise literary type escapes easy classification.

A lot of ink has been spilled on this question over the years. Professor Carol A Newsom's 2003 book *The Book of Job: A Contest of Moral Imaginations* is particularly sensitive to the issue of genre or type of literature that Job presents. Her approach is one that has gained a lot of prominence in the last twenty-five years, that is, to try to use contemporary literary theory, mostly from European literary critics or philosophers, to provide categories to help us understand what the author of Job might be doing. In her case, she relies heavily on the Russian critic Mikhail Bakhtin (1895-1975), who cut his teeth on exploring what he called the "polyphony" of Dostoevsky's presentation of characters. David Clines finds more comfort in the deconstruction theories of the French critic Jacques Derrida. I remain somewhat awed by their facile manipulation of seemingly obscure literary and philosophical texts to describe what scholars think is happening in Job; it just seems at times, however, that they are squeezing ten oranges to get one sip of juice...

*Second*, there is the issue of possible literary parallels to the Book of Job in other ancient cultures. One of the major developments in Biblical studies in the nineteenth and twentieth centuries was the unearthing of a wealth of materials from Ancient Egypt, Palestine and Mesopotamia which illumine the context in which early biblical narratives unfolded. Many, many texts have been suggested as bearing some resemblance to the book of Job but the contemporary consensus is that there is also no other ancient text that has the ambition or scope of the Book of Job. Occasional parallels in thought between two ancient texts neither indicate literary dependence one way or the other, nor do they even suggest that the texts shared the same thought world.

*Third,* we have the issue of possible stages of composition of the Book of Job. That is, though I prefer to look at the final or complete form of the Book of Job to make sense of it, many scholars are interested in trying to isolate various smaller units of text and positing a prior independent existence for this text before it was skillfully (or not) stitched together with other texts to make up the book we have. The most obvious example of this is the difference between the prose narrative in Job 1-2; 42:7-17 and the poetic narratives elsewhere. Some scholars argue that these portions probably were written in different circumstances, circulated independently for a while but then were put together probably late in the monarchical or exilic period of Israel (seventh-sixth centuries BCE) to yield the canonical Book of Job.

Other scholars go beyond that and suggest that the speeches of Elihu (Job 32-37) perhaps were written later than the rest of the Book of Job, and that they may function as a sort of 'first commentary' on the dialogue that has preceded them (Job 3-31). Emboldened by the effort of some to find smaller and smaller units of text that might have circulated independently before being combined into a final form, some have suggested that the wisdom poem in Job 28 or the divine speeches at the end of the book (Job 38-41) were written by someone other than the one who composed the dialogue sections.

This is all very fascinating and has resulted in the award of many Ph.D. degrees, I am sure, but no theory has managed to garner more than minimal support for a short period in scholarly circles. The best that can be said is that these scholars have pointed to legitimate concerns for those who, like me, try to look at the book as a literary whole and who ask how the language, and theology, functions in the final form of the book. Usually, however, I look at these efforts as intellectually stimulating but not very enlightening.

*Fourth,* there is a long-standing debate over the date and place of composition of the Book of Job. It is helpful to know these things, when available, so that we can talk about how concepts develop, or stay the same, over time. It is also helpful to know whether the book is dependent on an earlier source or initiates a fruitful debate in its wake. But we draw a blank on this one, too. Credible suggestions for the Book of Job's composition have ranged from the time of the earliest life of the people in the land of Canaan (before about 1000 BCE) to after the Babylonian exile (early sixth century BCE). A general rule of thumb in Biblical studies is that the more conservative you are theologically, the more you tend to use the word "early" a lot. Early date for the Patriarchs. Early date for Exodus. Early date of Daniel. Early date for Book of Job. There really isn't any reason for it other than to suggest that "early" must carry with it a sense of purity or being closer to the truth. I tend to look at the Book of Job as composed during the monarchic period of Israel (tenth-early sixth century BCE) and especially in response to the confident world-view of another wisdom book—The Book of Proverbs. Yet, at one point, I hypothesize an early date for Job, though turning the argument of conservative scholars on its head.

But liberal critics are often no better than conservatives. The facile assumption that the 'exilic period' (sixth century BCE) generally conceived was the time of greatest literary creativity for ancient Israel seemingly ignores the issue that most people aren't at their creative best when undergoing a 1000-mile trek over desert wastes under oppressive conditions. No doubt, the exilic period deeply shaped the people of Israel, as did the period of monarchy or a story of Exodus, but to see it as the great creative cauldron for production and editing of significant works is a bit too convenient. In short, we don't know *when* to place the book, and not too many issues really hang on that one.

As just mentioned, in this book I argue that the Book of Job is reacting to, rather than initiating a debate in Israel. That debate was provoked by the optimistic theology of Proverbs and especially by such verses as Proverbs 3:5-6. "Trust in the Lord with all your heart, and do not rely on your own understanding. In all your ways acknowledge him and he shall make your paths straight." Job trusted in God with all his heart, leaning not on his own understanding. He acknowledged God in all that he did, and his paths became very crooked, instead of straight. The Book of Job makes most sense to me if it responds to the philosophy of Proverbs captured in the verses just quoted.

In addition, as argued here and then laid out with more precision in my lengthy commentary on Job, Job seems often to be interacting with the Psalms or other Biblical literature, most of which owes its origins to the monarchic period (roughly tenth-early sixth century BCE). We cannot be more specific than that. I don't see the Book of Job antedating the Israelite monarchy, nor emerging in the exilic period. But more than that can't be said.

*Fifth*, we don't know *where* to place either the place of composition or the place where the debate/action of Job is happening. It is natural to think that since Job is arranged with the wisdom literature (also Proverbs and Ecclesiastes) of the Bible, that it might have emerged in a "wisdom school" or "wisdom context" in ancient Israel. But even that suggestion leads to a double imaginative process—imagining these "schools" (for which we have no independent evidence) and then imagining that there might have been someone at some time in these imagined institutions that could have written such a book. You see the issue, I am sure.

We are told clearly in Job 1 that Job is a leading figure in the "Land of Uz." But the word "Uz" is only attested elsewhere in the Bible as the name of a person about whom we know nothing else or a place whose exact location isn't indicated. Scholars generally say it takes place "near Edom" (south and east of Canaan) or somewhere "east of the Jordan" or some other such vague generalities. In a word, we don't know where Uz is. I think it is an accidental happy coincidence that L Frank Baum wrote a book called the *Wizard of Oz* over a century ago that became the staple of cultural formation in America in the twentieth century. Where was the land of Oz? Somewhere over the rainbow. Where is the land of Uz? Somewhere over the literary rainbow. It is as real as Shangri La was to James Hilton or Xanadu to Kublai Khan, but to us it is a place of imagination, where mingled pain, insight and unexpected resolution takes place.

*Finally,* we need a word on the language of the Book of Job. More than one hundred of its words appear no place else in the Bible (they are called *hapax legomena*), and often are very difficult to translate. In addition, many other passages are hard to render in English. Words are hard to translate and arguments don't flow smoothly. We don't know what it means, for example, when Job attacks his friends in Job 6 and then begins a section on caravans to Tema or travelers to Sheba (Job 6:19). We don't know why, for example, Eliphaz introduces five different words for "lion" in 4:10-11, when even introducing one wouldn't make much sense. Dozens of examples like this can be cited from the Book of Job—making it an almost impossible book just to sit down and read through without considerable confusion.

Scholars study literary patterns to try to tell us something about an author. In the case of Job, some scholars, among them Mitchell Dahood and Marvin Pope of the last generation, have credibly suggested that much of his language is indebted to ancient Ugaritic—a language which flourished in northern Israel/southern Syria from the thirteenth to eleventh centuries BCE, but only came to light in the twentieth century. Yet others have just as convincingly argued that some form of ancient Arabic or its predecessor languages that flourished in the south is most helpful in understanding the complex language of Job. We don't know.

In a word, then, Job is what I call a 'literary Melchizedek.' Melchizedek, the ancient king of Salem in Canaan, was later described by the author of Hebrews as "without father and mother or genealogy but continues as a priest forever" (Heb 7:3).

I see the Book of Job in that way—it has no (literary) father or mother or genealogy that we can tell, but continues forever, ever mediating knowledge of God, and ourselves, to us.

# PART III

## A Detailed Exposition of the Book of Job

# 5.

# Job 1-2, Getting Started

The story is familiar to many, but never gets old. We might outline Job 1-2 as follows:

Job 1:1-5, Job and His Family
Job 1:6-12, The Heavenly Conversation
Job 1:13-22, Job Loses Property and Children
Job 2:1-10, Attack on Job's Health
Job 2:11-13, A Visit from the Friends

## Job 1:1-5, Job and His Family

> 1 "There was once a man in the land of Uz whose name was Job. That man was blameless and upright, one who feared God and turned away from evil. 2 There were born to him seven sons and three daughters. 3 He had seven thousand sheep, three thousand camels, five

> hundred yoke of oxen, five hundred donkeys, and very many servants; so that this man was the greatest of all the people of the east. 4 His sons used to go and hold feasts in one another's houses in turn; and they would send and invite their three sisters to eat and drink with them. 5 And when the feast days had run their course, Job would send and sanctify them, and he would rise early in the morning and offer burnt offerings according to the number of them all; for Job said, "It may be that my children have sinned, and cursed God in their hearts." This is what Job always did.

A Jewish scholar once told me that when you encounter a Jewish story that starts with everyone happy, watch out! Trouble is right around the corner. So it is with the Book of Job. On one level the Book of Job may simply be seen as the exploration of an idea, in this case the problem of unexplained and extreme pain in human life. Yet, on another level, this exploration happens through the instrumentality of people rather than abstract argument. Normally when difficult philosophical issues are explored, such as the problem of evil or the nature of the human mind, they are discussed in dry and often obscure language, as if the difficulty of the problem precludes the writer from using clear language.

But the Book of Job explores a knotty problem through the means of human experience and conversation. This literary move by the author is brilliant, as it allows both the clear presentation of an issue as well as the living reality of a continuing conversation. That 'issue,' as I call it, is the seeming absurdity of extreme, and pointless, suffering in the life of a person who has done everything to cultivate a healthy and proper relationship with God. But since the Book of Job is told in the form of the story, the task of the rest of this essay is to retell the beginnings of that story.

Job was a man from the land of Uz, a rich man, indeed a very rich man. Maybe even richer than Edward Arlington Robinson's

"Richard Cory." First mentioned as evidence of his wealth are his seven sons and three daughters. The Psalmist perfectly captures the blessings of children: "Like arrows in the hand of a warrior are the children of one's youth. Blessed is the one whose quiver is full of them" (Ps 127:4-5). Job is blessed beyond this because of the extent of his holdings: thousands of useful oxen and regal camels and other animals. Last mentioned, but certainly not least important, were many servants. The conclusion quickly follows: he was "the greatest of all the people of the East" (1:3).

Added to the prosperity is the fact that his family seemingly lived in harmony. The children frequently went to each others' houses for meals. Ever the helicopter parent, Job even offered sacrifices for the children after these parties, lest they in their celebratory spirit unwittingly offended God. Job did this continually (1:5). To mangle Gilbert & Sullivan, he was the very model of the ancient major... domo... and much more.

## Job 1:6-12, The Heavenly Conversation

> 6 "One day the heavenly beings came to present themselves before the Lord, and Satan also came among them. 7 The Lord said to Satan, "Where have you come from?" Satan answered the Lord, "From going to and fro on the earth, and from walking up and down on it." 8 The Lord said to Satan, "Have you considered my servant Job? There is no one like him on the earth, a blameless and upright man who fears God and turns away from evil." 9 Then Satan answered the Lord, "Does Job fear God for nothing? 10 Have you not put a fence around him and his house and all that he has, on every side? You have blessed the work of his hands, and his possessions have increased in the land. 11 But stretch out your hand now, and touch all that he has, and he will curse you to your face." 12 The Lord said to Satan, "Very well, all that

> he has is in your power; only do not stretch out your hand against him!" So Satan went out from the presence of the Lord.

In a scene that at first seems strange but then becomes clear, God in heaven approaches a figure called "the Satan" and points out the exemplary character of Job. The Satan says that it is no doubt easy for Job to live so faithfully when everything is going well for him. But if Job's fortunes were reversed, the Satan believed that Job would curse God to his face. God gives the Satan power to act, with some limitations, to reverse Job's fortunes. The scene appears strange at first because it suggests that God might not know the outcome of the Satan's devastation of Job's life, and it seems to be quite a cost for Job to bear for God to figure this out, but then we return to the purpose of the story. The story's purpose to present a problem, using humans as the means for presenting the problem. In legal-speak, it is an extreme hypothetical, used to make the problem crystalline.

## Job 1:13-22, Job Loses Property and Children

> 13 'One day when his sons and daughters were eating and drinking wine in the eldest brother's house, 14 a messenger came to Job and said, "The oxen were plowing and the donkeys were feeding beside them, 15 and the Sabeans fell on them and carried them off, and killed the servants with the edge of the sword; I alone have escaped to tell you." 16 While he was still speaking, another came and said, "The fire of God fell from heaven and burned up the sheep and the servants, and consumed them; I alone have escaped to tell you." 17 While he was still speaking, another came and said, "The Chaldeans formed three columns, made a raid on the camels and carried them off, and killed the servants with the edge of the sword; I alone have escaped to tell

> you." 18 While he was still speaking, another came and said, "Your sons and daughters were eating and drinking wine in their eldest brother's house, 19 and suddenly a great wind came across the desert, struck the four corners of the house, and it fell on the young people, and they are dead; I alone have escaped to tell you."
>
> Then Job arose, tore his robe, shaved his head, and fell on the ground and worshiped. 21 He said, "Naked I came from my mother's womb, and naked shall I return there; the Lord gave, and the Lord has taken away; blessed be the name of the Lord." 22 In all this Job did not sin or charge God with wrongdoing."

The Satan wastes no time in acting. In a series of devastating blows to Job's possessions, including his servants, and his children, he loses everything. It is a most tragic story. But rather than cursing God to his face, as the Satan had predicted, Job continues to bless God (1:21-22). Chalk one up for God... and for Job.

## Job 2:1-10, Attack on Job's Health

> 1 "One day the heavenly beings came to present themselves before the Lord, and Satan also came among them to present himself before the Lord. 2 The Lord said to Satan, "Where have you come from?" Satan answered the Lord, "From going to and fro on the earth, and from walking up and down on it." 3 The Lord said to Satan, "Have you considered my servant Job? There is no one like him on the earth, a blameless and upright man who fears God and turns away from evil. He still persists in his integrity, although you incited me against him, to destroy him for no reason." 4 Then Satan answered the Lord, "Skin for skin! All that people have they will give to save their lives. 5 But stretch out your hand now and

> touch his bone and his flesh, and he will curse you to your face." 6 The Lord said to Satan, "Very well, he is in your power; only spare his life." 7 So Satan went out from the presence of the Lord, and inflicted loathsome sores on Job from the sole of his foot to the crown of his head. 8 Job took a potsherd with which to scrape himself, and sat among the ashes. 9 Then his wife said to him, "Do you still persist in your integrity? Curse God, and die." 10 But he said to her, "You speak as any foolish woman would speak. Shall we receive the good at the hand of God, and not receive the bad?" In all this Job did not sin with his lips.

Not satisfied with the result thus far, the Satan asks for further permission to wreak more havoc on Job, this time attacking his body. The combination of bodily and psychic pain can turn the most optimistic, positive person into a puling mass of slavering helplessness. So, the Satan attacks Job's body, inflicting "loathsome sores" on him (2:7). To make matters worse, Job's wife, who probably doesn't get the face time in this story that she deserves, urges Job to "curse God and die" (2:9). I will explore that verse in an essay in my longer commentary.

Yet, Job remains resolute, not sinning with his lips (2:10). Though some ancient Rabbis argued to the contrary, it is most natural to assume that Job also doesn't sin with his heart. That is, he remains blameless and upright, just as he is described in 1:1.

## Job 2:11-13, A Visit from the Friends

> 11 "Now when Job's three friends heard of all these troubles that had come upon him, each of them set out from his home—Eliphaz the Temanite, Bildad the Shuhite, and Zophar the Naamathite. They met together to go and console and comfort him. 12 When they saw him from a distance, they did not recognize him,

> and they raised their voices and wept aloud; they tore their robes and threw dust in the air upon their heads. 13 They sat with him on the ground seven days and seven nights, and no one spoke a word to him, for they saw that his suffering was very great."

The prose narrative concludes with a device that allows the narrative to turn into the poetry of Job 3-41. Three friends are introduced. They have come from afar to share his grief and try to extend some comfort. Though the passage of time in the Book of Job is only obliquely hinted at, we know that it must have taken a considerable time for knowledge of Job's distress to have traveled to each of the friends and then for them to have put it all together to come for a joint visit. Our scene closes with the three of them, Eliphaz, Bildad, and Zophar, quietly sitting with Job and not saying a word "because they knew that his suffering was very great" (2:13).

After this apparently controlled expression of emotion, all hell will break loose...

# 6.

## Job 3, The Dam Bursts

JOB 3 BEGINS THE LONG POETIC SECTION OF THE BOOK OF JOB (3-41). It also begins, in my outline of the book, the First Cycle of speeches. We will now have alternating speeches between Job and three friends for the next nine chapters until the cycle is complete: Job (3) and Eliphaz (4-5), then Job (6-7) and Bildad (8), then Job (9-10) and Zophar (11). Job gets more words than any one of his three friends, and the total number of his words exceeds even the total number of their words. It's Job's party and he can cry if he wants to...

One of the issues in understanding the relationship of Job and his friends in these speeches is whether they are talking *to* each other or *past* each other. Sometimes we get the impression that the friends are responding more to Job's condition than to his words. Other times we get the impression that Job is ignoring his friends' words and focusing solely on his own pain. To put it slightly differently, do the friends really contribute to the flow of the discussion or are they just 'background music' encouraging us to focus only on Job's words? My detailed commentary will take up these issues as they arise in the text; here I just note them.

Commentators differ on how best to divide Job's speech in Job 3. I suggest the following outline:

Job 3:1-12, Job's Torrent of Emotion
Job 3:13-19, A Reverie of Escape
Job 3:20-23, An Insistent Question
Job 3:24-26, Uneasy Resolution

## Job 3:1-12, Job's Torrent of Emotion

> 1 After this Job opened his mouth and cursed the day of his birth. 2 Job said:
> 3 "Let the day perish in which I was born,
>     and the night that said,
>       'A man-child is conceived.'
> 4 Let that day be darkness!
>     May God above not seek it,
>       or light shine on it.
> 5 Let gloom and deep darkness claim it.
>     Let clouds settle upon it;
>       let the blackness of the day terrify it.
> 6 That night—let thick darkness seize it!
>     let it not rejoice among the days of the year;
>       let it not come into the number of the months.
> 7 Yes, let that night be barren;
>     let no joyful cry be heard in it.
> 8 Let those curse it who curse the Sea,
>     those who are skilled to rouse up Leviathan.
> 9 Let the stars of its dawn be dark;
>     let it hope for light, but have none;
>       may it not see the eyelids of the morning—

> 10 because it did not shut the doors of my mother's womb,
>     and hide trouble from my eyes.
> 11 "Why did I not die at birth,
>     come forth from the womb and expire?
> 12 Why were there knees to receive me,
>     or breasts for me to suck?

After noting the equanimity with which Job greeted the multiple disasters that cascaded over him in Chapter 1-2, we are taken a bit aback at the onrush of feelings bursting from Job in this section. But after some thought, we recognize how true his words are to the actual experience of suffering extreme pain.

To give a trite example first: when I learned how to shave as a teen, I realized quickly that it was very easy to cut my face. What I didn't know then was that the superficial cuts were the ones which bled right away, but the deepest gashes often took longer to bleed. It was simple to stanch the former; the latter took gobs of toilet paper and several band-aids. Job's cut here is of the deep kind. It took a while to 'bleed,' and the cut is very deep.

Or to take two other examples. When an athlete suffers an injury, however serious, there immediately is a flow of adrenaline, nature's method of rushing a sort of false treatment, to the affected area. The rush of adrenaline sometimes leaves the person thinking at first that the injury is far less severe than it actually is. Again, automobile accident survivors often tell tales of feeling fine at first but then the deep tissue injuries and other maladies, so hard to heal, set in.

We can look at Job's torrent of emotions in Chapter 3 as related to that human phenomenon. The first inclination after suffering severe injury is to say, 'I'm OK; it's not all that bad.' But then, after you realize not only that the game is over for you, and that your season and perhaps even your career is jeopardized, the physical and psychic pain combine to produce a mingled reaction of bodily and emotional distress. That is what we have in Job 3.

Job's words in this section are put in the form of a curse. Indeed he wants to call on the experts in cursing to help him out as he struggles for words to express his anguish (3:8). Rather than cursing God directly, as the Satan says he will do if pushed to the limits (1:11), Job simply curses the fact that he was ever born. Is this a subtle way of cursing God—by cursing the day of his birth? Even in his pain, Job seems to pulls himself back from the brink of cursing God.

We see immediately, even in English translation, that we are in the presence of a great poet. Verses 3-5 begin with the desolate expression of the wish never to have been born. Rather than that night bringing the joyful shout of a child's birth, Job expresses the desire that that night should have swallowed up his birth and any trace of it. The overwhelming sense of these first twelve verses is one of darkness. 'Why wasn't the veil pulled over me at birth so that darkness, rather than light, would have been my experience? Why wasn't my mother's womb stopped up so I was confined in her stomach?' There is no answer because Job really doesn't want an answer at this point. All he feels is his pain. The repeated mention of darkness emphasizes that point.

## Job 3:13-19, A Reverie of Escape

> 13 "Now I would be lying down and quiet;
>    I would be asleep; then I would be at rest
> 14 with kings and counselors of the earth
>    who rebuild ruins for themselves,
> 15 or with princes who have gold,
>    who fill their houses with silver.
> 16 Or why was I not buried like a stillborn child,
>    like an infant that never sees the light?
> 17 There the wicked cease from troubling,

> and there the weary are at rest.
> 18 There the prisoners are at ease together;
> they do not hear the voice of the taskmaster.
> 19 The small and the great are there,
> and the slaves are free from their masters.

Even in our darkest moments, we need and seek an escape. People suffering from debilitating injuries or illnesses seek out mental or physical pleasures, sometimes of the most minimal kind, to escape the unremitting pain. A friend, dying from a multitude of ailments including pulmonary fibrosis, loves to indulge in eating some food that isn't the healthiest diet. Eating, he tells me, is one of his few remaining pleasures in life. I see a similar thing happening here. In an ironic sort of way, Job imagines what life would have been like had he never lived. Instead of the torment he now feels, he envisions peace and quiet (v 13) among the company of distinguished worthies who now are dead (vv 14-19). The thing he longs for most is what he doesn't have now: peace. This imagined existence will provide him the peace he do desperately desires.

## Job 3:20-23, An Insistent Question

> 20 "Why is light given to one in misery,
> and life to the bitter in soul,
> 21 who long for death, but it does not come,
> and dig for it more than for hidden treasures;
> 22 who rejoice exceedingly,
> and are glad when they find the grave?
> 23 Why is light given to one who cannot see the way,
> whom God has fenced in?

The reverie of escape gives him strength to raise one very long question. We get the first inkling here of what will become a staple of Job's method in speaking: using his pain to explore ideas hitherto closed to him. Pain is a great teacher, and one of the things it teaches is that the categories through which you have defined your previous life are more precarious than you ever thought. So, Job begins his questioning here. He really asks only one question: 'Why do people who want to die keep living (vv 20-23)?' It *isn't* just an academic question.

## Job 3:24-26, Uneasy Resolution

> 24 "For my sighing comes like my bread,
>    and my groanings are poured out like water.
> 25 Truly the thing that I fear comes upon me,
>    and what I dread befalls me.
> 26 I am not at ease, nor am I quiet;
>    I have no rest; but trouble comes."

Job is brought out of his reverie and his question, and he returns to the painful reality of his life. He both sighs and roars (3:24). He lets slip in verse 25 the thing that almost all wealthy people spend some time worrying about—the fear of losing everything. The section closes with four brilliantly hopeless two-word phrases (in Hebrew) describing his desolation. He has no ease, quiet or rest. Trouble comes. When he says the last words, you wonder if he has raised his eyes to look at his friends, now fidgeting and ready to speak. He thinks, 'This will be trouble.' He is right.

# 7.

# Job 4-5, Eliphaz's First Speech

SOMEONE HAS REMARKED THAT JOB'S FRIENDS, WHO NOW BEGIN TO speak, were never so eloquent as when they sat wordlessly comforting him (2:11-13). But Job's torrent of emotions in Chapter 3 functions as an invitation for the friends now to weigh in on his situation. It opens the door for their comments. Eliphaz's lengthy first speech covers a lot of ground but can be fairly easily outlined as follows:

>   Job 4:1-6, Time to Listen, Job!
>   Job 4:7-11, The "Rule" of Life
>   Job 4:12-21, A Vision in the Night
>   Job 5:1-7, Life's Pain
>   Job 5:8-16, Commit Yourself to God—That Is the Answer
>   Job 5:17-27, Better Days are Coming!

## Job 4:1-6, Time to Listen, Job!

> 1 Then Eliphaz the Temanite answered:
> 2 "If one ventures a word with you, will you be offended?
>     But who can keep from speaking?
> 3 See, you have instructed many;
>     you have strengthened the weak hands.
> 4 Your words have supported those who were stumbling,
>     and you have made firm the feeble knees.
> 5 But now it has come to you, and you are impatient;
>     it touches you, and you are dismayed.
> 6 Is not your fear of God your confidence,
>     and the integrity of your ways your hope?

For all the bad press that Job's friends have received in popular and scholarly commentary, we are somewhat astonished with the open and rather conciliatory tone with which Eliphaz begins. It is as if he is a rescue worker having arrived at the scene of a terrible crash, and he begins by gingerly sifting through the rubble to see if any of the mangled bodies lying around have life in them.

Eliphaz tiptoes in. Yet his words, which are usually translated as quite gentle are, on further reflection, more confrontative than gentle. The initial question may be translated, as most render it, "If one ventures a word with you, will you become impatient?" but an equally justified translation is, "If one were to test you, would you become impatient?" Then, he continues. He tells Job that Job has all along been the strong and reliable comforter of *others*, interpreting their distress no doubt in terms of the providential care of God. But now the shoe is on the other foot. Eliphaz says that Job needs to apply the same lessons to himself as he did to others. Is this inappropriate judgmentalism on Eliphaz's part? Gentle prodding? Appealing to the best angels of Job's nature? Tough love more than 2500 years ago? Human communication is such a fragile thing. Tone of voice and gesture, which we do not have, might tell us as much as words actually spoken. In any case,

Eliphaz is of the opinion that it is time for Job to listen rather than to speak.

## Job 4:7-11, The "Rule" of Life

> 7 "Think now, who that was innocent ever perished?
>   Or where were the upright cut off?
> 8 As I have seen, those who plow iniquity
>   and sow trouble reap the same.
> 9 By the breath of God they perish,
>   and by the blast of his anger they are consumed.
> 10 The roar of the lion, the voice of the fierce lion,
>   and the teeth of the young lions are broken.
> 11 The strong lion perishes for lack of prey,
>   and the whelps of the lioness are scattered.

After this somewhat auspicious beginning Eliphaz moves to where most religiously-oriented people would move in the conversation: to the basic rule of life which has guided and kept both him and Job safe over the years. Eliphaz appeals to an unquestioned basic principle. Though Eliphaz expresses it as a question, it can be stated declaratively: 'the innocent and upright aren't cut off in this life; the wicked receive their due punishment in this life. ' The basic rule of life is that righteousness/loyalty to God is rewarded here in this life and the wicked get repaid in kind. It is a well-worn, tested and reasonable approach to life. As we think of it for a minute, we have to appreciate Eliphaz's emphasis on the fundamentals here. It is better than saying, 'Which funeral home did you use for the kids?' or 'What are you doing with the four servants who escaped from the disasters to tell you the news?' Eliphaz majors here on the majors and asserts his principle that no innocent person is cut off unjustly in this life.

## Job 4:12-21, A Vision in the Night

> 12 "Now a word came stealing to me,
>    my ear received the whisper of it.
> 13 Amid thoughts from visions of the night,
>    when deep sleep falls on mortals,
> 14 dread came upon me, and trembling,
>    which made all my bones shake.
> 15 A spirit glided past my face;
>    the hair of my flesh bristled.
> 16 It stood still,
>    but I could not discern its appearance.
> A form was before my eyes;
>    there was silence, then I heard a voice:
> 17 'Can mortals be righteous before God?
>    Can human beings be pure before their Maker?
> 18 Even in his servants he puts no trust,
>    and his angels he charges with error;
> 19 how much more those who live in houses of clay,
>    whose foundation is in the dust,
>    who are crushed like a moth.
> 20 Between morning and evening they are destroyed;
>    they perish forever without any regarding it.
> 21 Their tent-cord is plucked up within them,
>    and they die devoid of wisdom.'

While Job longs for the quiet darkness of oblivion in Chapter 3, and later will complain about his sleepless and pain-filled nights (Job 6-7), Eliphaz here speaks of his own private revelatory experience in the night. It is a very moving passage in Hebrew, replete with mysterious language and fearful imagery. Perhaps while Job was cursing the darkness, Eliphaz was reveling in it. He suggests that he received a special visit from God through a vision, a vision that revealed to him the true state of humanity. That true state can be summed up in the rhetorical question, "Can human beings be pure before their Maker?" The answer expected is, 'Of course not!' It may be true that the just are rewarded and the unjust punished, but all humans share the common fate of impurity. This point will actually lead somewhere.

## Job 5:1-7, Life's Pain

> 1 "Call now; is there anyone who will answer you?
>    To which of the holy ones will you turn?
> 2 Surely vexation kills the fool,
>    and jealousy slays the simple.
> 3 I have seen fools taking root,
>    but suddenly I cursed their dwelling.
> 4 Their children are far from safety,
>    they are crushed in the gate,
>    and there is no one to deliver them.
> 5 The hungry eat their harvest,
>    and they take it even out of the thorns;
>    and the thirsty pant after their wealth.
> 6 For misery does not come from the earth,
>    nor does trouble sprout from the ground;
> 7 but human beings are born to trouble
>    just as sparks fly upward.

Eliphaz mingles two ideas here. Though he ended Chapter 4 by speaking about the common situation of humanity (we are impure), he begins here be referring to the fate of fools alone. Fools takes root in the ground, but things change suddenly. In language that Job must feel is increasingly directed towards him, Eliphaz says that "their children are far from safety...there is no one to deliver them" (v 4). How can Job *not* hear in this a word directed at him by his apparently magnanimous friend? Perhaps recognizing that he has overstated his case, Eliphaz then retreats to speaking about common human fate (vv 5-7). Humans in general are born to trouble just as sparks fly upward.

## Job 5:8-16, Commit Yourself to God—That is the Answer

> 8 "As for me, I would seek God,
>    and to God I would commit my cause.
> 9 He does great things and unsearchable,
>    marvelous things without number.
> 10 He gives rain on the earth
>    and sends waters on the fields;
> 11 he sets on high those who are lowly,
>    and those who mourn are lifted to safety.
> 12 He frustrates the devices of the crafty,
>    so that their hands achieve no success.
> 13 He takes the wise in their own craftiness;
>    and the schemes of the wily are brought to a quick end.
> 14 They meet with darkness in the daytime,
>    and grope at noonday as in the night.
> 15 But he saves the needy from the sword of their mouth,
>    from the hand of the mighty.
> 16 So the poor have hope,
>    and injustice shuts its mouth.

However we are to tease out the issue of the extent to which Eliphaz is *attacking* rather than trying to *comfort* Job at this point, Eliphaz quickly retreats to where religious people often feel most comfortable: exhorting other people to trust in God. Eliphaz is as glib as he thinks Job might have been in dispensing advice: "As for me, I would seek God." Of course, Job has never asked his friends what they would do were they in his place, but Eliphaz helpfully jumps into the breach on that one. Eliphaz then goes on theological auto-pilot; the words of sermons long-ago prepared easily fall from his lips. God is in charge. God will frustrate the crafty. God will save the needy. It's as comforting as most sermons are.

## Job 5:17-27, Better Days are Coming!

> 17 "How happy is the one whom God reproves;
>    therefore do not despise the discipline of the Almighty.
> 18 For he wounds, but he binds up;
>    he strikes, but his hands heal.
> 19 He will deliver you from six troubles;
>    in seven no harm shall touch you.
> 20 In famine he will redeem you from death,
>    and in war from the power of the sword.
> 21 You shall be hidden from the scourge of the tongue,
>    and shall not fear destruction when it comes.
> 22 At destruction and famine you shall laugh,
>    and shall not fear the wild animals of the earth.
> 23 For you shall be in league with the stones of the field,
>    and the wild animals shall be at peace with you.
> 24 You shall know that your tent is safe,
>    you shall inspect your fold and miss nothing.
> 25 You shall know that your descendants will be many,
>    and your offspring like the grass of the earth.
> 26 You shall come to your grave in ripe old age,
>    as a shock of grain comes up to the threshing floor in its season.
> 27 See, we have searched this out; it is true.
>    Hear, and know it for yourself."

Eliphaz subtly uses a hitherto unmentioned category in his theological armamentarium to close his speech: that of divine reproof or discipline. That is, rather than simply concluding that Job must be living in sin and that his children suffered for it, he holds out the olive branch of divine discipline. Perhaps God is engaged in the skillful divine chastising process right now. Eliphaz at this point never says directly that Job has sinned; perhaps what Job is suffering, then, is an expression of divine discipline. Eliphaz gets carried away with the brilliance of his own suggestion and then waxes quite eloquent on the ways that blessedness will return for one who meekly accepts the disciplining hand of God. We tend to smile until we realize that we have probably said the same thing, slightly altered, on more than one occasion.

# 8.

## Job 6-7, Job's Anger

I will cover Job's next speech, in Job 6-7, in two essays. This one will focus on Job 6.

We may profitably divide this chapter as follows:

Job 6:1-7, What Did You Expect from Me? Silence?
Job 6:8-13, Please Crush Me, God!
Job 6:14-23, The Treachery of "So-called" Friends
Job 6:24-30, Show Me How I Have Sinned in This Instance

## Job 6:1-7, What Did You Expect from Me? Silence?

> 1 Then Job answered:
> 2 "O that my vexation were weighed,
>   and all my calamity laid in the balances!
> 3 For then it would be heavier than the sand of the sea;
>   therefore my words have been rash.

> 4 For the arrows of the Almighty are in me;
>   my spirit drinks their poison;
>   the terrors of God are arrayed against me.
> 5 Does the wild ass bray over its grass,
>   or the ox low over its fodder?
> 6 Can that which is tasteless be eaten without salt,
>   or is there any flavor in the juice of mallows?
> 7 My appetite refuses to touch them;
>   they are like food that is loathsome to me.

The one Hebrew word that captures the entire spirit of these two chapters, as well as these seven verses, is *kaas* in verse 2. Using an image from purchasing goods in the marketplace, Job wishes that his *kaas* would be weighed in the scales. *kaas* has been variously translated as "anger" or "provocation" or "vexation" or "anguish" or "grief," but it is best to render it here as "grief-induced anger." When it is translated as "provocation" in the Bible, it is also closely associated with anger. For example, God is provoked (*kaas*) by the people's behavior and so gets angry (see, e.g., Deut 4:25; 9:18). Job's new reality has unleashed a cavalcade of emotions, which will run the full gamut over the next several chapters, but his anchor emotion in this chapter and this First Cycle of speeches is anger.

If Job 3 may be read as Job's undifferentiated scream of pain, Job 6 begins his more granular examination into the emotions that constitute that generic feeling of pain. Even though many feelings are present, we can fully understand how anger can be Job's anchor emotion. Rather than dissecting that emotion immediately, however, Job now speaks in metaphors. If his anger could be weighed in the scales, it would be heavier than the sand (v 3). Though Job never admits his words were mistaken, here he does recognize that they are "rash" or "wild" (*lau*, v 3), a rare and hard-to-translate Hebrew word.

The images tumble forth from his mouth. 'What do you friends expect from me? God's poisoned arrows are in me and the venom is slowly seeping into my bloodstream' (v 4). The Scriptures rarely present complaints with such startling directness. But Job doesn't stop even here. If animals are fed properly, they don't complain or bellow (v 5). We don't know exactly what he is complaining about in verse 6, but it seems like he is contrasting his 'improper' (i.e., insipid/without flavor) food with the food needed for healthy living. The food he now consumes is "sickness" to his flesh (v 7).

## Job 6:8-13, Please Crush Me, God!

> 8 "O that I might have my request,
>   and that God would grant my desire;
> 9 that it would please God to crush me,
>   that he would let loose his hand and cut me off!
> 10 This would be my consolation;
>   I would even exult in unrelenting pain;
>   for I have not denied the words of the Holy One.
> 11 What is my strength, that I should wait?
>   And what is my end, that I should be patient?
> 12 Is my strength the strength of stones,
>   or is my flesh bronze?
> 13 In truth I have no help in me,
>   and any resource is driven from me.

Job will ask for only *one thing* in the following six verses. When the Psalmist wants *one thing*, he says *"One thing* have I asked of the Lord." What is that *one thing?* That I might "dwell in the house of the Lord all the days of my life" (Ps 27:4). When Job asks for *one thing* here it is "that it would please God to crush me" (v 9). Rarely if ever does anyone speak like that about God in the Bible. Finish me off, God! We see in these stark words the hint that some of the central categories of the Bible will continue to be re-examined as the Book of Job unfolds.

Job doesn't let up. Instead of seeking comfort in God or in the community of faith, Job will have comfort in his being crushed (v 10). Rather than praying for pain to be assuaged, Job will "exult" in his pain. Though Job is characterized elsewhere in the Bible as a patient sufferer (James 5:11), here he casts that virtue to the wind: "What is my end, that I should be patient?" (v 11). In other words, why should I even want my life to be prolonged? Job has quickly entered into dangerous psychological space.

## Job 6:14-23, The Treachery of "So-called" Friends

> 14 "Those who withhold kindness from a friend
>    forsake the fear of the Almighty.
> 15 My companions are treacherous like a torrent-bed,
>    like freshets that pass away,
> 16 that run dark with ice,
>    turbid with melting snow.
> 17 In time of heat they disappear;
>    when it is hot, they vanish from their place.
> 18 The caravans turn aside from their course;
>    they go up into the waste, and perish.
> 19 The caravans of Tema look,
>    the travelers of Sheba hope.
> 20 They are disappointed because they were confident;
>    they come there and are confounded.
> 21 Such you have now become to me;[g]
>    you see my calamity, and are afraid.
> 22 Have I said, 'Make me a gift'?
>    Or, 'From your wealth offer a bribe for me'?
> 23 Or, 'Save me from an opponent's hand'?
>    Or, 'Ransom me from the hand of oppressors'?

We hear the slightest tone of mockery in these verses. In this case, it will be Job chiding or gently mocking the friends. This will be the first of many references to that important literary device in the Book of Job. Though mockery is present here, the dominant tone of these verses is of astonishment, of disbelief, of incomprehension. Rather than directing his thoughts here to God, Job turns to the friends. "My companions are treacherous as a torrent-bed, like freshets that pass away" (v 14). When Job needed to slake his thirst from refreshing waters of comfort, all he got in his "time of heat" was the dry wadi of the desert (vv 15-17).

Caravans traveling in the hot months count on plenteous supplies of water along the way, but even they would turn aside and perish. We don't understand the full power of Job's words, but the images are those of desiccation and death, of calamity and distress. He returns to the friends in verse 21. They have become like the seasonal wadis in the desert that dry up when the "heat is on" (v 21). Job has done nothing to deserve this (vv 22-23).

## Job 6:24-30, Show Me How I Have Sinned in This Instance

> 24 "Teach me, and I will be silent;
>   make me understand how I have gone wrong.
> 25 How forceful are honest words!
>   But your reproof, what does it reprove?
> 26 Do you think that you can reprove words,
>   as if the speech of the desperate were wind?
> 27 You would even cast lots over the orphan,
>   and bargain over your friend.
> 28 "But now, be pleased to look at me;
>   for I will not lie to your face.
> 29 Turn, I pray, let no wrong be done.
>   Turn now, my vindication is at stake.
> 30 Is there any wrong on my tongue?
>   Cannot my taste discern calamity?

One can now imagine Job's penetrating glance boring into his companions' souls. In words brimming with pain and longing, Job says, "Teach me, and I will be silent; make me understand how I have gone wrong" (v 24). Already, however, he suspects that his friends won't be helpful. "You would even cast lots over the orphan, and bargain over your friend" (v 27). We need seriously to entertain the notion that Job's spat with his friends is as much his as the friends' doing.

Job wants to know how he has sinned so badly *in this instance*. He isn't questioning the basic concept of his being a sinner. But now he is facing the biggest issue of his life. His vindication and righteousness is at stake (v 29). In more modern language, we might say that his entire reputation and belief system is now hanging in the balance. "Show me where I have gone wrong!" We don't have to think about it too long to realize it is an entirely reasonable request.

# 9.

# Job 7, Continuing the Barrage

T**HE TONE OF JOB'S WORDS IN CH 6 WAS ONE OF EXTREME ANGER AND** growing desperation. Like most people in deep pain, he has conflicting emotions. He wants God to crush him. He wants the poison of the divine arrows to seep into his bloodstream. But, then again, he wants to confront his companions and ask them to show him where he has gone wrong. He suspects, however, that these companions might not be of much help. They are fair-weather streams that dry up in the heat of the summer. He is beginning to feel what many sufferers feel—an increasing sense of profound aloneness.

> Job 7:1-6, A Window into Job's Desperate Life
> Job 7:7-10, Life Is a Vanishing Breath
> Job 7:11-16, Nothing to Lose!
> Job 7:17-21, Turning A Famous Scripture (Ps 8) on Its Head

## Job 7:1-6, A Window into Job's Desperate Life

> 1 "Do not human beings have a hard service on earth,
>    and are not their days like the days of a laborer?
> 2 Like a slave who longs for the shadow,
>    and like laborers who look for their wages,
> 3 so I am allotted months of emptiness,
>    and nights of misery are apportioned to me.
> 4 When I lie down I say, 'When shall I rise?'
>    But the night is long,
>    and I am full of tossing until dawn.
> 5 My flesh is clothed with worms and dirt;
>    my skin hardens, then breaks out again.
> 6 My days are swifter than a weaver's shuttle,
>    and come to their end without hope.

We are privileged, but almost feel ashamed, to enter into Job's intimate spaces now. Like the experience of being with a person suffering from suppurating lesions or loose bowels, we feel we should turn away and give them a little dignity in the midst of their suffering. Yet we are nevertheless drawn to Job, pulled in by the unflinching boldness of his language and thought. His words in this section have such an air of verisimilitude to them: "When I lie down, I say: 'When shall I arise? But the night is long, and I am full of tossing to and fro until the dawn" (v 4). How many millions of people have experienced the same thing when anguish physical or mental has so overwhelmed their lives that they find no relief, even in exhaustion?

His conflicting feelings continue. The nights are long, seemingly interminable. Yet "My days are swifter than a weaver's shuttle" (v 6). The sad conclusion, however, is "they come to their end without hope" (v 6). Though Job may have overstated the actual irreversibility of his situation, he doesn't overstate his feelings. When deluged by troubles, the light at the end of the tunnel, in the famous words of poet Robert Lowell, is probably the light of an oncoming train.

## Job 7:7-10, Life Is a Vanishing Breath

> 7 "Remember that my life is a breath;
> my eye will never again see good.
> 8 The eye that beholds me will see me no more;
> while your eyes are upon me, I shall be gone.
> 9 As the cloud fades and vanishes,
> so those who go down to Sheol do not come up;
> 10 they return no more to their houses,
> nor do their places know them any more.

He begins this brief section with a sense of finality that belies the fact that we are only in his second speech: "Remember that my life is a breath; my eye will never again see good" (v 7). Though we have an immediate word play on the word "eye" because he says that God's "eye" will look on him no more (v 8), he is more interested in developing the idea of the evanescence of life. Life disappears like a breath of air, like a cloud that quickly vanishes. There is almost a sense of defiant satisfaction, however, in Job's utterance of these words. When he says that his life is like the cloud that vanishes (v 9), like one who no longer returns to his house (v 10), there is the slightest sense that Job is pressing God's face right into this reality. In other words, he is saying, 'So, I will disappear and never return to my house. Is that what you really want, God?' His anger is transmuting now into defiance, a feeling which will be on full display in the next section.

## Job 7:11-16, Nothing to Lose!

> 11 "Therefore I will not restrain my mouth;
> I will speak in the anguish of my spirit;
> I will complain in the bitterness of my soul.

> 12 Am I the Sea, or the Dragon,
>     that you set a guard over me?
> 13 When I say, 'My bed will comfort me,
>     my couch will ease my complaint,'
> 14 then you scare me with dreams
>     and terrify me with visions,
> 15 so that I would choose strangling
>     and death rather than this body.
> 16 I loathe my life; I would not live forever.
>     Let me alone, for my days are a breath.

In this section, Job begins to realize a most precious lesson that will never depart from him for the rest of the book—that suffering will give him a kind of authority to speak, a kind of place to stand and survey the world and tell the world what he sees without fear of consequences. After all, once you have suffered the loss of everything, what more can God or life do to you? We need to understand this in order to grasp verse 11: "Therefore I will not restrain my mouth; I will speak in the anguish of my spirit; I will complain in the bitterness of my soul." In those words of breathtaking beauty and dramatic scope, Job enters a new chapter of his suffering. He will not be the patient, quiet, or even angry sufferer. Like a parent whose child has disappeared, who will never give up the search to find what happened to the child, Job will now go on the offensive, fearlessly seeking an explanation for his terrible torment.

For the first time we have the sense that God is now, in Job's mind, becoming Job's enemy. Job is not just suffering pain, but he has now concluded that this pain is brought on him by God's direct action (and he isn't very far off the mark). With biting, biting sarcasm he asks, "Am I the sea, or the Dragon, that you set a guard over me?" (v 12). In asking this, he is referring to the stories captured in other OT passages about God's taming unruly mythological creatures at the creation of the world. God is now, for Job, Job's active enemy. God "scares me with dreams" and "terrifies me with visions." (v 14). The end result is that Job hates the very air he breathes, despises the very life he lives, loathes everything about his existence.

## Job 7:17-21, Turning A Famous Scripture (Ps 8) on Its Head

> 17 "What are human beings, that you make so much of them,
>      that you set your mind on them,
> 18 visit them every morning,
>      test them every moment?
> 19 Will you not look away from me for a while,
>      let me alone until I swallow my spittle?
> 20 If I sin, what do I do to you, you watcher of humanity?
>      Why have you made me your target?
>      Why have I become a burden to you?
> 21 Why do you not pardon my transgression
>      and take away my iniquity?
>      For now I shall lie in the earth;
>      you will seek me, but I shall not be."

Job's distress has turned everything topsy-turvy for him. Yet it has also unleashed an onrush of literary creativity rarely seen in the Scriptures. In this section, he takes one of the most beloved Psalms (Ps 8), and uses its most revered words of wonderment, "What is man that you are mindful of him, and the son of man, that you care for him?" (Ps 8:4) to say the opposite: "What are human beings, that you make so much of them?" (7:17). In other words, Job's mocking now will turn into mocking the words of Scripture. In fact, all Job wants is a little relief so he can swallow his spittle (v 19). He closes with another defiant tweak at God, "Now I shall lie in the earth; you will seek me, but I shall not be" (v 21). Nah-nah, God!

# 10.

## Job 8, Bildad Chimes In

BEFORE EXAMINING BILDAD'S RESPONSE TO JOB AND HIS UNIQUE TAKE on Job's problems we ought to pause to reiterate where the debate is at this point. Job has just pointedly attacked three potential pillars of his intellectual and spiritual support. *First*, he has attacked God. I am sure Job would say that God started it all, and he will be correct on that one when all is said and done, but from the perspective of the narrative to this point, it is Job on the offensive. He has characterized God as a morally-obtuse bloodthirsty warrior who has nothing but enmity for Job. *Second*, he has described his friends as treacherous, like fake streams in a dry land. *Finally*, he has used the Scriptures in a mocking way that reverses their meaning. Note that he has done all this in two speeches! If Bildad, as I will go on to argue, shows less than the perfect patience of Eliphaz with Job, we should not be surprised. A red-hot debate is now in full swing.

Bildad's speech may conveniently be divided into four parts:

Job 8:1-7, Thrusting the Knife, Gently Retreating
Job 8:8-10, Learn from the Elders
Job 8:11-19, The Reality of Judgment
Job 8:20-22, Hope for the Innocent

## Job 8:1-7, Thrusting the Knife, Gently Retreating

> 1 Then Bildad the Shuhite answered:
> 2 "How long will you say these things,
>     and the words of your mouth be a great wind?
> 3 Does God pervert justice?
>     Or does the Almighty pervert the right?
> 4 If your children sinned against him,
>     he delivered them into the power of their transgression.
> 5 If you will seek God
>     and make supplication to the Almighty,
> 6 if you are pure and upright,
>     surely then he will rouse himself for you
>     and restore to you your rightful place.
> 7 Though your beginning was small,
>     your latter days will be very great.

Under the guise of defending God, Bildad's first words are like a knife thrust deeply into Job's psyche. It isn't hard to see the "guise" or "mask" here. Bildad seemingly wants to talk about the justice of God and the need for humans to seek that justice-loving God. But his questions in verse 3 are merely rhetorical: of course God *doesn't* pervert justice; God *doesn't* twist what is right. Before getting there, however, he seems to utter a throwaway line: "How long will you say these things, and the words of your mouth be a great wind" (v 2)? It appears to be the typical debating trick of characterizing your opponent as a blowhard or windbag... until we realize that his description matches the narrative description of 1:19, where a great wind destroyed the house of Job's children and crushed them to death. Granted, though it is "great" wind in both places the Hebrew word for "great" is different. But the reality is the same. 'You windy blowhard, Job! Ah, just like the wind that destroyed your family!' Clever, Bildad. And somewhat cruel.

Lest we think we are overreacting, Bildad thrusts again in verse 4. He couches his statement in a conditional phrase ("If"), but he has brought up the subject again. "If your children sinned against him, he delivered them into the power of their transgression." Wow, maybe Job's characterization of the friends isn't wrong. But Bildad then beats a hasty retreat, covering his merciless attack in pious rhetoric. He, like Eliphaz, hasn't yet accused Job of sin, but it is time for Job to seek God. If Job does this, all will work out well. Job's end will be greater than his beginning (v 7). It sounds a little like Eliphaz-lite.

## Job 8:8-10, Learn from the Elders

> 8 "For inquire now of bygone generations,
>     and consider what their ancestors have found;
> 9 for we are but of yesterday, and we know nothing,
>     for our days on earth are but a shadow.
> 10 Will they not teach you and tell you
>     and utter words out of their understanding?

Whereas Eliphaz appealed for authority to a dark dream in the night, where a gossamer spirit appeared to him and mentioned a very pedestrian thing (that people are sinners—4:17), Bildad now appeals to tradition. After all, these three friends and Job himself are deeply devoted to what one might call the international (and Israelite) tradition of wise sayings, prudent living, and honoring a God who stands behind it all. We live only a short time and know nothing (v 9) but the tradition of wisdom has existed for time out of mind. Let's listen to its teaching.

## Job 8:11-19, The Reality of Judgment

> 11 "Can papyrus grow where there is no marsh?
>     Can reeds flourish where there is no water?
> 12 While yet in flower and not cut down,
>     they wither before any other plant.
> 13 Such are the paths of all who forget God;
>     the hope of the godless shall perish.
> 14 Their confidence is gossamer,
>     a spider's house their trust.
> 15 If one leans against its house, it will not stand;
>     if one lays hold of it, it will not endure.
> 16 The wicked thrive before the sun,
>     and their shoots spread over the garden.
> 17 Their roots twine around the stoneheap;
>     they live among the rocks.
> 18 If they are destroyed from their place,
>     then it will deny them, saying, 'I have never seen you.'
> 19 See, these are their happy ways,
>     and out of the earth still others will spring.

Not waiting for Job to concur, Bildad plunges into what he considers the heart of that tradition. Here we see the impressive eloquence of Bildad, even though the difficulty of the language and appearance of rare words makes several verses unclear. His major point is the precariousness of life for those who forget God. Though they might appear to flourish as a green plant, they become like a papyrus plant removed from the water. Such a plant simply dies. Even though the plant isn't cut down, it withers and shrivels. That is the way it is with those who forget God. They eventually perish. Thought their house might appear to be firm (v 15) and though they seem to thrive under the sun (v 16), they will be destroyed, and either God or the place of their dwelling itself will say, "I have never seen you" (v 18). We get Bildad's drift. Perhaps he is deliberately trying to be obscure, even while his major point is clear: those who forget God (I wonder if he has anyone in mind?) become desiccated and dry up. Simple as that.

## Job 8:20-22, Hope for the Innocent

> 20 "See, God will not reject a blameless person,
>     nor take the hand of evildoers.
> 21 He will yet fill your mouth with laughter,
>     and your lips with shouts of joy.
> 22 Those who hate you will be clothed with shame,
>     and the tent of the wicked will be no more."

Like Eliphaz, Bildad will end his speech on an upbeat note. In words that seemingly bear little relationship to the devastating reality that Job now faces, Bildad speaks confidently about God's not rejecting a blameless person (v 20). But wait a second. At the beginning of the chapter, Bildad used language reminiscent of Job 1 to remind Job of his searing loss, but here he skillfully uses another word from Job 1-2 to give Job hope. God will not cast away the innocent (*tam,* v 20). Job is so characterized, not once, but *three* times, in Job 1-2 (1:1, 8; 2:3). Bildad's expression of hope, then, seems rooted in reality. But then, verse 21 comes. You wonder how someone could utter the following line with a straight face: "He will yet fill your mouth with laughter, and your lips with shouts of joy" (v 21), but this is not different in kind from the easy-to-procure advice in our own day about how to reverse our current fortunes. Those that hate Job will be clothed in shame (v 22). Hmm. You wonder if Bildad is unwittingly uttering a curse against himself...

# 11.

## Job 9-10, Job's Third Speech, Focusing on Job 9:1-12

THE KEY TO THE BRILLIANT LITERARY METHOD OF OUR AUTHOR IS both to reiterate some ideas and skillfully introduce new ones that keep the debate moving with a blazing intensity. In this two-chapter speech Job reiterates aspects of his sorry life, using new words, but then takes two dramatic leaps in his ideas that actually enable the book to spring into new territory. In the first new leap, he will temporarily shift the focus away from his pain and onto what he might call the reckless power and moral confusion of God. Second, he introduces, haltingly here, an idea that will absolutely dominate the middle part of the book—the call for a helper, umpire, Redeemer or some undefined character who will either go to bat for Job (as a witness or Redeemer) or do something else to protect him from this reckless power of God. Everything starts innocently enough… An outline for the entire chapter would be:

*Job 9-10, Job's Third Speech, Focusing on Job 9:1-12*

Job 9:1-12, The Torment of God's Greatness
Job 9:13-24, God's Anger and Moral Confusion
Job 9:25-35, Longing for an Umpire (Covered in the Next Essay)

# Job 9:1-12, The Torment of God's Greatness

> 1 Then Job answered:
> 2 "Indeed I know that this is so;
>   but how can a mortal be just before God?
> 3 If one wished to contend with him,
>   one could not answer him once in a thousand.
> 4 He is wise in heart, and mighty in strength
>   —who has resisted him, and succeeded?—
> 5 he who removes mountains, and they do not know it,
>   when he overturns them in his anger;
> 6 who shakes the earth out of its place,
>   and its pillars tremble;
> 7 who commands the sun, and it does not rise;
>   who seals up the stars;
> 8 who alone stretched out the heavens
>   and trampled the waves of the Sea;
> 9 who made the Bear and Orion,
>   the Pleiades and the chambers of the south;
> 10 who does great things beyond understanding,
>   and marvelous things without number.
> 11 Look, he passes by me, and I do not see him;
>   he moves on, but I do not perceive him.
> 12 He snatches away; who can stop him?
>   Who will say to him, 'What are you doing?'

Job begins by actually responding to Bildad. But that response is brief indeed. "Surely I know this is true" (v 2). It is the kind of dismissive, "Sure, guy," before going to where Job wants the debate to go. He asks a question that his three friends *think* they either have already answered or are quite able to answer: "How can a mortal be righteous/justified/just with God"? (v 2). Rather than letting them open their mouths, Job will now skillfully take that question in another direction. The problem, he says, is not with *him*; it is with *God*. *God* is the biggest obstacle to a mortal's (in this case Job's) being just before God. How can that be?

The basic problem, as Job identifies it in this section, is a disproportion in power between God and Job. In theory that ought not to make a difference or be a huge point: everyone knows that God has more power than a human. But Job will put a twist on the idea of divine power. He cautiously advances his new idea in verse 3 and then more fully develop it in verses 12-24. The problem will not be the *fact* of God's power but the way God *uses* the divine power. "If one wished to contend with him, one could not answer him once in a thousand" (v 3). The meaning is that God is not only powerful in the absolute sense, but God has the ability in debate to twist an opponent into a pretzel so as to cause the human to make foolish statements. It is all because of the dazzling power of God.

Job doesn't further develop this idea here. Rather, his thought goes in the following direction: There is a disproportion in power between God and humans. Normally that is a good thing, since God has control over much bigger questions and problems than do humans. And this power is sometimes vouchsafed to humans, in the form of visions, dreams or other modes of divine appearance that can sometimes disorient people. Yet it is an enriching disorientation. But Job feels that this amazing power of God is now being unleashed *against* him. Now the disorientation that will set in makes Job unable to hold onto anything firm anymore. His head will spin. God will, in Job's words, make him convict himself. It is a fearful thing to imagine that the God of the universe has set you up as the divine target and has deliberately disoriented your life. But that is how Job feels, and that is behind his words as this chapter opens.

Job's words in 9:3 presage, in an unexpectedly powerful way, what will happen in the divine speeches in Job 38-41. In other words, Job's fear expressed in 9:3 is that "one can't answer him once in a thousand," i.e., God will so overpower Job *with words* that he can't respond *at all*. To make matters utterly chilling, that is exactly what happens in Job 38-41. God comes in and speaks 1000 words in those 120 verses. And Job doesn't say a word—other than, 'I can't say anything' (40:4-5). Job has accurately predicted what God will do. Taking the chilling point even further: perhaps Job may know God better than or at least as well as God knows Himself. As the mother of a ten year-old daughter recently told me, 'I can't do anything without her noticing it and calling me on it.' In addition to that, Job is in considerable pain. Pain can sometimes give one amazing insights into life... and God.

But this is all in the future. What makes Job uneasy in Job 9:1-12 is God's greatness. Job can't at this point put his finger on why that makes him so uneasy, but it has something to do with the way that God uses the divine power. God arrays the heavens with dazzling brilliance and the earth with signs of his power (vv 5-10). Who could possibly succeed in resisting such a God (v 4)? A skeptical reader might ask, 'Why would you *want* to resist such a powerful God?' That is the issue that drives Job's quest. Why, indeed, would he want to resist such a God? But he does, and he feels he has to. He has to find out an answer to his question of why he is suffering so badly, so disproportionally to what he has done, in this instance. The friends aren't of much help so far. When he turns to God, he confronts the shocking reality that God might not be of much help either. He doesn't of course utter that thought yet, but it is in the back of his mind as this brilliant debate unfolds.

He concludes the section by expressing a thought similar to how he began it. God is a mysterious presence. Just as Job couldn't answer him one word for a thousand of the divine, so "He (God) passes by me and I do not see him; he moves on, but I do not perceive him" (v 11). The frustrating thing about God for Job is that Job just wants an explanation for what has happened to him. But God is so elusive. Job has already accused his friends of being afraid of Job's calamity (6:21). Could the reason for God's elusive behavior be that God, too, is afraid of Job? All kinds of conflicting thoughts roil Job's mind.

# 12.

## Job 9:13-24, God's Anger and Moral Confusion

13 "God will not turn back his anger;
   the helpers of Rahab bowed beneath him.
14 How then can I answer him,
   choosing my words with him?
15 Though I am innocent, I cannot answer him;
   I must appeal for mercy to my accuser.
16 If I summoned him and he answered me,
   I do not believe that he would listen to my voice.
17 For he crushes me with a tempest,
   and multiplies my wounds without cause;
18 he will not let me get my breath,
   but fills me with bitterness.
19 If it is a contest of strength, he is the strong one!
   If it is a matter of justice, who can summon him?[c]

> 20 Though I am innocent, my own mouth would condemn me;
>> though I am blameless, he would prove me perverse.
> 21 I am blameless; I do not know myself;
>> I loathe my life.
> 22 It is all one; therefore I say,
>> he destroys both the blameless and the wicked.
> 23 When disaster brings sudden death,
>> he mocks at the calamity of the innocent.
> 24 The earth is given into the hand of the wicked;
>> he covers the eyes of its judges—
>> if it is not he, who then is it?

Someone once said that when you only wield a hammer in life, everything around you looks like a nail. That Job is mired in feelings of overwhelming anger is confirmed by the fact that his characterization of God here is of a God controlled by anger. "God will not withdraw/turn back His anger" (9:13). Rather than God's anger being of recent origin, however, Job now sees anger as defining God since the beginning of time. God has acted this way since crushing the forces of the mythological sea creature Rahab in the beginning. In a curious but powerful sort of way, anger is also the controlling theme of one of the greatest books of Greek antiquity: Homer's *Iliad*. The first word in 1.1 is about the anger of Achilles, an anger that will take the rest of the book to resolve. Hm. Maybe these are the first two great literary attempts at 'anger management' in history.

The reality of divine anger presents a huge and insoluble dilemma for Job. Because anger has been God's *modus operandi* since time immemorial, how do you approach such a God? Job would just like an explanation for his situation and suffering, but he fears God's anger and uncontrolled power. If the great sea creatures couldn't stand against the divine anger, how is he to do any better?

But there also is a moral dimension to Job's complaint, which makes his situation different than that of the gigantic primeval marine creatures. Job wants an answer to his pain but the problem is that he has to appeal for mercy to the same Force who has brought him his pain (v 15). This issue is fundamental to the unfolding of the Book of Job and the development of Job's thought. He feels he has no place to go for an answer but to the source of his pain—God. This stark realization will drive him later in this chapter, and then again in Chapters 16 and 19, to posit the existence of another Force who will be on his side.

But his need for an answer causes additional problems. However skillful Job is with words, his words are nothing compared to the awesome power of God. And Job knows that. God wouldn't even have to listen to Job, trivial creature that he is. "If I summoned him and he answered me (i.e., responded to my summons), I wouldn't believe He was listening to my voice" (v 16). Some might say that the *glory* of God's omnipotence is that God can do whatever God wants. Job would say that the *perversity* of God's omnipotence is that God can seemingly do whatever God wants.

Job descends deeper into his own confusion and hopelessness. Breathing becomes difficult: "He will not let me get my breath, but fills me with bitterness" (v 18). God's power so perverts everything. Even though Job knows he is innocent, God would make his own mouth condemn him. "Though I am blameless (*tam* again), he would prove me perverse" (v 20). When too much power is vested in one source, it can do whatever it wants and then call it justice.

In his helplessness, Job utters three brief thoughts that don't seem at all related at first, but capture his utter despair: "I am innocent (*tam* yet again); I don't know my own soul; I despise my life" (v 21). We know he is innocent. God has said so repeatedly; Job believes it and says it. That is the issue. He is innocent. Yet he suffers terribly. The middle statement is obscure, but it is the conduit to the last one, i.e., Job hates/despises/rejects his life.

This section closes with Job's reflecting on God's confusion in managing the world. God has no problem snuffing out the lives both of the righteous (*tam* yet one more time) and the wicked (v 22). God is a God who mocks, rather than loves (v 23). Finally, God hoodwinks the judges. Rather than humans being able to dispense justice, God has covered the eyes of the judges (v 24). All of this is beginning to make sense for Job now, since he is convinced that in addition to anger, God is controlled by moral confusion. He feels God's moral confusion is evident in his own case, and he sees it practiced throughout the world. It is a sorry, sorry situation.

# 13.

## Job 9:25-35, Longing for an Umpire

JOB IS NOW IN DESPERATE STRAITS. HE SUFFERS TREMENDOUSLY. HE feels his friends are of no help. Worst of all, he now feels that God regards him with malevolence rather than mercy. Job just would like an audience with God, perhaps to get his pain removed but also to find an explanation for his pain. But the more he tries to find God, the more elusive God seems to become. Not only that. The disproportion in power between Job and God means that God can do anything God really wants. Job seemingly has no choice but to seek help or mercy from the one whom he feels is destroying him. God is angry and has been that way since the beginning of time; Job is simply the latest casualty of that anger. God is the author of a world of moral confusion. And Job is right in the middle of that confusion. That is why he can say, in three arresting phrases: "I am innocent; I don't know my own soul; I despise my life" (9:21). Confused. Knocked down but, apparently, not knocked out. So, he continues.

Though the section presents just one long argument, we can further subdivide it as follows:

Job 9:25-26, The Swiftness of Job's Days
Job 9:27-31, Failed Strategies
Job 9:32, The Problem in a Nutshell
Job 9:33-35, Longing for an Umpire

## Job 9:25-26, The Swiftness of Job's Days

> 25 "My days are swifter than a runner;
>   they flee away, they see no good.
> 26 They go by like skiffs of reed,
>   like an eagle swooping on the prey.

Space doesn't permit a verse-by-verse examination of this section. We will focus on the leading idea. If Job is an admirable figure for people, perhaps as emblem of doggedness or truth-seeking, that admiration really should be enhanced by this passage. Though only mentioned in the last three verses of this section (vv 33-35), Job will do in those verses what no character previously has done in the Bible, and that is to try to be faithful to God by seeking ultimate help from *another* or *different* source than God. But the idea is only adumbrated in verses 33-35 and is foreshadowed in an unclear form. Job will quickly draw back from the precipice of pursuing the idea fully. But the idea will have been raised, and it will then become the engine that drives much of the next ten chapters of the book.

We are getting slightly ahead of ourselves. Job explores three other ideas quickly before getting to verses 33-35. First, in verses 25-26, he reiterates a theme discussed in 7:6, the swift passage of his days. In 7:6 he used the image of a weaver's shuttle; now he talks about swift-passing skiffs on a river. His days pass away that quickly. The implication is that they are filled with meaninglessness. Or, even worse. Verse 26 closes with the ominous note that his days pass away "as the vulture swoops on the prey." Not only are his days quickly slipping from him; he is vulnerable to flesh-eating monsters.

## Job 9:27-31, Failed Strategies

> 27 "If I say, 'I will forget my complaint;
>   I will put off my sad countenance and be of good cheer,'
> 28 I become afraid of all my suffering,
>   for I know you will not hold me innocent.
> 29 I shall be condemned;
>   why then do I labor in vain?
> 30 If I wash myself with soap
>   and cleanse my hands with lye,
> 31 yet you will plunge me into filth,
>   and my own clothes will abhor me.

But he will soon run out of options, and that is the theme of the mini-section 9:27-31. We can see him racking his brain, trying to figure out what to do. Option 1: Act happy. Act like nothing is bothering him. But he quickly discards that idea, since the pain is too great and will betray him very quickly. Option 2: Try to clean himself up, both physically and metaphorically, so he doesn't present himself as a stench-filled, repulsive creature. But then, in one of the Scripture's saddest verses, Job says that even if he washes with soap and cleanses with lye, "yet you will plunge me into filth, and my own clothes will abhor me" (v 31). We can just see it. Job has decided to clean himself up, to make himself minimally presentable. But then, the God who has it out for him comes along and plunges him right back into the mire. Why even try?

## Job 9:32, The Problem in a Nutshell

> 32 "For he is not a mortal, as I am, that I might answer him,
>   that we should come to trial together.

Job states his problem again with stunning clarity: "(God) is not a mortal, as I am, that I might answer him, that we should come to trial together" (v 32). God runs the world and is seemingly unaccountable for the wreckage He mercilessly leaves in His wake. God can't be called to trial.

## Job 9:33-35, Longing for an Umpire

> 33 "There is no umpire between us,
>   who might lay his hand on us both.
> 34 If he would take his rod away from me,
>   and not let dread of him terrify me,
> 35 then I would speak without fear of him,
>   for I know I am not what I am thought to be."

Then, in verses 33-35, an idea flits across Job's mind. It is a kind of wish that, if it were true, might change everything. What about if there were another figure out/up there, a figure who could call 'time out!', a figure who would "lay his hand on us both" (v 33)? To use an image from a boxing match, what if there were some kind of referee who could step in between the two combatants to separate them, to enforce the rules, to let them each get some space before resuming the engagement?

But the one Job longs for here is not actually a boxing referee. It is more like a judge who could tell both parties to keep quiet and then let them each speak what is on their minds in freedom and without fear of reprisal. Job's biggest worry, just expressed, is that God will plunge him back into the mire when he is trying to clean himself up. But if the rules are different, Job will be happy. "If he would take his rod from me, and not let dread of him terrify me" (v 34), then Job could speak in freedom.

Job feels he cannot do this on his own. He needs a third party to intervene, to calm things down, to send the pugilists back to their corners or the competing sides back to their respective places, to let Job speak without fear of immediate and irreversible reprisal. But the chapter closes with a tone of incredible sadness when we look at the two possible ways of translating verse 33. It is either a simple statement of hopeless finality: "There is no arbiter between us" or a contrary-to-fact wish, "Oh that there would be an arbiter..." In this case, the result is the same. There is no person between Job and God who can say, "Stop!" and give Job a chance to speak. But even in Job's sadness, we realize that he has opened an intellectual door, a door that he will never really close.

Let's finish with a slightly irrelevant, but interesting (I hope!) digression on language. Job will try to speak freely with God now, without the help of an umpire or arbiter. Just a word on the English translation of "umpire/arbiter" in Job 9:33. The noble King James gave it a rendering that is no longer understood in English, but should be mentioned. "Neither is there any *daysman* betwixt us." The Oxford English Dictionary tells us that the term *daysman* was invented by William Tyndale, one of the earliest translators of the English Bible (1530) to describe an arbitrator or mediator. Yet the OED tells us that Tyndale only used it in his translation of Exodus 21:36 and not for Job 9:33. "Daysman" was first used to render the Hebrew *mokiach* in Job 9:33 by Miles Coverdale in his 1535 Bible. Then the KJV picked up on Coverdale's translation... Interestingly, the OED is wrong here. Tyndale uses the word "daysman" as "dayes men" not in rendering Exodus 21:36 but in translating Exodus 21:22. Irrelevant but fascinating—and you don't get to correct the OED every day.

# 14.

## Job 10:1-13, The Sadness of God's Fury at Job

THE BRILLIANT IDEA FLASHED ACROSS JOB'S MIND THAT IF THERE WAS an umpire between the two combatants, he then could be free to speak his concern to/against God. But there is no umpire. Yet, in Job 10, he tries to speak with this freedom anyway: "I will give free utterance to my complaint" (10:1). But his "free utterance" will soon turn to sadness and will provoke no immediate response from God, as the next essay will show. Why? Perhaps because he has no "umpire…"

We may divide this part of Job 10 into two sections:

**Job 10:1-7, Direct Address to God**
**Job 10:8-13, The Incredible Beauty of Creation**

## Job 10:1-7, Direct Address to God

> 1 "I loathe my life;
>   I will give free utterance to my complaint;
>   I will speak in the bitterness of my soul.
> 2 I will say to God, Do not condemn me;
>   let me know why you contend against me.
> 3 Does it seem good to you to oppress,
>   to despise the work of your hands
>   and favor the schemes of the wicked?
> 4 Do you have eyes of flesh?
>   Do you see as humans see?
> 5 Are your days like the days of mortals,
>   or your years like human years,
> 6 that you seek out my iniquity
>   and search for my sin,
> 7 although you know that I am not guilty,
>   and there is no one to deliver out of your hand?

Job continues his very long speech which began in 9:1. He will try to give free utterance to his complaint. He questions God in an accusing manner, "Does it seem good to you to oppress, to despise the work of your hands and favor the schemes of the wicked" (v 3)? Perhaps emboldened by asking this question of God, Job presses on. In a question whose meaning isn't fully clear, Job asks why God seeks out Job's sin even though God knows Job isn't guilty and that Job has no deliverer (v 7). Not only is God unnecessarily picking on Job, but God is acting like a human who wants to retaliate against another human. Yet, in this case, "you know I am not guilty" (v 7). God seems to oppress him just because He can get away with it. There is no accountability for God. *That* is a big problem for Job.

## Job 10:8-13, The Incredible Beauty of Creation

> 8 "Your hands fashioned and made me;
>     and now you turn and destroy me.
> 9 Remember that you fashioned me like clay;
>     and will you turn me to dust again?
> 10 Did you not pour me out like milk
>     and curdle me like cheese?
> 11 You clothed me with skin and flesh,
>     and knit me together with bones and sinews.
> 12 You have granted me life and steadfast love,
>     and your care has preserved my spirit.
> 13 Yet these things you hid in your heart;
>     I know that this was your purpose.

Job's relentless quest for some kind of audience with God is temporarily laid aside as Job now gives us a passage of delightful but sad beauty. These verses describe, with a kind of wistfulness, the care that God took in creating Job. But Job's sadness in recounting this story is driven by the realization that the God who took such care in fashioning him will also discard him peremptorily like a piece of garbage, or will plunge him back, face first, into the filthy mire.

Job begins with his dilemma: "Your hands fashioned and made me; and now you turn to destroy me" (v 8). He turns to that act of creation and, in three metaphors of stunning attractiveness, presents a tender side of God that we have not hitherto seen. It is almost as if Job is now pleading with God, rather than boldly confronting God, to understand what God is doing. The first image is taken from the creation story in Gen 2, "Remember that you fashioned me like clay." That act of making the human was an act of incredible hopefulness, launching us on the journey of life. Job seeks to remind God of that hopeful day. "Will you (now) turn me to dust again?" (v 9). It all seems so absurd.

Second, we have a metaphor from sexual contact between

men and women. In one of the potentially raciest passages of the Bible we have, "Did you not pour me out like milk and curdle me like cheese" (v 10)? As early commentators recognized, this is Job's way of pointing to God's ejaculatory fluid (white "like milk") that then becomes mingled with a woman's flow so that "cheese" is curdled and comes together for the making of a human. The amazing boldness and intimacy of this image should not be missed.

Finally, Job draws on an image from weaving or plaiting fabrics. "You clothed me with skin and flesh, and knit me together with bones and sinews" (v 11). We hear the echo of Psalm 139:13, "For it was you who formed my inward parts; you knit me together in my mother's womb." All of these divine creative processes involve patient, skillful and even loving labor.

The result is laid out in verse 12, "You have granted me steadfast love, and your care has preserved my spirit." Job knows God well enough to say, "I know that this was your purpose" (v 13).

We see in these verses a different kind of Job, a Job that is now pleading with God to recognize the effort *God* has put into the creative process. What sense does it make that a God who so lovingly lingered over the creatures would now summarily discard one who was a special creature, and discard him without explanation or recourse to an appeal or even an audience with God? It seems incomprehensible to Job and even a bit ludicrous. As one commentator has sagely said, what moves Job in this passage is not defiance but rather "puzzlement and hurt." He is utterly puzzled and hurt, and things aren't getting any better.

# 15.

# Job 10:14-22, Defiance and Resignation

Job's attempt at convincing himself, or God, that God *ought* to exercise more care with the special work of the divine hands, is a short-lived one. In the rest of the chapter Job returns to his complaint about God's attacking him before uttering a pathetic plea to be left alone, to fade away into the dark netherworld of the land of no-return.

> Job 10:14-17, Job as God's Target
> Job 10:18-22, Let Me Have Some Peace

## Job 10:14-17, Job as God's Target

> 14 "If I sin, you watch me,
>     and do not acquit me of my iniquity.
> 15 If I am wicked, woe to me!
>     If I am righteous, I cannot lift up my head,

> for I am filled with disgrace
> and look upon my affliction.
> 16 Bold as a lion you hunt me;
> you repeat your exploits against me.
> 17 You renew your witnesses against me,
> and increase your vexation toward me;
> you bring fresh troops against me.

We recognize immediately that Job's beautiful reflection on creation in verses 8-13 was simply a diverting plea, one that couldn't really take him away from the despair welling up in his heart. Two observations begin this mini-section, both of which point to Job's current hopelessness. If he happens to sin, he believes that God is keeping a tally, observing and marking his faults, so that he won't be able to escape (v 14). But even if he were righteous, he couldn't lift up his head because he is full of shame (v 15). We might think that the latter statement is a bit strong until we realize that the shame/dishonor/disgrace that Job feels is not only because of his loss of family and health, but also a loss of position and reputation. His gut-wrenching peroration in Chapters 29-30 goes into that in more detail.

But God does more than just keep a record of his sins. God also seeks him out, like a fierce lion, hunting him down (v 16). This is reminiscent of his words in 7:20 about God's making him the divine target. Using the language elsewhere used in the Bible to describe God's doing wonders *for* the people of Israel, Job says that God "shows himself awesome/does wonders"... *against* me. Just think—that power which did awesome wonders against the Egyptians, against others, is now directed against me. How special! Job has turned the sacred language on its head to describe his situation. Though verse 17 provides some translation difficulties, the sense is that God also raises up witnesses against Job. Ah, perhaps those "witnesses" are his so-called friends. Maybe this whole

## Job 10:18-22, Let Me Have Some Peace

> 18 "Why did you bring me forth from the womb?
>   Would that I had died before any eye had seen me,
> 19 and were as though I had not been,
>   carried from the womb to the grave.
> 20 Are not the days of my life few?
>   Let me alone, that I may find a little comfort
> 21 before I go, never to return,
>   to the land of gloom and deep darkness,
> 22 the land of gloom and chaos,
>   where light is like darkness."

We are more than a little happy when Job finally comes in for a bumpy landing in these verses. His language, heartfelt as it is, is demanding on us. The insistent jackhammer of complaint, accusation and anger erupting from a soul damaged and a body seemingly destroyed taxes *us.* But before ending and letting Zophar, the third friend, take the stage, Job reiterates some thoughts from earlier before closing with four different words to describe the darkness he is about to enter.

Verses 18-19 echo his earliest words in Job 3. Whereas his complaint in Chapter 3 was framed generically, "Why did I not come forth from the womb and die?" (3:11), it now is subtly changed to "Why did *you* bring me forth..?" (10:18) He has just talked about the intimacy of God's creative activity in 10:8-13, and his question in verse 18 reflects that intimacy. Verse 19 almost contradicts itself, even though we immediately understand it. Literally it is, "I should have been as though I had not been." He wishes he were carried right from the womb to the tomb.

Verses 20-22 present Job's plea to be left alone by God. We are starting to get used to Job's reversing the impact of crucial

Biblical concepts, but we are shocked nevertheless by these bold and bald words. The longing of the Psalmist, of those who served God as priests, of those who sought a divine word was to be *with God* or in God's presence, to luxuriate in the fullness of that relationship. Yet, Job needs a little peace to be *without God.* He believes he can find peace best without God around to harass him any longer. 'Leave me alone' is the flavor.

Our own disquiet rises if we take time with the choppy language of verse 20. Literally we have, "Aren't my days few? Cease. Depart from me. Then I will smile for a little." Very few translations bring out the full import of the rare verb translated "to smile/gleam forth." Job's gladness will come, the smile will return to his face, in the few moments of peace that he can now imagine—a few moments *apart* from God. But then, the last two verses plunge us and Job seemingly back into the mire that he accused God of plunging him at first (9:30-31). Using four words of ever-stronger intensity, Job talks about his descending into a world of darkness. It is "darkness" and the "shadow of death" in verse 21. It is "utter gloom" and "pitch darkness of the shadow of death" in verse 22.

Two points of incredible literary power are almost concealed in these most hopeless words. First, when Job twice mentions the land of the "shadow of death," he is echoing the language of that most beloved Psalm—Psalm 23. In Psalm 23 the believer is assured that even if s/he walks through the "shadow of death" there is no fear because God is with her/him. For Job, the shadow of death is the place of divine absence. Second, Job ends his words here with the comment that this dark region is where "light is like darkness." Light is swallowed up in darkness. Life is swallowed up in death. That thought, too, expressly contradicts another Scriptural idea: "Even the darkness isn't dark to you, and night will shine as the day" (Ps 139:12).

We are stunned, and even overwhelmed, by Job's passionate and hopeless eloquence.

# 16.

## Job 11, Zophar Replies

Not too many people try to defend the friends at this point. The friends are usually portrayed as narrow traditionalists or unfaithful, carping, and critical companions. Adding to the sense that they just ought to be dismissed is that fact that many people already know the ending of the Book of Job, where the words of the friends are disapproved by God (Job 42:7, 8). Though many readers also feel that Job may have gone too far in his attack on God, few are ready to stand up and say unequivocally, 'I stand with the friends in their words to Job!'

Yet Zophar is an immensely difficult position as he begins to speak. He feels that Job, by overstating his purity, has thereby impugned the integrity and dignity of God. If Job were to get the last word at this point, it would be as if people who see themselves supporting the tradition are meekly conceding the argument to this fiery complainer. Thus, he cannot let Job's words go unanswered. But Job's words have made it nearly impossible to carve out a middle ground now. Granted, Job has entertained the thought of an umpire or mediator to lay his hand on both parties (9:33-34), but his words have sharpened the edges between the two approaches. If we perceive some hardness or lack of compassion in Zophar's speech, as it is often characterized by scholars, it may be because Job has made *himself* so unattractive through his words and attacks.

> Job 11:1-6, Less than You Deserve
> Job 11:7-12, God is Smarter than You, Job
> Job 11:13-20, Hope for the Future

## Job 11:1-6, Less than You Deserve

> 1 Then Zophar the Naamathite answered:
> 2 "Should a multitude of words go unanswered,
>     and should one full of talk be vindicated?
> 3 Should your babble put others to silence,
>     and when you mock, shall no one shame you?
> 4 For you say, 'My conduct is pure,
>     and I am clean in God's sight.'
> 5 But O that God would speak,
>     and open his lips to you,
> 6 and that he would tell you the secrets of wisdom!
>     For wisdom is many-sided.
>     Know then that God exacts of you less than your
>     guilt deserves.

Rather than gingerly dipping his toes in the water like Eliphaz, Zophar plunges right in. He feels he has to respond to Job. Literally we have in verse 2, "Shall not the great number of words be answered? Should a man of lips be vindicated?" He calls Job a "man of lips," surely one of the most colorful names that Job has ever been called. He asserts that Job's empty talk/nonsense (v 3) has made people hold their peace, which isn't exactly true, but it is a popular debate ploy: Zophar claims that since no one has responded effectively to Job, he is the man for the job! He picks up on a word Job used in 9:23 ("mock"), which will grow in importance as the debate unfolds, and uses that word to describe Job's attack. Job is mocking them and God.

Zophar has much more to say. He begins by quoting Job, which is more than the other friends have done. Job actually never says the precise words, "My teaching is pure and I am clean," (v 4) but he has come close to saying this in his protestation of innocence (9:21). Job is not the only one who wants God to speak. Zophar wishes that God would speak, but for a different reason than Job. Zophar wants God to unleash "his lips" on Job (v 5, using the same word for lips as in v 2). When God does that, Job will discover that God exacts *less* of him than Job actually deserves. Now *that* is shocking. It makes Bildad's skillful play on the word "wind" in 8:2 look calm.

## Job 11:7-12, God is Smarter than You, Job

> 7 "Can you find out the deep things of God?
>   Can you find out the limit of the Almighty?
> 8 It is higher than heaven—what can you do?
>   Deeper than Sheol—what can you know?
> 9 Its measure is longer than the earth,
>   and broader than the sea.
> 10 If he passes through, and imprisons,
>   and assembles for judgment, who can hinder him?
> 11 For he knows those who are worthless;
>   when he sees iniquity, will he not consider it?
> 12 But a stupid person will get understanding,
>   when a wild ass is born human.

Zophar has just expressed the wish that God would let Job know the "secrets of wisdom" (v 6). Now his eloquence reaches impressive heights as he points out the difference between the divine wisdom and human limitations. In a series of rhetorical questions that sound ominously like the catechism that God will use to instruct Job in Chapters 38-41, Zophar speaks of the greatness and wonder of God. His point in verses 7-9 is that God's greatness is basically unfathomable and beyond the comprehension of humans. Who would disagree? But part of the divine method may be to "change" or "hem in" or "gather in" (three suggestive verbs in v 10), and who really can tell God to act differently? Then, he closes this sub-section on a scary note. Judgment is real (v 11). God knows human vanity. Then, with another portentous rhetorical question he asks, "When God sees evil, won't he understand/consider it?" (v 11). Zophar closes with a somewhat gratuitous slam against Job, "But an empty person (i.e., Job) will get understanding when a wild ass's colt is born to a human" (v 12). Now you don't see *that* every day...

## Job 11:13-20, Hope for the Future

> 13 "If you direct your heart rightly,
>   you will stretch out your hands toward him.
> 14 If iniquity is in your hand, put it far away,
>   and do not let wickedness reside in your tents.
> 15 Surely then you will lift up your face without blemish;
>   you will be secure, and will not fear.
> 16 You will forget your misery;
>   you will remember it as waters that have passed away.
> 17 And your life will be brighter than the noonday;
>   its darkness will be like the morning.
> 18 And you will have confidence, because there is hope;
>   you will be protected and take your rest in safety.
> 19 You will lie down, and no one will make you afraid;
>   many will entreat your favor.
> 20 But the eyes of the wicked will fail;
>   all way of escape will be lost to them,
>   and their hope is to breathe their last."

Despite the seemingly hopeless words of verse 12, this section holds out some hope for Job. Like his predecessors Eliphaz and Bildad, Zophar will briefly sketch a glowing future for Job. Surely these friends are portrayed as a caricature of what we in the twenty-first century might call the clueless life coach, happily and quite ignorantly pointing to the certainly of future blessing to draw a person out of the current dilemma. But just as a sermon rarely leaves the hearers in the pit of despair (at least according to the way I was taught to preach in seminary), so Zophar wants to hold out reason for hope. He exhorts ("put iniquity far from you," v 14) and he expresses hope ("surely you shall lift up your face," v 15). Misery will be a thing of the past (v 16).

Zophar not only wants to encourage; he also carefully picks up on Job's descent into darkness at the end of Chapter 10 by holding out hope that Job's life will be "clearer than the noonday" and his "darkness will becomes as the morning" (v 17). Zophar closes with terminology of safety and security (v 18). Like the sheep of God who pasture in safety in Psalm 23, so Job will lie down with none to make him afraid (v 19). But remember, he says in closing, the wicked will really get it (v 20)!

# 17.

## Interlude. Job 12-14 and Beginning the Second Cycle of Speeches

JOB'S SPEECH INITIATING THE SECOND CYCLE OF SPEECHES WILL BE three chapters in length (Job 12-14). This brief essay provides some background to the Second Cycle. The next essay will begin the exposition of this section. The principal point to note is that in this Second Cycle Job acts differently than the first in at least two ways. First is a change in his anchor emotion. I argued above that his first speeches are rooted in anger, the bitter, stinging feeling resulting from the realization that he is being unfairly singled out for punishment by God. It is the emotion emerging from a deep sense of injustice suffered.

But here his anchor emotion is grief. Grief differs from anger in that it is more of a passive or inward emotion, one that draws all the feelings inside and directs their result to the self. It stands in contrast to anger, which directs all the feelings either towards the self or the other. Grief results when the energy of anger subsides and one realizes that anger, no matter how righteous, how eloquently expressed, how convincingly articulated, is ignored. If there is one thing that anger *can't* stand, it is to be ignored.

But that is precisely what is happening to Job. Though his friends give him attention, they don't really recognize the validity of his anger. And God, the seemingly Great One, is silent. Deafeningly so.

Second, in the midst of his feeling of grief, Job develops a strategy of counterattack, not on the friends but on God. It is captured most eloquently in a verse in this long speech, "I have indeed prepared my case; I know that I will be vindicated" (13:18). The second cycle sees Job preparing his case for presentation before the divine tribunal. One of the most powerful aspects of this case presentation is Job's ultimate appeal to a Redeemer (19:25-27) who will act for him in his dilemma.

# 18.

## Job 12, Gathering the Resources

Job 12 may conveniently be divided as follows:

Job 12:1-6, A Laughingstock Indeed!
Job 12:7-12, God is Responsible for Everything, Including My Misfortune
Job 12:13-25, Correct Theology, Miserable Life

## Job 12:1-6, A Laughingstock Indeed!

> 1 Then Job answered:
> 2 "No doubt you are the people,
>   and wisdom will die with you.
> 3 But I have understanding as well as you;
>   I am not inferior to you.
>   Who does not know such things as these?
> 4 I am a laughingstock to my friends;

> I, who called upon God and he answered me,
>     a just and blameless man, I am a laughingstock.
> 5 Those at ease have contempt for misfortune,
>     but it is ready for those whose feet are unstable.
> 6 The tents of robbers are at peace,
>     and those who provoke God are secure,
>     who bring their god in their hands.

Job feels that he now fighting a war on two fronts. He suspects that God has mysteriously and secretly plotted to wreck his life. But he also feels that his friends are of no help. Job 12 starts out with Job's own brand of cynicism but also with a kind of unexpected defensiveness. The cynicism is captured in 12:2, "No doubt you are the people and wisdom will die with you," a kind of mocking retort to the invective dumped on him especially by Bildad and Zophar. But his words, "I am not inferior to you" (12:3), repeated in 13:2, hint at something akin to self-protectiveness that we haven't previously seen from Job.

Perhaps the words of friends have gotten to him, and he wonders for a minute about the rightness of his cause. Their words must have stung, since he twice uses the word "laughingstock" or "joke" in 12:4 to capture his feelings. "I am now a joke to you." This really stings because one of the things that Job carefully cultivated in his position of honored elder was an aura of invincibility and respect. We have already seen that he doesn't want his anger to be ignored, but he also definitely doesn't want his honor to be besmirched through laughter. As one author has said about humiliation, "The fiercest pain is nothing compared to it." That is how he feels now. Confirming the truth of Zophar's quoted words in 11:4, Job says that he is "just and blameless" (v 4).

Verses 5-6 are difficult to understand, but they seem to be a criticism of his friends, perhaps a riposte to Zophar's enigmatic "wild ass born of human" comment in 11:6. Job can also play the game of subtle rejoinder, even as his subtlety mostly escapes us.

## Job 12:7-12, God is Responsible for Everything, Including My Misfortune

> 7 "But ask the animals, and they will teach you;
>     the birds of the air, and they will tell you;
> 8 ask the plants of the earth, and they will teach you;
>     and the fish of the sea will declare to you.
> 9 Who among all these does not know
>     that the hand of the Lord has done this?
> 10 In his hand is the life of every living thing
>     and the breath of every human being.
> 11 Does not the ear test words
>     as the palate tastes food?
> 12 Is wisdom with the aged,
>     and understanding in length of days?

His tone changes now to one of pleading. We almost imagine Job stretching out his hands and appealing to the seemingly dumb animal creation to support him in his complaint. Verses 7-9 have a poignant appeal to them. We almost hear an echo of God's creative activity in Gen 1, where God made the animals, the birds of the air, the plants of the earth, the fish of the sea in a powerful display of divine creativity. Now Job wants to call on each of those creatures to defend him. But there also is the idea that Job may be calling on the entire creation just to praise God for his wondrous works. That will be the idea in the rest of the chapter. So, a bit of ambiguity is created in these verses, which form a transition between a focus on Job as laughingstock and God as majestic creator. My reading is that the stronger emphasis is on Job's calling on creation to support him in his cause. Rather than the created order giving praise to God just by existing, Job wants that same created order to act his witnesses now *against God* as he puts his case together. "Who among all of these (creatures) doesn't know that the hand of the Lord has done this?" (v 9). Job's incredulity and incomprehension knows no bounds.

Verses 10-12 act as a kind of transition to the next section, one of the most dramatic of the dramatic ones we have seen in the book, a hymn to divine wisdom. It isn't as if Job doesn't know his theology. It is simply that the theology won't help him out at this point.

## Job 12:13-25, Correct Theology, Miserable Life

> 13 "With God are wisdom and strength;
>   he has counsel and understanding.
> 14 If he tears down, no one can rebuild;
>   if he shuts someone in, no one can open up.
> 15 If he withholds the waters, they dry up;
>   if he sends them out, they overwhelm the land.
> 16 With him are strength and wisdom;
>   the deceived and the deceiver are his.
> 17 He leads counselors away stripped,
>   and makes fools of judges.
> 18 He looses the sash of kings,
>   and binds a waistcloth on their loins.
> 19 He leads priests away stripped,
>   and overthrows the mighty.
> 20 He deprives of speech those who are trusted,
>   and takes away the discernment of the elders.
> 21 He pours contempt on princes,
>   and looses the belt of the strong.
> 22 He uncovers the deeps out of darkness,
>   and brings deep darkness to light.
> 23 He makes nations great, then destroys them;
>   he enlarges nations, then leads them away.
> 24 He strips understanding from the leaders of the earth,
>   and makes them wander in a pathless waste.
> 25 They grope in the dark without light;
>   he makes them stagger like a drunkard."

## Job 12, Gathering the Resources

This long section at first might seem strange to us. We have seen an angry and increasingly grief-stricken Job complain about God to friends and to anyone else who will listen. He feels that God has made him a special target (7:6) and that God will plunge him into filth (9:30-31). Later he will say that God has made him into the divine enemy (19:11). So, what is Job doing in this section, where he seemingly sings the virtues of God's wisdom and strength (v 13)? Some scholars have tried to explain this passage as full of irony, that Job is speaking tongue-in-cheek as he sings the wonderful strength of God in this passage. Others argue that God's great power that is described here is an amoral power, one that treats "deceived and deceiver" the same way (v 16).

But I see this as a fully sincere statement of Job's belief. He is not inferior to his friends (12:3) in understanding. In fact, the problem Job faces is *because* he continues to hold on to his traditional categories of an all-powerful God. If he could simply argue that God was a malevolent or impotent divinity, then he would only have the problem of why he had trusted this impotence or malevolence for so long. But his problem emerges precisely *because* he still believes in the all-powerful and good God.

The language of this section is suffused with echoes of Psalms 104 and 107, some of the more powerful Psalms singing God's glory in nature and history. Only one verse from Psalm 104 will be quoted at this point, and it seems to summarize this entire section. "When you hide your face, they are dismayed; when you take away their breath, they die and return to their dust" (Ps 104:29). Isn't that what God does in the rest of Job 12? God upends all the pride of humans, leading counselors and judges away. The wise are shown to be foolish (v 17). The religious authorities are shamed (v 19). Kings are deposed (v 18).

Job knows the tune and all the verses. But his life is still miserable.

# 19.

## Job 13, Preparing His Case

JOB HAS COME TO THE POINT WHERE IS HE READY TO APPROACH GOD not simply with his angry cry of pain but with an argument that needs to be answered. He approaches God because the friends have shown themselves to be unhelpful. Job even calls them treacherous (6:15). Each has a slightly different approach to his source of authority (Eliphaz's is a night vision; Bildad's is the elders; Zophar's is knowledge of God's immensity) and each of them holds out hope for Job, but each has missed the fundamental point that Job tries to communicate. He is suffering unjustly, well out of proportion to whatever bad acts he has done. The friends are clueless on that point. Perhaps they don't understand because of their fear ("You see my calamity and are afraid," 6:21), but Job realizes that he must now approach God. He prepares his case in Job 13.

We may divide Job 13 as follows:

Job 13:1-12, Attacking the Friends
Job 13:13-19, I Will Speak, Come What May
Job 13:20-28, Rules of Engagement

# Job 13:1-12, Attacking the Friends

> 1 "Look, my eye has seen all this,
>   my ear has heard and understood it.
> 2 What you know, I also know;
>   I am not inferior to you.
> 3 But I would speak to the Almighty,
>   and I desire to argue my case with God.
> 4 As for you, you whitewash with lies;
>   all of you are worthless physicians.
> 5 If you would only keep silent,
>   that would be your wisdom!
> 6 Hear now my reasoning,
>   and listen to the pleadings of my lips.
> 7 Will you speak falsely for God,
>   and speak deceitfully for him?
> 8 Will you show partiality toward him,
>   will you plead the case for God?
> 9 Will it be well with you when he searches you out?
>   Or can you deceive him, as one person deceives another?
> 10 He will surely rebuke you
>   if in secret you show partiality.
> 11 Will not his majesty terrify you,
>   and the dread of him fall upon you?
> 12 Your maxims are proverbs of ashes,
>   your defenses are defenses of clay.

Job's has just sung the mighty power of God, a power that reverses the fortunes of even the most exalted of humans. In 13:1-2 he gives us a clue as to the reason for that awesome monologue in 12:13-25. It was to show his friends, and us as readers, that Job really *hasn't* gone overboard theologically. "My eye has seen all this" (v 1). Again he repeats the idea that he is in no way "inferior" to them (v 2). The Hebrew is more picturesque: "I do not fall below/from you." Because of the friends' unhelpfulness, and because of the severity of his need, he says, "I will speak to the Almighty" (v 3). Despite his racking pain, Job articulates his desire in impressive and balanced couplets.

Yet Job can't resist a few digs at the friends before he turns to God. He both opens (v 4) and closes (v 12) his words with biting comments. You are "plasterers of lies" (v 4), a phrase captured nicely in the English phrase, "You have smeared me." They are worthless physicians (v 4). At the end of this section he says that the things they leave behind (literally, their "memorials") are proverbs of dust (v 12). We speak in English about the wind taking our words, but the meaning is the same. The companions are as helpful as the dust ; in a few chapters he will call them "miserable comforters" (16:2).

Yet Job doesn't just attack the friends. He asks them several questions in verses 7-11 which really amount to one question: 'What would you do if God were after *you?*' He says, "Would it be good if He should search you out?" (v 9). "Shall not His majesty terrify you, and His dread fall upon you?" (v 11). If it is a fearful thing to fall into the hands of the living God, then why don't you, friends, try it? Job is immensely exasperated with them.

## Job 13:13-19, I Will Speak, Come What May

> 13 "Let me have silence, and I will speak,
>    and let come on me what may.
> 14 I will take my flesh in my teeth,
>    and put my life in my hand.
> 15 See, he will kill me; I have no hope;
>    but I will defend my ways to his face.

> 16 This will be my salvation,
>     that the godless shall not come before him.
> 17 Listen carefully to my words,
>     and let my declaration be in your ears.
> 18 I have indeed prepared my case;
>     I know that I shall be vindicated.
> 19 Who is there that will contend with me?
>     For then I would be silent and die.

We have a phrase in English we often use in desperate situations: "My only hope is that…." I was originally going to write that Job now feels his only hope is in God, but I'm not sure that Job feels that way at this point. I think he feels that he *must* approach God simply because there is no other source that might hear and possibly help him. He has (at least for the moment) given up on the idea of an umpire or mediator who could lay his hand on both parties (9:33-35). So, Job has to approach God with his naked plea.

But he is terrified to do so, and this passage brings out that terror. It is captured in verses 14-15, verses that aren't crystal clear but literally say,

> "Whatever (the risks)!/Come what may! I will take my flesh in my teeth and place my life in my hand. He will slay me; I will not wait/I have no hope, but I will argue my ways before his face."

The traditional translation of 13:15, "Though he slay me I will trust in him," is not supported by the text, and most contemporary scholars have abandoned it. See my commentary for a more detailed treatment. The only point to add here is that it would be highly unlikely that a person who has been attacking God with such fervor in his last few speeches would then meekly say "Though he slay me I will trust in him." Thus, both philology and theology don't give much support to the traditional translation.

As to verse 14, we have no other record of an ancient Israelite proverb that might say "I take my flesh in my teeth." The meaning, however, should be clear. Job is facing the most precarious situation of his life. He believes that God has demonstrated ill-will towards him. He believes that God is all powerful and can snuff him out in a heartbeat. He has suffered all this loss when he was being obedient; how much more dangerous will his life be if he actually *challenges* God and *attacks* God in turn? Our phrase, "To take one's life in one's hands," captures it.

Yet, Job will not only argue his case before God. He is confident that in the end he will be vindicated (v 18). The section closes with a slightly ambiguous verse 19, which seems to suggest that even though Job is confident he will be vindicated, *if* there happens to be someone to shows up to contend with him, who could show him to be at fault, Job would certainly be silent and die (v 19). There is a lot of death talk here. Job isn't contemplating doing self-damage; he is afraid that he just might be crossing over an ill-defined line that will cause God to snap and unceremoniously obliterate him.

## Job 13:20-28, Rules of Engagement

> 20 "Only grant two things to me,
>   then I will not hide myself from your face:
> 21 withdraw your hand far from me,
>   and do not let dread of you terrify me.
> 22 Then call, and I will answer;
>   or let me speak, and you reply to me.
> 23 How many are my iniquities and my sins?
>   Make me know my transgression and my sin.
> 24 Why do you hide your face,
>   and count me as your enemy?
> 25 Will you frighten a windblown leaf
>   and pursue dry chaff?
> 26 For you write bitter things against me,

> and make me reap the iniquities of my youth.
> 27 You put my feet in the stocks,
> and watch all my paths;
> you set a bound to the soles of my feet.
> 28 One wastes away like a rotten thing,
> like a garment that is moth-eaten."

Job does have some requests, however. Crucial to understand before presenting any legal case are the rules of the judicial forum in which you will be arguing. Job suggests two possible rules in verses 21-22,

> "Withdraw your hand far from me; let not your terror make me afraid.
> Then you can call and I will answer; or let me speak and you answer."

That is, first, take away the blinding pain that I now feel and don't threaten me when I am trying to present my case. Second, either you, God, can call and I will answer or I will present my case followed by your answer. Even before awaiting the divine response, Job quickly goes on to present his case in a nutshell in the next few verses. His greatest fear is that when God actually does intervene that God would just clobber him unmercifully. We will have to determine, when reading Chapters 38-41, if God simply does what Job most fears. As we will see in those chapters, God doesn't seem to want a calm conversation with the creatures He has made.

Job's case follows in three rapid questions or statements: verse 23: "Make me to know my transgression and my sin;" verse 24: "Why do you hide your face from me?" (Is God, like the friends, afraid also?); verses 25-27: "Why do you harass a driven leaf?" (i.e., me). Job's final words are meant to capture his weakness and vulnerability. 'I am like a moth-eaten garment, but yet you do all these things to me. Why? Why? Why?'

# 20.

## Job 14, The Music of Job's Grief, Introduction

THE BOOK OF JOB NOT ONLY GIVES US NEATLY-CRAFTED AND TOUCHING individual speeches; the overall design of the book shows signs of enormous literary skill. If we were to divide the book into thirds, instead of looking simply at the cycles of speeches, Job 14 represents the completion of the first third, Job 28 the second third and Job 42 the completion of the entire book. Job 14 provides a reflection on grief and the transitory nature of life; Job 28 is an interlude on the nature and inaccessibility of wisdom; Job 42 is the powerful coda to the whole. Rather than an ancient Greek chorus, which gives the actors and audience a "break" from the onslaught of the action by simply repeating or reflecting the flow of the drama to that point, Job 14 and 28 both give the reader a break, but add deep and resonant substance to the argument.

We saw Job express his fears about approaching God. He

presented the rudiments of his case in Job 13. He is confident of victory. But, nothing happens. He has prepared his case and asked three hard-hitting but reasonable questions (about his sins; God's absence; the divine harassment). Silence. We have no idea how much time passes between the impassioned plea of Job 13 and Job's resigned hopelessness of Job 14, but Job's mood has changed dramatically between these two chapters. Gone is the fighting spirit and the confidence that he will be justified. As we will now see, "he only feels the pain of his own body" (14:22).

# 21.

# Job 14, The Music of Job's Grief, Analysis

W<small>E MAY DIVIDE JOB 14 AS FOLLOWS:</small>

Job 14:1-6, The Pain of Mortal Life
Job 14:7-17, Hope for a Tree
Job 14:18-22, But Not for Me

## Job 14:1-6, The Pain of Mortal Life

> 1 "A mortal, born of woman, few of days and full of trouble,
> 2 comes up like a flower and withers,
>    flees like a shadow and does not last.
> 3 Do you fix your eyes on such a one?
>    Do you bring me into judgment with you?
> 4 Who can bring a clean thing out of an unclean?
>    No one can.

> 5 Since their days are determined,
>     and the number of their months is known to you,
>     and you have appointed the bounds that they cannot pass,
> 6 look away from them, and desist,
>     that they may enjoy, like laborers, their days.

Almost any summary of this poem does some injustice to its sublime and majestic heights. Our days are short, and they are full of trouble. The noun for "trouble" (*rogez*) is used 7x in the Bible; five of them are in Job. Death was called a ceasing from *rogez* in 3:17; when the friends were ready to speak, Job said, "but *rogez* comes" (3:26); now he speaks of life as brief but *rogez*, "full of trouble" or "filled with turmoil." We burst forth with the energy and brilliance of a spring flower, but we soon flee away like a shadow (v 2). Shakespeare often spoke eloquently about the transience of human life, but never so memorably as in Sonnet 65:

> "O, how shall summer's honey breath old out
> Against the wrackful siege of batt'ring days,
> When rocks impregnable are not so stout,
> Nor gates of steel so strong, but time decays?"

Because our days are so numbered, what should we do? Eat, drink and be merry? Not for this author. But rather than say that "a day in Your (God's) courts is better than 1000 elsewhere" (Ps 84:10), Job says in verse 6, "look away from them/leave them alone." If any comfort is to be found in life, it is *away* from God's searching eyes.

## Job 14:7-17, Hope for a Tree

> 7 "For there is hope for a tree,
>     if it is cut down, that it will sprout again,
>     and that its shoots will not cease.

> 8 Though its root grows old in the earth,
>     and its stump dies in the ground,
> 9 yet at the scent of water it will bud
>     and put forth branches like a young plant.
> 10 But mortals die, and are laid low;
>     humans expire, and where are they?
> 11 As waters fail from a lake,
>     and a river wastes away and dries up,
> 12 so mortals lie down and do not rise again;
>     until the heavens are no more, they will not awake
>     or be roused out of their sleep.
> 13 O that you would hide me in Sheol,
>     that you would conceal me until your wrath is past,
>     that you would appoint me a set time, and remember me!
> 14 If mortals die, will they live again?
>     All the days of my service I would wait
>     until my release should come.
> 15 You would call, and I would answer you;
>     you would long for the work of your hands.
> 16 For then you would not number my steps,
>     you would not keep watch over my sin;
> 17 my transgression would be sealed up in a bag,
>     and you would cover over my iniquity.

This long middle section of the poem may further be divided into verses 7-12 and 13-17. In the first six verses, the author's grief-filled incredulity and pain reach their acme. He now draws himself back from his own situation to consider the life of a tree. Consider the tree. There is hope (*tiqvah,* a beautiful contemporary girl's name in Hebrew). If is is cut down, it grows back (literally, "it changes again"). Then come rich verses describing how a tree revives when receiving water. In contrast, humans die and where are they? (v 10) Unlike the tree, humans lie down and don't rise again. It all seems so final.

Job's pain is driving him into dimensions of thought hitherto unexplored in ancient Israel. First, we saw him exploring the idea of a heavenly umpire different from God. Now the thought of the disparity between the life of a tree and a human opens up the possibility of idea of a future life, a life after death, for humans. But he doesn't go down either road at this point.

With these realities dominating Job's mind, he (and God) need a timeout. Verses 13-17 express the desire for that timeout. The flow of these five verses is that God's anger has gotten the better of Him; it would be best if He just hides Job away for now, out of the path of the divine anger, until it has blown over. Then, after the storm has passed, Job would want to be reunited with God. Job pleads, 'Please remember me! I would respond to your call. You, God, would again long greatly for the work of your hands (i.e., ME!). But now, you scrutinize my every move; you "heap up my sins" (v 17).' God has had a terrible, horrible, no good, really bad day, but Job is confident that God can work through it and restore their relationship.

## Job 14:18-22, But Not for Me

> 18 "But the mountain falls and crumbles away,
>    and the rock is removed from its place;
> 19 the waters wear away the stones;
>    the torrents wash away the soil of the earth;
>    so you destroy the hope of mortals.
> 20 You prevail forever against them, and they pass away;
>    you change their countenance, and send them away.
> 21 Their children come to honor, and they do not know it;
>    they are brought low, and it goes unnoticed.
> 22 They feel only the pain of their own bodies,
>    and mourn only for themselves."

Reality hits Job again. Though he can escape for a minute into his poetic reverie, as he did in 3:13-19, he has to return to the painful realities right before him. If nature teaches a lesson of *hope*—that there is life again for the tree— it also teaches *hopelessness*. "Waters wear away stones" and "rocks are removed out of their place" (v 18). Nature gives and nature takes away. The thing nature takes away, most chillingly, is human hope (v 19). Humans are brought low, they fade away and, in the meantime, they only feel the pain of their bodies (v 22). The last word of the chapter is the verb *abal*, "to grieve" or "to mourn." Job 14 leaves us in the somber depths of seemingly irreversible grief. It is a place that many, many humans inhabit.

# 22.

# Job 15, Eliphaz II, Back on the Offensive

IF ELIPHAZ'S TONE IN HIS FIRST SPEECH (JOB 4-5) COULD BE CHARACterized as gentle reproof combined with encouragement of Job, this speech is much harsher. After listening to Job for several chapters, Eliphaz now feels that Job is seriously misguided and even suffering from self-delusion. He believes that Job's words actually hinder his own and others' understanding of the fear of God. The gulf between the friends and Job is well-nigh unbridgeable at this point. One wonders for a moment if the friends will continue to add much to the development of the ideas of the book or whether they will serve primarily as a foil for Job's own thought development. We will see.

We may divide this chapter as follows:

Job 15:1-6, Your Words Convict You, Job
Job 15:7-16, You Aren't So Special, Job
Job 15:17-35. Let Me Teach You a Thing or Two

## Job 15:1-6, Your Words Convict You, Job

> 1 Then Eliphaz the Temanite answered:
> 2 "Should the wise answer with windy knowledge,
>     and fill themselves with the east wind?
> 3 Should they argue in unprofitable talk,
>     or in words with which they can do no good?
> 4 But you are doing away with the fear of God,
>     and hindering meditation before God.
> 5 For your iniquity teaches your mouth,
>     and you choose the tongue of the crafty.
> 6 Your own mouth condemns you, and not I;
>     your own lips testify against you.

Rather than beginning with a congratulatory, 'Hey, Job, that was about the most eloquent speech I have ever heard, even if eloquently misguided...' Eliphaz plunges right into an attack on Job. Taking a page out of Bildad's playbook, when Bildad talked about Job's words being a "great wind" (8:2), Eliphaz begins with a rhetorical question about the wind. Using seven words, with the word *ruach* ("wind/spirit") being the fulcrum fourth word, Eliphaz asks whether a wise person should answer with such "windy" knowledge and fill his belly with the "east" wind (v 2). By placing "wind" so prominently in his opening question, and emphasizing the source of the wind, Eliphaz is even more cruel than Bildad. It was undoubtedly such a wind sweeping with its dust-laden force across the eastern spaces that led to the collapse of the children's house, snuffing out ten promising lives in Job 1. This is not "touché!" but rather "deep rapier thrust."

Eliphaz's major point is that Job's words are dangerous. They endanger faith, both Job's and others. In verse 3 Eliphaz characterizes them as "unprofitable" and "not conferring a benefit," but he gets to his major point in verse 4: you are "bringing to nought/utterly frustrating" the fear of God; you are "diminishing/restraining" prayer to God (v 4). Eliphaz's point has merit. He feels that Job's blatant attacks on God will deter others from expressing proper respect towards God. The problem is, as Eliphaz goes on to explain, that Job's sin is the root of the problem (v 5). His sin has "taught" his mouth, and his tongue chooses words of craftiness (v 5). It's fascinating that the word for "crafty" that Eliphaz selects here is the same word to describe the serpent in Gen 3:1. As I argued in my commentary on Genesis, one might see the serpent in Gen 3 in a few different ways because of the suppleness of that term *arum*, "crafty/prudent," but I tend to see the serpent as a wisdom teacher. Yet the word *arum* isn't meant positively here. Thus, Eliphaz concludes that Job's own crafty words condemn him (v 6).

## Job 15:7-16, You Are Not So Smart, Job

> 7 "Are you the firstborn of the human race?
>     Were you brought forth before the hills?
> 8 Have you listened in the council of God?
>     And do you limit wisdom to yourself?
> 9 What do you know that we do not know?
>     What do you understand that is not clear to us?
> 10 The gray-haired and the aged are on our side,
>     those older than your father.
> 11 Are the consolations of God too small for you,
>     or the word that deals gently with you?
> 12 Why does your heart carry you away,
>     and why do your eyes flash,
> 13 so that you turn your spirit against God,
>     and let such words go out of your mouth?
> 14 What are mortals, that they can be clean?
>     Or those born of woman, that they can be righteous?
> 15 God puts no trust even in his holy ones,
>     and the heavens are not clean in his sight;
> 16 how much less one who is abominable and corrupt,
>     one who drinks iniquity like water!

Assumed but never really said in Job's speeches is that his distress is worse and different in kind than other people's; his distress gives him authority to speak and complain in the way he does. Eliphaz's point here is that Job is not only not so special in what he suffers, but has no unique sources either of personal knowledge or special revelation to allow him to make special demands on God. In a word, God's "consolations" should be sufficient for Job (v 11).

The point is significant. One of the functions of religion is to give explanations for life, explanations that cover all the possibilities of imagined or real human experience. If, for example, a religion only had convincing explanations for experiences of joy, then it would not be a very useful religion. Or if its explanations only covered those in the middle of the 'bell curve'—i.e., only those 70 percent of rather 'normal' people who face the rather 'normal' distresses of life, then it likewise wouldn't have much to say to the soaring mystics or profound sufferers. Religion's effectiveness relates to its ability to give convincing explanations to people feeling the full panoply of human emotion. Eliphaz's point is that Job is acting as if the explanations or the "consolations" of God (v 11) are too small for him. He needs other words, other explanations. He is the special case, the unique sufferer, the one who wants personalized treatment by God.

'Well, buddy,' opines Eliphaz, 'that isn't the way life or God works.' That is Eliphaz's point in a nutshell. Look, he says, on "our side" (i.e., Eliphaz's side) are the hoary heads of tradition (v 10). People much older than Job's father would agree with Eliphaz. And, in addition, Job has no special revelation vouchsafed to him. He didn't "hearken in the counsel of God" (v 8). Job's heart has, in a sense, carried him away (v 12), which results in Job's turning away from God (v 13). Eliphaz's basic point is that humans are sinful; they can't be clean (v 14). It is as if Eliphaz is saying, 'You, Job, don't deserve any special treatment. It would be best for you to realize that.'

*Job 15, Eliphaz II, Back on the Offensive*

## Job 15:17-35, Let Me Teach You a Thing or Two

> 17 "I will show you; listen to me;
>   what I have seen I will declare—
> 18 what sages have told,
>   and their ancestors have not hidden,
> 19 to whom alone the land was given,
>   and no stranger passed among them.
> 20 The wicked writhe in pain all their days,
>   through all the years that are laid up for the ruthless.
> 21 Terrifying sounds are in their ears;
>   in prosperity the destroyer will come upon them.
> 22 They despair of returning from darkness,
>   and they are destined for the sword.
> 23 They wander abroad for bread, saying, 'Where is it?'
>   They know that a day of darkness is ready at hand;
> 24 distress and anguish terrify them;
>   they prevail against them, like a king prepared for battle.
> 25 Because they stretched out their hands against God,
>   and bid defiance to the Almighty,
> 26 running stubbornly against him
>   with a thick-bossed shield;
> 27 because they have covered their faces with their fat,
>   and gathered fat upon their loins,
> 28 they will live in desolate cities,
>   in houses that no one should inhabit,
>   houses destined to become heaps of ruins;
> 29 they will not be rich, and their wealth will not endure,
>   nor will they strike root in the earth;
> 30 they will not escape from darkness;
>   the flame will dry up their shoots,
>   and their blossom will be swept away by the wind.
> 31 Let them not trust in emptiness, deceiving themselves;
>   for emptiness will be their recompense.

> 32 It will be paid in full before their time,
>    and their branch will not be green.
> 33 They will shake off their unripe grape, like the vine,
>    and cast off their blossoms, like the olive tree.
> 34 For the company of the godless is barren,
>    and fire consumes the tents of bribery.
> 35 They conceive mischief and bring forth evil
>    and their heart prepares deceit."

Once the foregoing is clear, this long and complex soliloquy neatly falls into place. Eliphaz will then become the 'teacher' of Job in these last 19 verses, helping him realize that he doesn't deserve special treatment. Eliphaz will declare what the tradition has taught him about the fate of people like Job. Perhaps not unexpectedly he then speaks with quite some passion, even though his words in Hebrew are hard to understand at various points, especially when he speaks about the miserable life and painful doom awaiting the wicked. "They will not be rich" (v 29—is he poking at Job here, who has experienced a reversal of economic fortunes?); "they will not escape from darkness" (recall the four words Job used to describe darkness at the end of Job 10); "emptiness will be their recompense" (v 31, what better way to describe Job's current condition?). Deception is their life (v 35). On that note, he stops.

# 23.

## Job 16-17, Job Responds

JOB'S TWO-CHAPTER RESPONSE BOTH BRINGS US NEW LANGUAGE describing the divine savagery against Job as well as the firm hope Job has of a "witness" in heaven on his behalf (16:19). What was only hinted at previously about an "umpire" has now matured into an actual belief in a heavenly witness. But, as we are already expecting with the Book of Job, there is most likely an interesting twist as to who this witness actually is.

This essay will only summarize Job 16:1-17. The next essay will briefly discuss Job's appeal to a heavenly witness in 16:18-22. A third essay will deal with Job 17.

> Job 16:1-5, You are the Ones Speaking Windy Words!
> Job 16:6-17, A Description of God's Savage Attack on Job

## Job 16:1-5, You are the Ones Speaking Windy Words!

> 1 Then Job answered:
> 2 "I have heard many such things;
>     miserable comforters are you all.
> 3 Have windy words no limit?
>     Or what provokes you that you keep on talking?
> 4 I also could talk as you do,
>     if you were in my place;
>     I could join words together against you,
>     and shake my head at you.
> 5 I could encourage you with my mouth,
>     and the solace of my lips would assuage your pain.

Picking up on a word just used by Eliphaz in 15:35 (*amal*, "trouble"), Job says that the friends are "comforters of trouble" in 16:2. That is, they bring trouble rather than consolation in their wake. Turning back on Eliphaz the allegation of "windiness," Job bitingly asks if his "words of wind" (*ruach*) will ever end (v 3). But then Job not so gently turns the tables on the companions. "I could also speak as you do, if you were in my position" (v 4). But, in contrast to the brutal and judgmental words of his fearful friends, Job would speak genuine words of comfort if his friends were afflicted. Literally, "the movement of my lips would restrain" your grief (v 5).

## Job 16:6-17, A Description of God's Savage Attack on Job

> 6 "If I speak, my pain is not assuaged,
>     and if I forbear, how much of it leaves me?
> 7 Surely now God has worn me out;
>     he has made desolate all my company.
> 8 And he has shriveled me up,

> which is a witness against me;
> my leanness has risen up against me,
> and it testifies to my face.
> 9 He has torn me in his wrath, and hated me;
> he has gnashed his teeth at me;
> my adversary sharpens his eyes against me.
> 10 They have gaped at me with their mouths;
> they have struck me insolently on the cheek;
> they mass themselves together against me.
> 11 God gives me up to the ungodly,
> and casts me into the hands of the wicked.
> 12 I was at ease, and he broke me in two;
> he seized me by the neck and dashed me to pieces;
> he set me up as his target;
> 13 his archers surround me.
> He slashes open my kidneys, and shows no mercy;
> he pours out my gall on the ground.
> 14 He bursts upon me again and again;
> he rushes at me like a warrior.
> 15 I have sewed sackcloth upon my skin,
> and have laid my strength in the dust.
> 16 My face is red with weeping,
> and deep darkness is on my eyelids,
> 17 though there is no violence in my hands,
> and my prayer is pure.

The words of these twelve verses are unprecedented in fury and pathetic in scope. Job decides to go for broke, literally speaking, because his pain is not assuaged either if he is silent or if he speaks (v 6). He might as well speak his mind. So his mind begins to overflow like a spewing sewer pipe, expelling with great force all the muck and grime which has caked his heart since the combined force of his distresses landed on him. The images tumble over each other with such profusion that we have to struggle just to keep up with them.

First, God has exhausted Job (v 7), though the verb can also be translated "has made me impatient." God has taken away all his company/companions (v 7). His body, which we infer was once strong and supple, is now shriveled (v 8). But then God is described as a ravenous wild beast. God has "torn me to shreds" (v 9), using the same word Jacob plaintively used twice in Gen 37:33 to describe what he felt a wild beast had done to Joseph. God hates him (v 9). He grinds his teeth against Job (v 9). He makes his gaze as if it is a sharp laser, slicing Job in half (v 9).

Sometimes Job has difficulty differentiating what is an attack of people and what is from God. Sometimes when he uses "they" to describe a human attack we aren't sure if he is referring to the three companions here or to the marauders who despoiled his property or to the store of accumulated hurts visited on him by enemies over the years. But his mind isn't in the mood for granular discriminations at this point. He is suffering the combined weight of all the collapses now (v 10).

But then, just as we think he will describe the enemies in more detail, he returns to an even more blistering description of God's attack on him in verses 12-17. "I was living a peaceful and quiet life, and God took me by the neck and shattered me" (v 12). The Hebrew verb is almost onomatopoetic: *yepatspatsni;* we can almost hear the crunching of his bones in the repeated *patspats*. Then, changing the metaphor once again, Job speaks of God as making him his special target (v 12).

The language of brutality continues in verses 13-17, but it becomes more interior, focusing on the pouring out of guts and viscera. God's archers pierced his kidneys/heart/innards (v 13); Job's bile/gall is pouring out on the ground (v 13). We see in our mind's eye a wounded animal, penetrated by lethal and probably poisoned arrows, heaving in distress as its entrails and bowels come gushing out. Three times in verse 14 the verb or noun *parats* (break through/make a breach) appears. It is as if God has breached all of Job's defenses, leaving him a huddled mass of quivering flesh.

What does Job do in this situation? All he can do is show obvious signs of grief, such as the donning of sackcloth (v 15), and then weep his eyes out (v 16). But then, he closes this description of the divine assault with the thought he has consistently uttered: "There is no violence in my hand, and my prayer is pure" (*zakah*, v 17). Bildad had said that there was hope if Job was pure (*zakah*, 8:6); Job is saying that he is pure. God has recognized as much in Job 1 and 2. Job has presented a compelling case of divine cruelty towards a faithful servant of God. What has happened to him makes no sense at all.

# 24.

## Job 16:18-22, Job's Appeal to a Heavenly Witness

> 18 "O earth, do not cover my blood;
>     let my outcry find no resting place.
> 19 Even now, in fact, my witness is in heaven,
>     and he that vouches for me is on high.
> 20 My friends scorn me;
>     my eye pours out tears to God,
> 21 that he would maintain the right of a mortal with God,
>     as one does for a neighbor.
> 22 For when a few years have come,
>     I shall go the way from which I shall not return."

This essay will be brief, and it only deals with one subject. Who is the one called "my witness" whom Job says he knows is in heaven testifying now for him (v 19)? Is it the God whom he has been speaking about all along or is it another party?

First, let's set the context for the question a bit more precisely. Job has just described God's repeated and unmerciful assaults against him. In a previous passage where Job had reached similar rhetorical heights (Job 9), Job sadly concluded that there was no one really to give him the help he needed in his sorry situation. He had no umpire, no referee, no mediator to put hands on both parties (God and Job), to calm them both down and let Job finally speak his words without fear of divine reprisal (9:33-35). Even though there was no mediator who could play this role, Job had momentarily entertained the idea of a power or force apart from God who might be able to help him in Job 9. Then he dropped the idea.

He develops the thought here which we thought he had buried in Job 9. But now what he seeks is not a mediator who will allow both sides to speak, but a witness who will speak up on his behalf in heaven, holding forth for him. Most commentators immediately conclude that this must mean that Job is appealing to God, almost as if he is asking for God to be a witness against the divine, adumbrating perhaps a dual character to the Godhead that will receive its fullest expression in the Christian doctrine of the Trinity.

Any reader who has gotten this far in these essays will easily understand how I would consider that a real s-t-r-e-t-c-h. Job is not friendly to God here because he believes that God has been unfriendly to him. Job has just unleashed his most colorful and rhetorically stunning description of God's assault on him for the world to see. The God whom he has faithfully served has not just treated Job as a punching bag but as thrusting practice for the divine collection of rapiers, swords, daggers, halberds and knives. God has pounced on him unmercifully, tearing him apart as a lion does its prey.

Does that sound like a prelude to asking God for help? The most convincing explanation consistent with the literary flow of Job 16 is that this witness is someone *other* than God, someone who actually sides with Job *against* God as Job makes his case. Job knows that his strength is insufficient to sustain the case on his own. God is too wily, too powerful, too elusive, too deceptive for him. He needs help to make sure that the points he knows are correct and which he has so lovingly cultivated over time are not lost but are perfectly presented before the divine tribunal.

Job never gives up the idea of a just God. The thing that drives him to this point, however, is his incomprehension at God's terrible cruelty to him. In order to make his case, he not only needs to marshal all his personal resources but to have the aid of a heavenly advocate or witness. He now knows that witness exists. Such a witness *must* exist. The character of God demands that there be another heavenly force now opposing God.

# 25.

## Job 17, Exhausted!

JOB 17 IS A BIT OF A CIPHER. IT IS NOT THAT THE THOUGHTS EXPRESSED here and there in it are strange or atypical for Job. Several of them are fully consistent with what we have already heard from Job's lips. It is just that they seem so jumbled here, so disconnected from each other that we feel that this is a point where we needed to be *with* Job, to hear his breathing, see his expression, feel his emotion in order to understand fully what he was saying. Jumbled and tumbled thoughts. Consult 20 scholars, get 20 different outlines of how the chapter holds together.

Rather, then, than giving you a 21st outline, though I am not averse to pointing out a consistent flow of a few verses here or there, I will present what I consider the main theme, buttressed by three verses that emphasize that theme. In a word, the chapter reflects Job's physical and mental *exhaustion*.

Consider what Job has just done. He has moved from utter despair to expression of wild hope in the space of a few verses

(16:18-22). The potent verses describing God's slashing attack on Job in the previous chapter (16:7-17) were crowned by the most unexpected declaration that there is another force, a *witness in heaven*, who will speak for Job (16:19). All of a sudden we feel that the intellectual tectonic plates of the book have just shifted. Rather than Job's growing desperation and hopelessness as he continues to bash the treachery of friends and the hostility of God, we have a sturdy, though undeveloped, hope in a different kind of friend. It is far more than the mediator of 9:33-35, a mediator who really doesn't exist. Now we have the makings of an idea that will launch Job into a new level of confidence and freedom. As I will argue in treating Job 19, this "witness" then will morph or mature into his "Redeemer," a Redeemer who will not simply state Job's case for him but will bring him out of his mess.

Job is beginning to learn a potent but most frightening lesson: that his freedom might reside not simply in the rhetorical spaces of sentences such as 'Leave me alone so I can find some peace,' found at the end of Job 10 and Job 14:6, but in the actual reality of a full life of freedom *apart* from God.

But this is all too much to bear for Job at the moment. He is thoroughly spent by his ordeal to date; even the mere mention of the revolutionary idea of a witness in heaven who isn't God and who will testify in his upcoming lawsuit against God is frightening and debilitating. We see the full results of that debility in Job 17.

Three verses capture Job's enervation: 17:1, 7, 11. Though much more could be said about the chapter, I will just focus on these three. First, though, is the entire chapter.

> 1 "My spirit is broken, my days are extinct,
>     the grave is ready for me.
> 2 Surely there are mockers around me,
>     and my eye dwells on their provocation.
> 3 "Lay down a pledge for me with yourself;
>     who is there that will give surety for me?

> 4 Since you have closed their minds to understanding,
>     therefore you will not let them triumph.
> 5 Those who denounce friends for reward—
>     the eyes of their children will fail.
> 6 "He has made me a byword of the peoples,
>     and I am one before whom people spit.
> 7 My eye has grown dim from grief,
>     and all my members are like a shadow.
> 8 The upright are appalled at this,
>     and the innocent stir themselves up against the godless.
> 9 Yet the righteous hold to their way,
>     and they that have clean hands grow stronger and stronger.
> 10 But you, come back now, all of you,
>     and I shall not find a sensible person among you.
> 11 My days are past, my plans are broken off,
>     the desires of my heart.
> 12 They make night into day;
>     'The light,' they say, 'is near to the darkness.'
> 13 If I look for Sheol as my house,
>     if I spread my couch in darkness,
> 14 if I say to the Pit, 'You are my father,'
>     and to the worm, 'My mother,' or 'My sister,'
> 15 where then is my hope?
>     Who will see my hope?
> 16 Will it go down to the bars of Sheol?
>     Shall we descend together into the dust?"

## "My spirit is broken, my days are extinct, the grave is ready for me," (17:1)

Job utters three two-word phrases (in Hebrew) in staccato-like fashion, as if his breath is so labored that he is simply overwhelmed. The first phrase can be variously translated: "My spirit (*ruach*, the same word repeatedly used for the "wind" that killed Job's children in Job 1) is broken" or, similarly, "my spirit is spent," or, differently, "my breath is corrupt." The last would emphasize the offensiveness of his very breath to those around him, perhaps because of its odor or the fact that he still is alive and breathing. I'll go with the majority which favors "my spirit broken" or even "ruined." The verb for "extinct" or "extinguished" (*zaak*) is a *hapax* in the Bible (appears only one time), but most scholars see it as a corruption of *daak,* a much more common verb in Semitic languages for "extinguish" or "quench." This supposition is confirmed by the fact that Bildad uses the verb *daak* twice in his rejoinder to Job in 18:5, 6, to slam Job once again. All that is left for Job is the grave. He will die just as millions of other invisible sufferers.

## "My eyes have grown dim from grief, and all my members are like a shadow," (17:7).

People who feel their existence is slipping away or who have never fully felt like a human often express their feelings in words like 17:7. A young friend of mine, suffering from severe life-long depression, told me that in his youth he invented a game he called "Ghosts," where he would play with his friends and be invisible but somehow present. Job seems to reflect that spirit here. Literally we have, "My eye grows dim/faint because of my provocation (*kaas*)," where *kaas* is the same word translated as "provocation" or "anger-induced provocation" in 6:2. Perhaps now we are to see it as anger shading off into grief, consistent with the movement of this part of the book. Dimness of vision is associated with Isaac (Gen 27:1) as a sign of debility and old age. Moses was said to have died *without* dimness of vision (Deut 34:7). "Dimness of eyes" is the prelude to death.

## "My days are past, my plans are broken off, the desires of my heart," (17:11).

Again Job gives us three two-word phrases to capture his brokenness. Every one is heart-rending. I will just translate them literally. "My days have *passed by*." The verb is the very common *abar*, most frequently used when one is crossing a river or going through a territory. "My plans/devices are crushed." Rather than "broken off," the verb *nataq* suggests a process of crushing, tearing apart or even breaking in pieces. Most memorably, the verb is used in Lev 22:24 to describe one of the ways a man may be disqualified from the priesthood. If his genitals are "crushed," he can't approach God in serving the people. Job's final two words of the chapter are simply, "the desires of my heart." These "desires" are in fact the "possessions" (*yarash*, the underlying verb, means "to possess"). Every vital thing of Job has been torn away from him. He is ready for the grave, a grave however that won't really welcome him (17:12-16).

# 26.

## Job 18, Bildad Rides Again

IF JOB'S LAST SPEECH PRESENTED US WITH A MEDLEY OF MIXED VERSES, Bildad's second speech, presented here, gives us a contrasting feel. Even though he doesn't advance the debate much in this passage, his speech has such resonant clarity and even eloquence that we are immediately grateful. At least we aren't going to have to scratch our heads to figure out what he is saying!

We may divide this chapter as follows:

Job 18:1-4, Skillfully Slamming Job
Job 18:5-21, The Fate of the Wicked—Again

## Job 18:1-4, Skillfully Slamming Job

> 1 Then Bildad the Shuhite answered:
> 2 "How long will you hunt for words?
>     Consider, and then we shall speak.

> 3 Why are we counted as cattle?
>     Why are we stupid in your sight?
> 4 You who tear yourself in your anger—
>     shall the earth be forsaken because of you,
>     or the rock be removed out of its place?

I say that Bildad is particularly skillful here because of the way he subtly uses words or concepts Job used so dramatically and effectively in Job 16 in order to turn them back on Job. We were awed by Job's description of the brutal savagery of God against him in 16:8ff. For example, Job characterized God as hunting him down, like a marksmen seeking his prey in 16:12-13. Bildad's opening words in 18:2 are "How long will you hunt for words/lay a trap for words?"—trying to liken Job's devastating accusation against God into Job's futile search for words. 'It isn't about what God has done to you, Job; it is about your fumbling attempt to find language.'

To show that this isn't just a fluke, Bildad also says in 18:4, "You tear yourself in your anger...," using the same verb (*taraph*, "to tear") which Job had used to describe God's cruel attack on him in 16:8, "He has torn me (*taraph*) in his wrath and hated me." What Bildad is saying to Job is, 'Job you are *tearing* yourself; God is not *tearing* you.' It is the about the most rhetorically powerful way of handling a pretty effective attack on God that one can imagine. Yet, Bildad's words here are generally forgotten, while very few can forget Job's words in Chapter 16.

## Job 18:5-21, The Fate of the Wicked—Again

> 5 "Surely the light of the wicked is put out,
>     and the flame of their fire does not shine.
> 6 The light is dark in their tent,
>     and the lamp above them is put out.
> 7 Their strong steps are shortened,
>     and their own schemes throw them down.

> 8 For they are thrust into a net by their own feet,
>     and they walk into a pitfall.
> 9 A trap seizes them by the heel;
>     a snare lays hold of them.
> 10 A rope is hid for them in the ground,
>     a trap for them in the path.
> 11 Terrors frighten them on every side,
>     and chase them at their heels.
> 12 Their strength is consumed by hunger,[a]
>     and calamity is ready for their stumbling.
> 13 By disease their skin is consumed,[b]
>     the firstborn of Death consumes their limbs.
> 14 They are torn from the tent in which they trusted,
>     and are brought to the king of terrors.
> 15 In their tents nothing remains;
>     sulfur is scattered upon their habitations.
> 16 Their roots dry up beneath,
>     and their branches wither above.
> 17 Their memory perishes from the earth,
>     and they have no name in the street.
> 18 They are thrust from light into darkness,
>     and driven out of the world.
> 19 They have no offspring or descendant among their people,
>     and no survivor where they used to live.
> 20 They of the west are appalled at their fate,
>     and horror seizes those of the east.
> 21 Surely such are the dwellings of the ungodly,
>     such is the place of those who do not know God."

This is one very long presentation of the sorry state, present and future, of the wicked (*rashim*, v 5). But even in beginning his speech, Bildad takes yet another dig at Job. Bildad says, "Surely, the light of the wicked is put out" (v 5). The verb "to put out" or "extinguish" is the somewhat rare (9x-appearing) verb *daak*. Perhaps you recall that when Job uttered one of his more memorable verses in Job 17, it was the utterly forlorn statement, "My spirit is consumed, my days are extinguished, the grave awaits me" (17:1). The verb for "extinguish" there is *zaak*, a *hapax* which most scholars see as another way of writing *daak*. Bildad would be saying here, 'Hmm...poor Job, your days are extinguished. Well, guess what, it is the light of the wicked that is extinguished (18:5). Put two and two together, Job, and you will see your fate!'

By this time of the conversation, then, we see that the personal animosity has so poisoned the friends' communication that subtle and not-so-subtle insults fill the speeches. But Bildad continues, with another dig at Job in 18:6. Using the vivid metaphor of light and darkness to describe the fate of the wicked, Bildad says, "The light is dark in their tent" (18:6). The word for "dark" is *choshek*, the same word Job used when he began his descent into his own private darkness in 10:21 and then again in 17:13. 'Ah... that darkness you say you are descending into, Job... well, it is the darkness of the wicked.' Make no mistake about it. Bildad uses brilliant and beautiful rhetoric to condemn Job.

The truly scary thought in all this is not that Bildad speaks this way against Job. Job is able to withstand the attack and even come up with his most brilliant and controversial concept (the Redeemer) in Job 19, the chapter after Bildad's attack. But it will presage an even more devastating rhetorical fusillade against Job launched by God in Job 38. My theory, to be developed below, is that by the time that God enters the arena with the carping and critical divine words in Job 38, the environment has been so poisoned that Job may not be able to hear the Word of God. He will, in a word, have already 'checked out' mentally. But where does Job go if he 'checks out' from God? Well, you have to read on..

Bildad goes toe-to-toe with Job in Job 18. As we have seen, Job pointed out about eight things that God did to upend his life in

Job 16. In the remainder of his speech, Bildad will point to about eight ways that the fate of the wicked is miserable.

1. Their own schemes bring them down (v 7)

2. Their light is extinguished (vv 5-6)

3. A snare lays hold on them (vv 9-10).

4. Terrors frighten them and chase them (v 11)

5. They go hungry (v 12)

6. Their skin is consumed by disease (v 13). Can anyone not be reminded of the sad picture of Job scratching his sores in ch 2?

7. Nothing remains in their tents (v 15). Ah, all of Job's possessions have disappeared.

   Then, most devastating,

8. They have no offspring or descendants among the people, and no survivor where they used to live (v 19).

Not even Zophar's untimely remark in 11:6 matches the cruelty of these words of Bildad. Bildad probably even looks at Job a bit triumphantly as he utters his last line, "Surely such are the dwellings of the ungodly, such is the place of those who do not know God" (v 21). It is a rhetorical tour-de-force, matching Job's slashing attack on God tit-for-tat.

But someone has to begin to raise the question at this point: 'Is there any way out of this mess?' Job will make a suggestion in that regard in the next chapter...

# 27.

# Job 19:1-12, The Redeemer, a Preparation

JOB WILL EXPLORE HIS MOST RADICAL AND TRANSFORMATIVE IDEA IN this chapter. It will be so powerful that after he says it in verse 25, he will become disoriented, almost as if the mere mention of a Redeemer or a Vindicator sends his mind and heart into overdrive so that it "faints" within him. But before we get to that verse, Job prepares us by some further words describing his sorry condition.

> Job 19:1-6, Repeated Humiliation by Friends
> Job 19:7-12, God's Reproach

## Job 19:1-6, Repeated Humiliation by Friends

> 1 Then Job answered:
> 2 "How long will you torment me,
>     and break me in pieces with words?
> 3 These ten times you have cast reproach upon me;

> are you not ashamed to wrong me?
> 4 And even if it is true that I have erred,
>   my error remains with me.
> 5 If indeed you magnify yourselves against me,
>   and make my humiliation an argument against me,
> 6 know then that God has put me in the wrong,
>   and closed his net around me.

We have seen a lot of language in the past few chapters about tearing, hunting, ripping, destroying. Job follows up on that now with an image of "crushing." Verse 2 literally says, "How long will you torment me and crush me with words?" Though the friends have only made a total of five speeches so far, Job says, "Ten times you have dishonored/insulted me" (v 3). Perhaps each attack feels like a double attack. Job will then seemingly let down his guard for a moment, but he actually does so for only one verse, and he doesn't give his friends a chance to respond (v 4). In words reminiscent of 6:3, where he excused his "rash" language because of the extremity of his suffering, Job here says, somewhat enigmatically, "Even if it is true that I have erred, my error remains with me" (v 4). This seems to mean that if Job bears any fault in this sorry mess it is through what lawyers call a 'procedural' rather than a 'substantive' error. That is, his error is more in the 'process' (i.e., he spoke with too loud a voice; perhaps he chose some words that were over-the-top), but it was not an error in 'substance' (which would relate to his sin or mistake actually deserving the punishment he received). In words that again bring up the image of hunting and nets, he says that God has hunted him down and enclosed him with the divine net (v 6). All this talk about nets and being caught…if some psychologist could go beyond the obvious observation that Job feels 'trapped' here, we would be most grateful. The theme of these verses is now familiar to us: the friends have mercilessly attacked him; God has trapped him.

## Job 19:7-12, God's Reproach

> 7 "Even when I cry out, 'Violence!' I am not answered;
>    I call aloud, but there is no justice.
> 8 He has walled up my way so that I cannot pass,
>    and he has set darkness upon my paths.
> 9 He has stripped my glory from me,
>    and taken the crown from my head.
> 10 He breaks me down on every side, and I am gone,
>    he has uprooted my hope like a tree.
> 11 He has kindled his wrath against me,
>    and counts me as his adversary.
> 12 His troops come on together;
>    they have thrown up siegeworks against me,
>    and encamp around my tent.

But now Job does what he does best: show how God has thoroughly obliterated him. You kind of wonder after reading this section how long Job actually will wait for God to answer him. An idea that I don't see in the Job commentaries is the notion that perhaps God might have waited too long before answering His child. Every parent knows that it is good sometimes to let the children "stew" in their anger or dissatisfaction, but every good parent also knows that sometimes you can answer too late, and you just might lose your child forever...

Even though Job hasn't yet finished speaking (that won't happen until Job 31), we get the sense that by now he must just about have exhausted the lexicon to describe the divine savagery. But he finds even more words here to express his distress. After a question opening this section, Job will utter five unforgettable allegations against God that will make us forget all of Bildad's nicely constructed phrases of the previous chapter. Verse 7 acts like a one word summary or title to the entire subsection: "I cry out, 'Violence' but I am not answered; I shout for help but there is no judgment." How long must he shout? God's ways may not be human ways but if they are too different, humans will fade away from this God...

Fresh images now emerge. God has walled Job in, fenced up his way so he cannot pass (v 8). Darkness (*choshek* again) is on his paths. To be noticed is the way that Job's language subverts the wisdom tradition of Israel, of which the Book of Job is one familiar exemplar. In Proverbs, for example, God makes the paths straight (Prov 3:6); now God makes them dark. Reversal and subversion. Then, God strips Job of his glory (v 9). The verb is very visual (*pashat*), suggesting either a process of raiding a city, gently removing garments or flaying an animal's skin (Lev 1:6). I think Job feels more like the last is happening to him.

Then, God tears Job down on every side, using the special verb *natsab*, often used in the Hebrew tradition for tearing down idols and dangerous altars (see, e.g., Ex 34:13). But the image of tearing down is neatly placed right next to one of uprooting. "He plucks me up/uproots me like a tree" (v 10). We see the utter turmoil and topsy-turvy nature of Job's life in these two verbs. On the one hand he feels as if he is being torn *down*; on the other hand he is being *up*rooted. What is left? Just a quivering useless mass of decaying branches on the ground.

In verse 11 the image changes to God's having kindled His wrath against Job and to God's considering him an enemy. We have seen Job refer to the divine anger previously (e.g., Job 9:13). Our section closes with the divine attack likened to troops uniting to come against Job and camping against him. We hear the distant echo of that most comforting Psalm in our mind, "The angel of the Lord sets up a camp around those who fear God, and delivers them" (Ps 34:7). But here it is God setting up the camp around Job to destroy him. Job has utterly charmed us now by his eloquent description of abject hopelessness, even as he turns the Scripture on its head for his advantage. And, he isn't yet finished with his description. He now turns to how this works itself out in his daily life...

# 28.

## Job 19:13-22, Job the Repulsive

IN THIS PASSAGE JOB PROVIDES A SLIGHT VARIATION ON AND DEVELOP-ment of the theme of rejection by friends. Here, however, we have a more thorough catalogue of those who reject Job, as well as a reference to his sorry physical condition. Though this section is only ten verses in length, it may be further subdivided into three mini-sections:

Job 19:13-15, Repulsive to Those Far and Near
Job 19:16-20, Repulsive to Low and High
Job 19:21-22, Have Pity on Me, a Repulsive Person

## Job 19:13-15, Repulsive to Those Far and Near

> 13 "He has put my family far from me,
>    and my acquaintances are wholly estranged from me.
> 14 My relatives and my close friends have failed me;

> 15 the guests in my house have forgotten me;
> my serving girls count me as a stranger;
> I have become an alien in their eyes.

The text has previously mentioned very few people beyond Job, his family and friends. Except for the marauders that ravished Job's property in Job 1, the people we meet are all on the same social level with Job. But in this and the next subsection, we will be introduced to serving girls, other servants, and young children. All of them, whose opinions really didn't much matter in the world Job inhabited, are brought in to register the same verdict: Job is repulsive. When servants don't respond to their master it is a the telltale sign that they find their master repellent. When this happens, you *know* the master has sunk into the abyss.

The contrasts are evident in the Hebrew text of 19:13. It begins with "brothers." Normally one would like to think of brothers in close proximity, but here they are "far off" (*rachaq* is verb). Normally one thinks of "acquaintances" (here we have the participial form of "to know," thus meaning, "those whom I know") in familiar terms—you "know" them, but the text says that they are "strangers" (verb is *zur*). I highlight the term *zur* because it will appear four times in the rest of Job 19 (vv 13, 15, 17, 27). Estrangement is the theme.

Verse 14 continues the catalogue of those who have rejected Job, including relatives (literally, "those who are near") and more "acquaintances." They have either "ceased/stopped" (*chadal*) from seeing him or have "forgotten" him (the familiar verb *shakach*). Even while he is at home, he is a stranger (*zur* again) or an alien in people's eyes, especially to the eyes of his maidservants and others.

## Job 19:16-20, Repulsive to Low and High

> 16 "I call to my servant, but he gives me no answer;
> I must myself plead with him.
> 17 My breath is repulsive to my wife;

> I am loathsome to my own family.
> 18 Even young children despise me;
>    when I rise, they talk against me.
> 19 All my intimate friends abhor me,
>    and those whom I loved have turned against me.
> 20 My bones cling to my skin and to my flesh,
>    and I have escaped by the skin of my teeth.

If *zur* or "stranger" captured the feel of the previous section, we now have a fourfold appearance of another verb (*chanan*) in verses 16-21. It can mean "to beg," as in verse 16, or to "have mercy" in verse 21 of the next subsection, but it also has an interesting, vivid and somewhat controversial meaning in verse 17 which normally is missed. To set the context: Job's world has been so upended that he finds himself calling to servants who don't answer him (v 16). This is the height of humiliation. Just imagine the servants in the kitchen and Job in another room. His voice weakly cries out, "Servant!" The servants huddle in the kitchen and say, "I didn't hear anything, did you?" All nod their heads. Servants don't respond to masters when they think that masters have lost their power and status. Job even is driven to beseeching/begging (*chanan*) them (v 16), but to no avail. We can imagine them trying to keep a straight face with their master who had fallen so low.

Almost all translations of verse 17 elide a fascinating translation difficulty. The NRSV is typical: "My breath is repulsive to my wife; I am loathsome to my own family." Others render it: "my own family finds me repulsive; I am loathsome to my own brothers." But *chanan* appears in verse 17 again, and if we translate it "loathsome," it would be the only place in the Bible where that is the case. Let's keep it as "implore" or "beseech" or "beg." Then, the final words are, literally, "the sons/children of my own body." But how can one "beg" the "sons of one's body"? I think Job is laying out a most pitiable thought: Because he is rejected by all the *living* people in his world, he must repair to the realm of the dead. Nothing is more pathetic than to imagine a broken man, Job, fallen from such great heights, pouring out his soul to his deceased children, as if they can hear and help him.

The young children (a rare word *avil,* derived probably from *ul,* a "sucking child/little one") "reject/abhor" (the very strong *maas*) Job. But another pathetic mini-picture follows: when Job rises up, they speak against him (v 18). We *know* that because of the previous dignity Job enjoyed that people would fall silent when he stood up (see 29:8-9). A hush allowed the great man to speak. But now the din rises as Job rises. The multiple humiliations, added to the bodily torment, make his life unbearable.

Speaking of bodily torment, Job gives us the memorable words of verse 20, "My bones cling to my skin and to my flesh." He escapes only, as both we and the Hebrew say, "by the skin of his teeth." The verb for "cling" is especially suggestive: *dabaq,* the verb first used in Gen 2:24 to express the "clinging" relationship between Adam and Eve. But Job's wife, the other half of the "clinging" couple, finds even his breath repulsive (v 17).

## Job 19:21-22, Have Pity on Me, a Repulsive Person

> 21 "Have pity on me, have pity on me, O you my friends,
>    for the hand of God has touched me!
> 22 Why do you, like God, pursue me,
>    never satisfied with my flesh?

Job is left as a blubbering mess to appeal for mercy to those who have shown him little mercy. To be fair to the friends, Job has really not given them many reasons to sidle up to him with compassion. He closes this small section with a plaintive cry to them. It is the hand of God, he says, which has "struck" (word is *naga,* which can be "touch," but often is "strike," which appears more appropriate here) him.

# 29.

# Job 19:23-29, The Appeal to a Redeemer

IN MY READING OF THE BOOK OF JOB, THE APPEAL TO A REDEEMER IN this passage is the pinnacle of his thought thus far. That actual appeal is in verses 25-27. Before he gets there, we have two verses of ever-increasing intensity (vv 23-24) as Job utters his wish for his words to be permanently recorded.

> 23 "O that my words were written down!
>   O that they were inscribed in a book!
> 24 O that with an iron pen and with lead
>   they were engraved on a rock forever!

Note the way that his thoughts ramp up in intensity in verses 23-24. He wants his words recorded and saved for posterity. But rather than just saying that or calling for a faithful amanuensis to take notes, he first wants his words *written* (the regular verb for writing—*kathab*); then he wants them *inscribed* in a book (using a much stronger verb—*chaqaq*, which means to "carve" or "cut in" or even "decree"). The noun form of *chaqaq* is *choq*, one of the eight terms used synonymously for the "law of God" in Psalm 119. So, Job wants his words both recorded but also inscribed in a book. It is sort of like writing with more permanent ink. But then, in verse 24, he rises to new rhetorical heights. He wants his words *engraved permanently* in a rock with an *iron stylus*. The verb I render "engrave" is *chatsab*, which is normally used to describe the process of cutting metals out of the earth. Job wants his words this deeply carved into all of our permanent memories.

Well, he got his wish! We should all be so fortunate.

> 25 "For I know that my Redeemer lives,
>    and that at the last he will stand upon the earth;
> 26 and after my skin has been thus destroyed,
>    then in my flesh I shall see God,
> 27 whom I shall see on my side,
>    and my eyes shall behold, and not another.
>    My heart faints within me!

But then the three verses of 19:25-27 follow, the most important verses in the Book of Job in many ways. The first verse is easy to translate and interpret; the second is much harder but probably still clear; the third is almost impossible to understand. I think the gradual progression (or regression, if you will) into unclarity is studied; i.e., it has a purpose. Job will be voicing a revolutionary thought, a thought whose radical character dawns on him as he is saying it, and it leaves him breathless. Most versions have him almost fainting at the end of verse 27. That may indeed be his reaction, but the reason for his fainting is not clearly stated. I don't believe it is the return of his exhaustion. Rather, something about his thought is so daring, so unprecedented that it, as it were, takes his breath away.

The first verse (v 25) is easy to translate, even though it is a blockbuster thought: "I know that my Redeemer (some render it

Vindicator) lives and that afterwards/at the end he shall stand on the dust (i.e., the earth)." This thought needs to be understood in the context of the evolution of Job's ideas about mediators and witnesses in 9:33-35 and 16:19. Job has been searching for some kind of help in making his case against God. There is no umpire, he sadly said, in Job 9, but he never really abandoned the thought of some kind of intermediary who would help him out.

In a dramatic jump in idea formation, the "mediator" who *didn't exist* in Job 9 became the witness in heaven who *did exist* and who spoke/will speak for Job. I argued that the natural sense of the argument in Job 16 was that this witness had to be someone other than God. You don't trash a figure as unmercifully as Job did to God in Job 16 and then calmly say, 'Oh, by the way, God, I know you are my witness.' The witness in Job 16 is a figure *apart* from God, who will speak *for* Job in the case he is preparing (13:18).

But by Job 19, this witness in heaven has morphed a bit more. All good ideas take time and many efforts to get right, and Job's thought on a Redeemer/Vindicator is no different. What he does in 19:25 is to reach back into the traditions of the Hebrew people for a term (*goel*) that already has rich salvific connotations and bring it to bear in this case. The *goel* in the Hebrew tradition may either be God or a human savior. In the latter instance it is probably a blood relative who "redeems" an oppressed family member from a difficult situation. God as *goel* is a very popular subject especially in the prophetic literature.

Again, it makes much more sense to see this figure in 19:25 as someone apart from and different from God. It is an independent entity who will stand on the earth (v 25). Notice the witness in heaven has evolved into a Redeemer on earth. Then we have the idea of Job's skin has been "rounded off" (v 26, the literal meaning of *naqaph*), a thought that isn't immediately clear but probably doesn't mean "after I die." It probably has more to do with restoration of health than destruction of the body. But then, Job will "see God" (v 26). The notion of "seeing God" or "seeing" appears three times, and must be seen as central to the development of the passage. With the Redeemer now on Job's side, he can "see" God. But the image is left undeveloped. Will Job "see God" in order to be awed by God? Will he "see God" in order to look at God rather triumphantly, because now he has a Redeemer standing next to him, delivering him *from* God?

It is the thought of actually facing God, which he has been calling for already for several chapters, that overwhelms Job emotionally in verse 27. The actual thought of seeing God makes his heart "yearn" or "faint" (*kalah*). Again, the language is maddeningly elusive. Yet, the verb *kalah* is enormously suggestive in verse 27. Normally it means "to complete" or "finish," as when God finished/completed the work of creation (Gen 2:1, 2). If we kept that sense here, Job would be uttering the thought that his life is somehow finished/complete when he can see God. Not a bad thought.

But we ought not to leave this essay without recognizing the revolutionary nature of what Job has just done. He has now more firmly than ever uttered the hope for a figure *separate from God* who will save him. Christian theologians run to Jesus as the one whom Job must have been unconsciously adumbrating. Yet, that isn't satisfactory. Job 19 has a meaning as uttered, in the world in which it was uttered, and that utterance is defined by the way words and concepts were used at the time it was uttered. Job 19 differs from Job 16 by using a term well-known in Hebrew thought, a term that has a long history as a human deliverer when a person is oppressed.

To read Job as being in any situation other than at enmity with God at this point is to be untrue to the text. He did, of course, entertain the notion in 14:13ff that God was just going through a bad spot, a fit of anger perhaps, and that after God had put aside his anger Job would come back to be with God. But that hasn't happened. No way has that happened. Job has dug in his heels more firmly as time goes on. He has prepared his case. He is ready to argue it. But now he has a Redeemer, a genuine savior, on his side. God may have been silent for too long...

The truly scary thought that Job has opened at this point is whether one really *needs* God once the hope for a Redeemer is mentioned. As I will argue in my treatment of Elihu's usually ignored speeches (Job 32-37), Elihu inadvertently gives Job a method of living his life happily without God. And, to make things even more unexpected, Job will take Elihu up on it. But that gets us, once again, ahead of ourselves. As Job 19 draws to a close, we have a more confident Job, a Job who has used the time of divine silence to develop his own take on life, a take that will be increasingly powerful and convincing as the text unfolds, and a take that increasingly doesn't really need God.

> 28 If you say, 'How we will persecute him!'
>     and, 'The root of the matter is found in him';
> 29 be afraid of the sword,
>     for wrath brings the punishment of the sword,
>     so that you may know there is a judgment."

Except as indicated in the next paragraph, I have nothing to say here about the confusing final verses of the chapter (Job 19:28-29), though I try to make sense of them in my detailed commentary.

# 30.

## Job 20, Zophar Once More

AFTER JOB'S LIFE-REORIENTING REALIZATION OF A REDEEMER OR VINdicator who will one day stand upon the earth, he utters two verses (19:28-29) that appear to have no relationship to the preceding thoughts. They seem to be a criticism of the friends, suggesting that the punishment the friends think is reserved for Job will be visited upon them. This is important in order to understand the tone of Zophar's speech in Job 20, though Zophar quickly deflects the criticism in order to focus on his (and his friends') favorite topic: the grisly punishment awaiting the wicked.

We might outline this long chapter as follows:

Job 20:1-11, The Fate of the Wicked, Part I
Job 20:12-18, The Poisonous Bite of Asps and Cobras
Job 20:19-29, The Fate of the Wicked, Part II

# Job 20:1-11, The Fate of the Wicked, Part I

> 1 Then Zophar the Naamathite answered:
> 2 "Pay attention! My thoughts urge me to answer,
>   because of the agitation within me.
> 3 I hear censure that insults me,
>   and a spirit beyond my understanding answers me.
> 4 Do you not know this from of old,
>   ever since mortals were placed on earth,
> 5 that the exulting of the wicked is short,
>   and the joy of the godless is but for a moment?
> 6 Even though they mount up high as the heavens,
>   and their head reaches to the clouds,
> 7 they will perish forever like their own dung;
>   those who have seen them will say, 'Where are they?'
> 8 They will fly away like a dream, and not be found;
>   they will be chased away like a vision of the night.
> 9 The eye that saw them will see them no more,
>   nor will their place behold them any longer.
> 10 Their children will seek the favor of the poor,
>   and their hands will give back their wealth.
> 11 Their bodies, once full of youth,
>   will lie down in the dust with them.

Zophar and his two friends, Eliphaz and Bildad, spend a lot of time talking about the punishment the wicked will endure. Does that reflect a lack of creativity on their part or the author's part, as if the only really important thing for the Book of Job is the development of Job's thought, with the friends being mere 'background noise' until Job reaches the Redeemer or other ideas? Or, does the repetition of ideas mirror life pretty accurately— that most of us have our bedrock beliefs that we return to again and again in our speech?

The author is careful to point out distinctions among the friends in manner of presentation and idea development, especially in the First Cycle of speeches, but by the time we are in the Second and Third Cycles, the individuality of the friends recedes more and more into the background so that they become stock characters. They repeat hackneyed phrases, even though Zophar tries, mostly unsuccessfully, to rise to great rhetorical heights when he describes how snake poison will kill the wicked (vv 12-16).

Though the friends' ideas may recede in importance, the author gives Zophar 29 verses here, much more than the 20 verses of Job 11. Even if we are to look at the final speech in Job 27 as a combined Job/Zophar speech, with the two speaking over each other and with Job speaking in a mocking tone and Zophar deadly serious, this speech exceeds the latter in length by several verses. Job 20 is hard to outline because it presents only one idea (the certainty of punishment for the wicked), but the outline suggested above is serviceable.

Zophar begins by acknowledging the tone of Job's last words in Job 19 before turning to the topic at hand. Job 20:2-3 are difficult to translate. "Therefore my opinions return to me, on account of which my agitation is in me." Huh? It seems that he is stirred up by Job's last words. But he plows on, "I have heard the judgment/reproof shaming me, and the spirit of my understanding answers me" (v 3). Zophar will never receive the Nobel Prize for Clarity here, but he seems to be suggesting that his "mind" or "understanding" rather than the emotion provoked by Job's words, will now control what he says. We just wish he could have been a bit clearer on that one...

The rest of the subsection (vv 4-11) proceeds without a hitch. Once you become familiar with your favorite topic, you can speak 1000 words on it without thinking. Your mouth almost becomes twisted into various predictable forms to enable the usual words to come forth. For Zophar, these words relate to the nasty fate awaiting the wicked. It has been a rule since time immemorial (v 4) that the triumph of the wicked is short (v 5). They may seem to have it all going for them, with even their "excellency/haughtiness" (Zophar can be hard to translate—the word is a *hapax, si)* reaching heaven, but soon they will perish like their own dung (v 7). I think Zophar is trying to make the wicked sound dirty and despicable, though if you think about it, dung can last a long time and has a quite useful afterlife as fertilizer. So, he changes his image and talks about the wicked flying away like a dream (v 8). But Zophar can't end on that note of clarity. He returns to the obscure, "His children shall appease/receive the poor favorably" and "his hands shall restore his wealth" (v 10). Huh? He may be suggesting that God's justice works so well in this life that even before the wicked die his children shall seek some kind of reconciliation with those oppressed by the wicked. The wicked person himself may even restore the wealth stolen. But by now Zophar has descended into his own netherworld of confusion, and then he changes the topic a bit.

## Job 20:12-18, The Poisonous Bite of Asps and Cobras

> 12 "Though wickedness is sweet in their mouth,
>   though they hide it under their tongues,
> 13 though they are loath to let it go,
>   and hold it in their mouths,
> 14 yet their food is turned in their stomachs;
>   it is the venom of asps within them.
> 15 They swallow down riches and vomit them up again;
>   God casts them out of their bellies.
> 16 They will suck the poison of asps;
>   the tongue of a viper will kill them.
> 17 They will not look on the rivers,
>   the streams flowing with honey and curds.
> 18 They will give back the fruit of their toil,
>   and will not swallow it down;
>   from the profit of their trading
>   they will get no enjoyment.

Zophar is still talking about the fate of the wicked, but now he tries to describe the actual pains they will suffer. But his attempt is like an apprentice trying to imitate a Rembrandt. There might be some resemblance to the work of the great artist, but mostly it is 'student work.' Zophar will describe how the sin of the wicked starts in the mouth (v 12), is hidden under his tongue but then it turns into the poison of asps in his bowels (v 14). An image of vomiting follows (v 15), with more references to sucking poison of asps, cobras or vipers (v 16). We give him light applause, but he really needed to learn how to describe exactly how guts spill out and poison distorts features, takes away breath, makes eyes bulge and all other kinds of gory details. We thank Zophar for his attempt at describing poison, but he quickly retreats in verses 19-29 to the fate of the wicked again. Perhaps he realizes also that his brief foray into describing poison's effects wasn't too successful.

## Job 20:19-29, The Fate of the Wicked, Part II

> 19 "For they have crushed and abandoned the poor,
>    they have seized a house that they did not build.
> 20 They knew no quiet in their bellies;
>    in their greed they let nothing escape.
> 21 There was nothing left after they had eaten;
>    therefore their prosperity will not endure.
> 22 In full sufficiency they will be in distress;
>    all the force of misery will come upon them.
> 23 To fill their belly to the full
>    God will send his fierce anger into them,
>    and rain it upon them as their food.
> 24 They will flee from an iron weapon;
>    a bronze arrow will strike them through.
> 25 It is drawn forth and comes out of their body,
>    and the glittering point comes out of their gall;
>    terrors come upon them.
> 26 Utter darkness is laid up for their treasures;
>    a fire fanned by no one will devour them;

>    what is left in their tent will be consumed.
> 27 The heavens will reveal their iniquity,
>    and the earth will rise up against them.
> 28 The possessions of their house will be carried away,
>    dragged off in the day of God's wrath.
> 29 This is the portion of the wicked from God,
>    the heritage decreed for them by God."

Zophar keeps hammering away at the hapless victim of his soliloquy—the wicked. You wonder if he is looking directly at Job when he is saying this, though too "polite" to say "You are the man!" to Job, or whether he is just spouting theological verities and expecting Job to apply the lesson to his own heart. In any case, he finishes his labored description here. He actually begins with a useful thought: "For he (the wicked) oppresses and forsakes the poor; he has violently taken a house and shall not build it up" (v 19). There is a very strong and useful tradition in ancient Israelite thought about the judgment awaiting those who oppress the helpless and the poor, and Zophar continues that theme. Again, his words are useful: "Because he knows no ease/quietness in his own breast" (v 20). These thoughts could become a theology analyzing oppression, but instead Zophar concludes his thoughts by returning to a species of goriness we haven't heard from him: instead of snakebites killing the wicked, the wicked now will have iron weapons thrust through his midsection (vv 24-25). The "glittering point" of the arrow will come out of the stomach. Great. But the image quickly changes to a fire that will consume the wicked person (v 26). His goods will all flow away from him in the day of his (God's) wrath (v 28). Then, just as if he has put together a tidy and well-argued disquisition, he concludes, "This is the portion of the wicked from God; the inheritance of his matter/word from God" (v 29). Zophar rests his case: wicked clobbered.

# 31.

# Job 21-27, Introduction to the Third Cycle of Speeches

We now begin the Third Cycle of speeches (Job 21-27). The cycle starts predictably enough. Job first speaks, then Eliphaz; Job then speaks again, followed by Bildad. But Bildad's third speech in is only six verses in length (25:1-6). It seems that Bildad is just getting warmed up in characterizing humans as "maggots" and "worms" when someone pulls the plug. Then, all serious students of the book have noted what appears to be a truncation of this cycle in Chapters 26 and 27. Only Job is said to speak in these chapters. I will still stay with the suggestion I advanced in the introduction: that Job 26 is Job's third speech of the cycle, and that Job 27, beginning with verse 13, reflects the *combined* voice of Job and Zophar. Job is said to be speaking it, but it really reflects Zophar's theology. My suggestion is to see the two speakers talking over each other, perhaps with Job's voice being the louder. But Job speaks in a mocking tone and Zophar is deadly serious. That, at least at this point, is still my thesis for the Third Cycle. It really *is* a complete cycle, and reading it as I have done lets the author present it in an artistically imaginative way.

I identified Job's two anchor emotions in Job 3-20 as anger and grief. Many ideas emerged from those anchor emotions, but the primary focus was on the effect of Job's suffering on himself. It is a very natural or realistic way of presenting suffering. We first feel the pain of our own bodies, and then react to that pain. That is what Job does.

But now, in the Third Cycle, Job changes his focus. While still referring occasionally to his pain, and especially in Job 23 to the case he is presenting against God, he focuses more on the myriad ways that the wicked oppress others and seem to get off without serious repercussions.

# 32.

# Job 21, No Judgment on the Wicked

In Job 21, Job turns to the fate of the wicked, a topic also of great interest to the three conversation partners. It is a fairly straightforward speech, one of Job's clearest. Yet, as Job speaks, he will turn the ideas of his friends upside down. Rather than being punished, the wicked flourish. We can outline this chapter as follows:

> Job 21:1-16, Mock on, Friends!
> Job 21:17-26, The Wicked Suffer No Loss, Part I
> Job 21:27-34, The Wicked Suffer No Loss, Part II

## Job 21:1-16, Mock on, Friends!

> 1 Then Job answered:
> 2 "Listen carefully to my words,
>   and let this be your consolation.
> 3 Bear with me, and I will speak;

> then after I have spoken, mock on.
> 4 As for me, is my complaint addressed to mortals?
>   Why should I not be impatient?
> 5 Look at me, and be appalled,
>   and lay your hand upon your mouth.
> 6 When I think of it I am dismayed,
>   and shuddering seizes my flesh.
> 7 Why do the wicked live on,
>   reach old age, and grow mighty in power?
> 8 Their children are established in their presence,
>   and their offspring before their eyes.
> 9 Their houses are safe from fear,
>   and no rod of God is upon them.
> 10 Their bull breeds without fail;
>   their cow calves and never miscarries.
> 11 They send out their little ones like a flock,
>   and their children dance around.
> 12 They sing to the tambourine and the lyre,
>   and rejoice to the sound of the pipe.
> 13 They spend their days in prosperity,
>   and in peace they go down to Sheol.
> 14 They say to God, 'Leave us alone!
>   We do not desire to know your ways.
> 15 What is the Almighty, that we should serve him?
>   And what profit do we get if we pray to him?'
> 16 Is not their prosperity indeed their own achievement?
>   The plans of the wicked are repugnant to me.

Job will not actually get to the major point of his speech until verse 7, when he specifically addresses the fate of the wicked, but in the meantime (vv 2-6) he both addresses the three friends and then, as it were, says he really isn't talking to them. We may see some irony in verse 2 when Job urges the friends to listen, and "this will be your consolation." But we may also take that phrase to mean that *their* act of being silent will be a consolation *to Job*. It will be a consolation because their silence is golden; he won't have to respond to baseless charges and hyperventilating attacks.

Job's tone turns derisive. "Bear with me, and I will speak. Then, you can mock on" (v 3). He says nothing about their possible sincerely-held beliefs or commitment to basic principles of Israelite religion. To Job, his friends are now just mockers. Then, to bury them further into oblivion, he says, "In fact, do I complain to people?" (answer assumed: NO!). Job is *so* done with them. He really just wants to talk with God (he will say this more explicitly in Job 23). He asks, "Why shouldn't I be impatient?" (v 4). This question, literally, reads, "Why shouldn't I cut short my spirit?" with the verb for "cut short" (*qatsar*) being the regular verb for cutting the fields at harvest. Job's condition is really a horrible one (v 6).

But now Job turns to the nub of his complaint, a complaint that will occupy him for the rest of the chapter. In a word it is that God really doesn't punish the wicked. All that talk about the wicked dying a miserable death, with arrows piercing their viscera, their guts pouring out, and asps poisoning them, really isn't happening. Job states his case for this in verses 7-16. His question in verse 7 implies a lifetime of safety, rather than of danger, for the wicked. They live and grow old, but they are also mighty in power. Rather than being visited with miserable sufferings, the wicked are born in safety, live in prosperity and become old in power. And, not only that. They have children that grow up right before their eyes (v 8), who live in security and prosperity (vv 9-10). They have periodic parties, singing to the tune of timbrel and harp (v 11). You wonder if when Job uttered this he had the sad memory of his children, festively celebrating when the roof collapsed on them. Yet, even as the wicked prosper, they reject God (vv 14-16). They have all they need without God; why bring in God to muck things up?

# Job 21:17-26, The Wicked Suffer No Loss, Part I

> 17 "How often is the lamp of the wicked put out?
> How often does calamity come upon them?
> How often does God distribute pains in his anger?
> 18 How often are they like straw before the wind,
> and like chaff that the storm carries away?
> 19 You say, 'God stores up their iniquity for their children.'
> Let it be paid back to them, so that they may know it.
> 20 Let their own eyes see their destruction,
> and let them drink of the wrath of the Almighty.
> 21 For what do they care for their household after them,
> when the number of their months is cut off?
> 22 Will any teach God knowledge,
> seeing that he judges those that are on high?
> 23 One dies in full prosperity,
> being wholly at ease and secure,
> 24 his loins full of milk
> and the marrow of his bones moist.
> 25 Another dies in bitterness of soul,
> never having tasted of good.
> 26 They lie down alike in the dust,
> and the worms cover them.

We really don't have neatly separated sections of this chapter. The thought is one and the same: the wicked, whom the friends love to bash, are really the blessed ones in life. They live in peace; they are prosperous; their children have children; their animals don't miscarry; they live a full life. In this section Job begins by posing a few questions: "How often is the lamp of the wicked *extinguished?*" (turning back on Bildad the same verb, *daak,* that he used in 18:5, 6 to describe the certainty of the wicked's fall). Does calamity come upon them? (v 17). The answer, of course, is

'No!' If indeed God is laying up punishment for them, let it come! Why keep threatening it? Why not actually show it?

Verse 22 acts to soften Job's seemingly certain tone of the previous verses. He expects a negative answer to the question in verse 22, "Will any teach God knowledge, seeing that he judges those that are on high?" Job recognizes his own limited knowledge and that God judges angels (and perhaps the heavenly bodies) on high. Rather than saying that the wicked always prosper, it might be better to say that Job admits he hasn't discerned all the principles of divine judgment. His certainty thus morphs in verses 23-26 into "one dies" in full ease and quiet while "another dies" in bitterness of soul. God may have something in mind in all of this, but from the human perspective it just seems that there are no definite rules of life.

## Job 21:27-34, The Wicked Suffer No Loss, Part II

> 27 "Oh, I know your thoughts,
>   and your schemes to wrong me.
> 28 For you say, 'Where is the house of the prince?
>   Where is the tent in which the wicked lived?'
> 29 Have you not asked those who travel the roads,
>   and do you not accept their testimony,
> 30 that the wicked are spared in the day of calamity,
>   and are rescued in the day of wrath?
> 31 Who declares their way to their face,
>   and who repays them for what they have done?
> 32 When they are carried to the grave,
>   a watch is kept over their tomb.
> 33 The clods of the valley are sweet to them;
>   everyone will follow after,
>   and those who went before are innumerable.
> 34 How then will you comfort me with empty nothings?
>   There is nothing left of your answers but falsehood."

Verses 27-28 are most likely quite subtle. Job says that he knows the thoughts of his friends (v 27), but then we have, "For you say, 'Where is the house of the prince? And where is the tent where the wicked dwell?" (v 28). Job is probably suggesting that this refers to him: the friends are using *him* as Exhibit A for the truth of the principle of divine justice: Job got clobbered, ergo Job is a bad sinner. But Job quickly turns that argument back on the friends. All you have to do is ask those who walk on the road—they will tell you differently—that the wicked are spared in the day of calamity. The final words are that the "clods/mud" of the earth will be sweet to him (the wicked). His funeral train will have innumerable people following along (v 33). The friends' words are false and vain (v 34). Job is a still very much a fighting man.

# 33.

# Job 22, Eliphaz's Allegations Against Job

OF ALL THE THREE FRIENDS, ELIPHAZ DEVELOPS AND CHANGES HIS arguments most significantly over the course of Job 3-27. His first speech, in Job 4-5, was a model of decorum and calm encouragement of Job. Rather than concluding that Job was a sinner or expositing the full scope of the doctrine of retribution, Eliphaz laid out some basic principles about human impurity and then gently tried to interpret Job's distress as an expression of God's discipline (5:17-27). Discipline is not a bad thing. God uses it for our good. Job may be on the verge of descending into foolishness (5:1-7), but Job's task was to commit himself anew to God (5:8-16). That was the tone and content of Eliphaz's first speech.

Eliphaz changed his tone considerably in his second speech, Job 15. Picking up on Bildad's subtle hint of Job's "windiness" (8:2) possibly being related to the "wind" of God that tumbled the house that killed Job's children, Eliphaz also became more biting and judgmental. He also talked about Job's filling himself with the (dangerous) "east wind" (15:1). He accused Job of hindering faith—his and others (15:4) and being driven by his own craftiness (15:5). Job is not unique, but he acts like he is. Finally, Eliphaz concluded Job 15 by painting the final fate of the wicked with savage colors and brutal brush strokes. The wicked writhe amid terrors all their years (15:19-20). Certainly Job is in danger of joining their company.

Thus, when a prominent commentator begins his remarks on Job 22 with the statement, "Eliphaz is a good man," (Francis Anderson, *Job: An Introduction and Commentary*, 202), I scratch my head. He is definitely has more diplomatic skills than his two compatriots, but he is cut from the same cloth. He still holds out hope for Job's confession and "returning to the Almighty" (22:23), but he will utter that hope after laying out a catalogue of damning allegations against Job without any supporting evidence. He is no less judgmental than his friends; he only knows how to conceal it with prettier words. We see this all the time in our day.

We can divide Eliphaz's words in Job 22 as follows:

Job 22:1-11, Introduction and Job's Moral Lapses
Job 22:12-20, God is Truly in Charge
Job 22:21-30, One Last Chance to Repent

## Job 22:1-11, Introduction and Job's Moral Lapses

> 1 Then Eliphaz the Temanite answered:
> 2 "Can a mortal be of use to God?
>     Can even the wisest be of service to him?
> 3 Is it any pleasure to the Almighty if you are righteous,
>     or is it gain to him if you make your ways blameless?
> 4 Is it for your piety that he reproves you,
>     and enters into judgment with you?
> 5 Is not your wickedness great?
>     There is no end to your iniquities.

> 6 For you have exacted pledges from your family for no reason,
>     and stripped the naked of their clothing.
> 7 You have given no water to the weary to drink,
>     and you have withheld bread from the hungry.
> 8 The powerful possess the land,
>     and the favored live in it.
> 9 You have sent widows away empty-handed,
>     and the arms of the orphans you have crushed.
> 10 Therefore snares are around you,
>     and sudden terror overwhelms you,
> 11 or darkness so that you cannot see;
>     a flood of water covers you.

Eliphaz at first tries a different approach to penetrate the bastions of Job's defenses, though he will quickly abandon it. Rather than Job being at the center of a cosmic drama, which Job seemingly believes, Eliphaz asserts that Job is really insignificant. "Is it any pleasure to the Almighty if you are righteous?" (v 3). That is, God is unmoved by your writhing in pain and will also take no notice of your goodness. 'God really has better things to do than pay attention to you, Job.' Perhaps Eliphaz is thinking that Job will thereby be humbled, see the error of his ways, confess to God and be restored.

But as with many argumentative trial balloons, this one also comes crashing down. By verse 5 Eliphaz gets to where he feels more comfortable: criticizing Job for his moral lapses. Job has great wickedness; there is no end to his sin (v 5). Eliphaz's criticism turns more granular: Job has taken pledges of people without returning them in a timely fashion (violating the biblical injunction in Ex 22:26); he has not fed the hungry; he has sent widows away empty; he has crushed the orphans (vv 5-9). It is a catalogue of severe allegations, accusing Job of singling out the most vulnerable people in society and either ignoring them or making their lives worse. Therefore, Job is now reaping what he has sown. "Therefore snares are around you" (v 10). The very darkness into which Job wanted to descend (10:21-22) has now fully enveloped him, according to Eliphaz (v 11). Eliphaz has one more allegation to hurl Job's way. Eliphaz says that Job believes that God has hidden Himself in the clouds and really is ignorant of what is happening on earth (v 13). These allegations are of such severity and specificity that Job will feel he needs to respond to some of them in his final speech in Job 29-31.

## Job 22:12-20, God is Truly in Charge

> 12 "Is not God high in the heavens?
>   See the highest stars, how lofty they are!
> 13 Therefore you say, 'What does God know?
>   Can he judge through the deep darkness?
> 14 Thick clouds enwrap him, so that he does not see,
>   and he walks on the dome of heaven.'
> 15 Will you keep to the old way
>   that the wicked have trod?
> 16 They were snatched away before their time;
>   their foundation was washed away by a flood.
> 17 They said to God, 'Leave us alone,'
>   and 'What can the Almighty do to us?'
> 18 Yet he filled their houses with good things—
>   but the plans of the wicked are repugnant to me.
> 19 The righteous see it and are glad;
>   the innocent laugh them to scorn,
> 20 saying, 'Surely our adversaries are cut off,
>   and what they left, the fire has consumed.'

Eliphaz accuses Job of thinking that God just doesn't see what is going on in the world (v 14). We actually can comment on this one. *Au contraire!* Job's problem with God is *not* that God is too distant but that God is too close. When someone, like Eliphaz here, makes a statement that is so obviously very wide of the mark, we wonder if the person's judgment in general is impaired or that he has just missed the point here. In fact, Eliphaz then descends into unclear words in the rest of this mini-section. His reference to people of old being "snatched away" before their time may refer to the Great Flood (v 16), but he doesn't help us out by connecting his words with Job's actions. Eliphaz characterizes these old-time people as saying to God, "Leave us alone" (v 17), presumably to tie them to Job's words to God to leave him alone (10:20), but he doesn't make a skillful connection. The only intelligible thing he has said in these nine verses is in the first verse—"Is not God in the heavens?" (v 12). He should have stopped there.

## Job 22:21-30, One Last Chance to Repent

> 21 "Agree with God, and be at peace;
>     in this way good will come to you.
> 22 Receive instruction from his mouth,
>     and lay up his words in your heart.
> 23 If you return to the Almighty, you will be restored,
>     if you remove unrighteousness from your tents,
> 24 if you treat gold like dust,
>     and gold of Ophir like the stones of the torrent-bed,
> 25 and if the Almighty is your gold
>     and your precious silver,
> 26 then you will delight yourself in the Almighty,
>     and lift up your face to God.
> 27 You will pray to him, and he will hear you,
>     and you will pay your vows.
> 28 You will decide on a matter, and it will be established for you,
>     and light will shine on your ways.
> 29 When others are humiliated, you say it is pride;
>     for he saves the humble.

> 30 He will deliver even those who are guilty;
> they will escape because of the cleanness of your
> hands."

Even though Eliphaz has compromised himself intellectually by this point, he still has one more thing to say. He urges Job to get himself "right" with God. "If you return to the Almighty, you will be built up" (v 23). Though some of his words aren't crystal clear, the tone is clear enough. If you, Job, delight yourself in the Almighty and lift up your face in prayer, then God will hear you (v 27). Light will flood your path (v 28). God delivers people even if they are guilty (v 30). Good liquid can come from cracked vessels, to be sure, though most of the liquid might run have run out by the time you actually want a drink...

# 34.

## Job 23, Job Is Back on the Offensive

ONE MAJOR DEVELOPMENT IN JOB'S THOUGHT IN THE SECOND CYCLE of speeches was his framing of his complaint in the form of a lawsuit against God. "I have indeed prepared my case; I know that I shall be vindicated" (13:18). Job spends a good part of his second series of three speeches (12-14; 16-17; 19) also doing a few other things (mourning because of his injuries, complaining about God's attack) but he really is interested in preparing his case. He feels he has an airtight case against God. Job has done nothing deserving the kind of vicious treatment that God has meted out to him. He will show God how this is true.

We return to the idea of Job's making the case against God in Job 23-24. Job won't put his finishing touches on the case until Job 31 when he actually signs the document ("Here is my signature! Let the Almighty answer me" (31:35)), but here we see further thoughts on the development of his case. Lawsuits require a lot of preparation, especially if you expect to win them. But here we not only have what one might call the content of the case ("I am innocent") but also Job's fears about court procedure. One fear is that he doesn't know in fact where to find God; the other fear is that when he actually *does* find God, God will terrify him. Job doesn't have the protections that are vested in the American court system, where parties are put at separate tables and each can, at best, calmly present the case before judge or jury. So, he expresses both his hopes and fears in Chapter 23.

> Job 23:1-7, Laying Out the Case Before God
> Job 23:8-12, I am Innocent... But
> Job 23:13-17, ... Terrified

## Job 23:1-7, Laying Out the Case Before God

> 1 Then Job answered:
> 2 "Today also my complaint is bitter;
>     his hand is heavy despite my groaning.
> 3 Oh, that I knew where I might find him,
>     that I might come even to his dwelling!
> 4 I would lay my case before him,
>     and fill my mouth with arguments.
> 5 I would learn what he would answer me,
>     and understand what he would say to me.
> 6 Would he contend with me in the greatness of his power?
>     No; but he would give heed to me.
> 7 There an upright person could reason with him,
>     and I should be acquitted forever by my judge.

As Job prepares to submit his case, his tone is confident. There is only one hitch that might derail things. He can't find God, the defendant. He starts out with unexpectedly rich eloquence: "My complaint is bitter; sighing has made my hand listless" or "My hand is heavy because of my groaning" (v 2). We want to get lost in his rhetoric, but he quickly moves on: "Oh that I knew where

I could find him" (v 3). You would think that God would *want* to be accessible to His children. But Job has found it otherwise. The form of the Book of Job confirms Job's feeling. God is silent from Job 3-37. Job is confident, however, that he already knows how his lawsuit will turn out. He would fill his mouth with arguments (v 4). He would make his case; he could even predict how God would respond (v 5). The result would be, in a surprisingly difficult verb to translate despite the simplicity of its basic meaning (the common verb *sim* ("to put/place")) that God would "take note of me" or "give heed" or "put strength" in me (v 6). Maybe Job is still a bit too fearful to state exactly how he believes God will deal with him, even though we get the impression that Job feels God would listen and acquit him. "An upright person could reason with him." Job is confident that "I should be acquitted forever by my judge" (v 7).

When a lawsuit is in preparation by an attorney, the client goes through immense emotional swings. On the one hand, the client feels that the case is a 'slam dunk.' But then doubts creep in and, on other occasions, the client feels that it is a lost cause. Job reflects both of those feelings. Here he is confident. Later in the chapter he will be very worried.

## Job 23:8-12, I am Innocent... But

> 8 "If I go forward, he is not there;
> or backward, I cannot perceive him;
> 9 on the left he hides, and I cannot behold him;
> I turn to the right, but I cannot see him.
> 10 But he knows the way that I take;
> when he has tested me, I shall come out like gold.
> 11 My foot has held fast to his steps;
> I have kept his way and have not turned aside.
> 12 I have not departed from the commandment of his lips;
> I have treasured in my bosom the words of his mouth.

In between these two emotions of confidence and terror is Job's belief that he is innocent. Even though God seems to be hiding, God knows Job's steps. When Job is tested, he shall come out like gold (v 10). We get another unexpectedly rich literary description of God's absence in verses 8-9. It is almost as if Job is rummaging about for something he has misplaced: "If I go forward, he is not there; or backward, I cannot perceive him; or on the left he hides, and I cannot behold him; I turn to the right, but I cannot see him" (vv 8-9). The nub of his case is in verses 11-12. "My foot has held fast to his steps; I have kept his way and have not turned aside." We are touched by Job's clarity, directness and confidence.

## Job 23:13-17, ... Terrified

> 13 "But he stands alone and who can dissuade him?
>  What he desires, that he does.
> 14 For he will complete what he appoints for me;
>  and many such things are in his mind.
> 15 Therefore I am terrified at his presence;
>  when I consider, I am in dread of him.
> 16 God has made my heart faint;
>  the Almighty has terrified me;
> 17 If only I could vanish in darkness,
>  and thick darkness would cover my face!"

Though Job is confident that he has an air-tight case, he is worried that he might be suing someone who doesn't play by basic rules of fairness. Job expresses his uncertainty, and even his despair, in verse 13, "But he (God) stands alone and who can dissuade him? What he desires, that he does." Job's worry here is the concern of every vulnerable plaintiff. 'What if the defendant pulls a fast one on me? What about if the rules of justice don't apply to my opponent?' Ultimately this fear will get the better of Job. Though he wonders if God will sit down and speak rationally to him, his stronger suspicion is that God will pull rank and be governed by irrationality and anger and just do whatever God wants. That is why Job says that "I am terrified at his presence; when I consider, I am in dread of him" (v 15).

Job has put his finger on a significant issue here. I argued previously that his discovery of or positing a Redeemer or Vindicator in 19:25 was the most audacious intellectual move in the Book of Job. His most audacious tactical move is suggested in this inner soliloquy about his terror. That is, I will argue that his tactical move here, of stating his fear at God's potential irrationality, will give him justification later in the book actually to leave God, to leave faith, if God acts in a way that may be characterized as irrational or unreasonable. Make no mistake about it. Job feels he has a case. He wants someone to speak rationally to him and consider his complaint. He is afraid that God will pull rank and just obliterate him. That is, many think, exactly what God will do starting in Job 38. By that time, however, Job will be *so* done with God's antics that God's words in Job 38-41 give him ample and good grounds to reject faith. But that is getting ahead of ourselves. We have many more chapters to treat before that case can fully be made.

# 35.

# Job 24, Continuing Job's Complaint

JOB 23 CONTAINS LINES OF POETIC BEAUTY AND SEARING PAIN. JOB 24, in contrast, presents us with problems. One problem is that the underlying Hebrew is frequently unclear; another is that some of Job's lines, especially in verses 18-25, seem more appropriate in the friends' mouths than in Job's. We can tell that the debate is running out of steam, even as the author seems determined to fill out the Third Cycle of speeches. Recognizing that Job 24 will rarely be the topic of a personal or group Bible study, I still try to supply a defensible outline:

Job 24:1, A Helpful Transition—On Holding Court
Job 24:2-4, The Conduct of the Wicked
Job 24:5-12, The Life of the Poor and Vulnerable
Job 24:13-17, Doing the Deeds in Darkness
Job 24:18-25, Judgment on the Wicked

## Job 24:1, A Helpful Transition—On Holding Court

> 1 "Why are times not kept by the Almighty,
>     and why do those who know him never see his days?

The meaning of the Hebrew text isn't crystal clear, but I suggest reading this verse in connection with the preceding chapter. There, as we recall, Job longed for an audience with God so he could present his case. In the early verses of Job 23 he even expressed confidence that God would hear and vindicate him. Yet, this confidence didn't last long. Two problems developed. First, he didn't know where to find God. Second, even if he managed to get God to answer him, he was worried that God would 'pull rank' and not respond to him justly. This terrified Job.

The opening verse of Job 24 needs to be read in connection with the foregoing. It expresses Job's (unfulfilled) desire that God would just keep "times." What that means is that God would have regular hours or places where one could predictably bring a complaint and have it adjudicated. Job no doubt is thinking of his role as distinguished elder among the people when he says this. He would sit with his fellow elders at the town gate; people would bring their complaints; he would make decisions; people would bow and retreat. That is the way justice is *supposed* to work, isn't it? Why can't God just follow this kind of simple procedure? Life would be *so* much better for all concerned if that were the case.

## Job 24:2-4, The Conduct of the Wicked

> 2 "The wicked remove landmarks;
>     they seize flocks and pasture them.
> 3 They drive away the donkey of the orphan;
>     they take the widow's ox for a pledge.
> 4 They thrust the needy off the road;
>     the poor of the earth all hide themselves.

Yet, God doesn't hold "times" or "days" (v 1) and so the wicked just keep going on in their wicked ways, plundering, marauding, oppressing, taking advantage of the weak, and not facing any kind of comeuppance, any kind of divine judgment. Job's complaint in Job 21 related to the *private* conduct of the wicked; the complaint in Job 24 now relates to their *public* conduct. Space doesn't permit a discussion of each bad act of the wicked. Suffice it to say that the first one, removing landmarks, is especially egregious because if someone takes your landmarks overnight you can wake up the next morning without your land. That is why this practice is condemned in Deut 19:14. This is only one of about five or six bad acts the wicked perform.

## Job 24:5-12, The Life of the Poor and Vulnerable

> 5 "Like wild asses in the desert
>   they go out to their toil,
>   scavenging in the wasteland
>   food for their young.
> 6 They reap in a field not their own
>   and they glean in the vineyard of the wicked.
> 7 They lie all night naked, without clothing,
>   and have no covering in the cold.
> 8 They are wet with the rain of the mountains,
>   and cling to the rock for want of shelter.
> 9 "There are those who snatch the orphan child from the breast,
>   and take as a pledge the infant of the poor.
> 10 They go about naked, without clothing;
>   though hungry, they carry the sheaves;
> 11 between their terraces they press out oil;
>   they tread the wine presses, but suffer thirst.
> 12 From the city the dying groan,
>   and the throat of the wounded cries for help;
>   yet God pays no attention to their prayer.

The language and meaning of many of these verses aren't crystalline. When it says that "they lie all night naked" (v 7) or "they are wet with the rain of the mountains" (v 8), we are probably to think of the vulnerability and exposure of the poor to the elements as they serve wicked and greedy people. The sad thing about all this is that those who are wounded by the wicked's depredations cry to God, "yet God pays no attention to their prayer" (v 12). Job may even have specific people in mind (is he speaking about himself?) as he speaks these verses. God, for His part, is silent.

## Job 24:13-17, Doing the Deeds in Darkness

> 13 "There are those who rebel against the light,
>   who are not acquainted with its ways,
>   and do not stay in its paths.
> 14 The murderer rises at dusk
>   to kill the poor and needy,
>   and in the night is like a thief.
> 15 The eye of the adulterer also waits for the twilight,
>   saying, 'No eye will see me';
>   and he disguises his face.
> 16 In the dark they dig through houses;
>   by day they shut themselves up;
>   they do not know the light.
> 17 For deep darkness is morning to all of them;
>   for they are friends with the terrors of deep darkness.

Murderers, adulterers, thieves all act at night when they perform their acts. They say, "No eye will see me" (v 15). They put on disguises, digging through houses. They reverse the order of nature: "deep darkness is morning to all of them" (v 17). Job's moral universe has been upended; the wicked want to upend even the cycles of labor and time. They will receive judgment in 24:18-25, but for now we just have a catalogue of their rapacity.

Shakespeare captured both the idea of evening as time of bad deeds, and the eventual downfall of wicked people in unforgettable lines from Act III, Scene 2 of *Richard II:*

> "Then thieves and robbers range abroad unseen,
> in murders and in outrage....
> But when from under this terrestrial ball
> He fires the proud tops of the eastern pines,
> And darts his light through every guilty hole,
> Then murders, treason, and detested sins,
> The cloak of night being plucked from off their backs,
> Stand bare and naked, trembling at themselves."

## Job 24:18-25, Judgment on the Wicked

> 18 "Swift are they on the face of the waters;
>     their portion in the land is cursed;
>     no treader turns toward their vineyards.
> 19 Drought and heat snatch away the snow waters;
>     so does Sheol those who have sinned.
> 20 The womb forgets them;
>     the worm finds them sweet;
>     they are no longer remembered;
>     so wickedness is broken like a tree.
> 21 They harm the childless woman,
>     and do no good to the widow.
> 22 Yet God prolongs the life of the mighty by his power;
>     they rise up when they despair of life.
> 23 He gives them security, and they are supported;
>     his eyes are upon their ways.
> 24 They are exalted a little while, and then are gone;
>     they wither and fade like the mallow;
>     they are cut off like the heads of grain.
> 25 If it is not so, who will prove me a liar,
>     and show that there is nothing in what I say?"

This passage is unexpected, and the Hebrew is a bit unclear, too. "He is swift upon the face of the waters; their portion is cursed in the earth; he doesn't turn (to) the way of the vineyards" (v 18). *That* is the transition verse to the final section. We *think* it must be referring to the same people who marauded under cover of darkness in the preceding section, but we go from "he" to "they" as the verse develops; we go from the seemingly unrelated ideas of waters to vineyards. If we assume that the text makes sense, it probably points to a reversal of fortunes for the wicked. Shakespeare was more eloquent..

Now in verses 19-20 a series of judgments comes down on the people who are "swift upon the face of the waters." But then, in verse 21, we seem to go back to the devouring ways of the marauder. But then, in verses 24-25, their eventual destruction is assured. "They are brought low, they are gathered in as all the others, and wither as the tops of the ears of corn" (v 24). If this section really does emphasize the judgment on the wicked, it stands in tension both with Job 21 and earlier words in this chapter. Yet, it might not be inconsistent with Job 21:18-25, where Job probably recognized that the divine ways of judgment were beyond his full understanding. Thus, Job may believe *both* propositions: the wicked get off scot-free, but sometimes they end up paying for it.

Let's just thank Job for his brilliant clarity of Job 23, his heartfelt appeal to God for an audience and the terror that grips his heart. Let him utter a few lines that don't seemingly make much sense. He has made his major points. Job needs a break, but he won't get one for a little longer. He is running on empty, and that emptiness will also be evident in his last speech(es) of this cycle (Job 26; 27).

# 36.

## Job 25, Bildad's Last Words

BILDAD'S FINAL SPEECH IS UNCHARACTERISTICALLY BRIEF (SIX VERSES). He just seems to be getting warmed up, with the germ of an idea, when the mic goes dead. No technician is in the house, and so he ends with the sound of the word "worm" or "maggot" (*toleah*) dying out before them. There may be some humor here. The author is poking fun at pretentious people. How would you like it if the last word that was ever associated with your name in a holy source is the word "maggot"?

But on a more serious note, the author may pull the plug on Bildad because he is trying to suggest that the friends' conversation has descended to such negativity (calling people "worms" and "maggots") that they are worthless conversation partners. When your conversation circles back to the fate of the wicked and the fact that humans are maggots, you aren't getting anywhere. Thus, the friends aren't advancing the issue at hand at all. They don't help Job understand if he has sinned in this instance;

they don't help Job come up with a useful explanation for how he is to go forward in life. They don't say to Job, "We are with you... God owes you an explanation." They just talk about the fate of the wicked. Thus, cutting Bildad off after six verses can be seen as a brilliant literary device that serves multiple purposes.

My review of the contents of his six-verse speech will be brief, but it may be helpful first to review Bildad's total contribution to the debate. He only gets 50 verses; Eliphaz, by contrast, got over 110 verses of air time. Eliphaz has three full speeches; Bildah has about 2 1/3. Bildad began with two thinly veiled insults in 8:1-4 before retreating to the safe haven of spiritual advice in 8:5. He spent the next dozen or so verses speaking with some eloquence on the fate of the wicked. Their confidence is "gossamer" and their trust a "spider's web" (8:14). They lean against houses only to see them collapse (8:15). Bildad held out some hope for Job, in the three last verses of Job 8, but Bildad has to pack so much into those three verses that the laughter he says will characterize the innocent (8:21) seems oddly out of place. It is like rushing in with a helping of joy to the 9/11 rescue workers three hours after the towers had collapsed.

We have recently considered Bildad's second speech in Job 18. From the perspective of vocabulary and development of a speech, he was brilliant. He deftly parried the thrust of Job in 18:2-4 before returning to the fate of the wicked. Job 18 depicted the fate of the wicked in even more lurid hues than in Job 8, and there is no concluding section of hope in Job 18. We meet darkness, deceptive counsel, nets that snare, nooses that are hidden, overwhelming terrors and enormous calamities. Rather than being brought to a righteous or good Judge, the wicked is brought to the "king of terrors" (18:14), a phrase that has such a felicitous ring until we realize that all we have here is a dazzling verbal display. If someone ever wanted to put together a children's picture book of Biblical terrors, Job 18 would be a good place to start. Maybe even hire Edward Gorey's granddaughter as the artist...

> 1 Then Bildad the Shuhite answered:
> 2 "Dominion and fear are with God;

> he makes peace in his high heaven.
> 3 Is there any number to his armies?
>   Upon whom does his light not arise?
> 4 How then can a mortal be righteous before God?
>   How can one born of woman be pure?
> 5 If even the moon is not bright
>   and the stars are not pure in his sight,
> 6 how much less a mortal, who is a maggot,
>   and a human being, who is a worm!"

As for the contents of Job 25, three points should briefly be mentioned. First, Bildad begins with reference to the greatness or immensity of God (v 2). It is a theme eloquently sung by Job in 9:5ff and less so by Zophar in Job 11. We think, 'Perhaps Bildad will use that as his starting point to try to come at Job again...'

Second, there is the contrast between the purity of God and the impurity of even the heavenly bodies (v 5). Job said that God will judge "those on high" in 21:22, and perhaps this is the same thought as in 25:5. But Bildad wants to use an *a fortiori* argument: if God judges the heavenly bodies and creatures, which by definition are purer and more "heavenly" than humans, how can humans stand a chance? We are brought into his mental workshop as he is trying to build his next argument. It doesn't, however, look like a very promising beginning.

Finally he comes crashing down with his third point in 25:6. Humans are less clean than the heavenly bodies; thus, they are "worms" and "maggots." We have two Hebrew words here: *rimah* and *toleah*. There may be very little difference between them actually. Job loves using the former word: 5/7 of its appearances in the Bible are in the Book of Job. Only in one other instance, however, are humans likened to maggots, and that use is metaphorical (17:14). Bildad is going nowhere. It is a act of mercy that the author cuts him off here.

# 37.

## Job 26, Job's Third Speech in the Third Cycle

JOB 26 PRESENTS A MARVELOUS RESPONSE TO THE FRIENDS AS WELL AS a ringing declaration of Job's continuing belief and trust in the God of Israel. What contributes to the poignancy of Job's speeches to this point in the book is that he has not abandoned his belief in God. It is *because* he continues to believe that his pain is so severe. He just can't understand how the powerful and good God in whom he believes would allow or even actively bring about the pain that he now suffers. He would like an explanation; even more, he believes he deserves an explanation. But he is also deeply committed to his blamelessness in this instance, an opinion which God, too, seems to share (Job 1:8; 2:3). He is putting together what he believes is an air-tight case, a case to which he will proudly affix his signature in 31:35.

Job 26 is only fourteen verses in length but it accomplishes two things: 1) through the mocking tone of verses 2-4, it demonstrates Job's complete alienation from his friends; and 2) through soaring and imaginative poetry in verses 5-14, it shows that Job's belief system is still intact. But verses 5-14 have, I believe, a subsidiary function. They show that Job will not only try to be straightforward and clear in his complaint but that he has really done all that he could to elicit *some* response from God.

Whenever an issue of immense social importance is broached through the legal system (the example of discrimination on the basis of color in America comes immediately to mind), the goal of the plaintiff's attorney is to find a model client. You have to find a client who has a clean criminal record, who leads a blameless or relatively blameless life, who is just the kind of person you would want your children to become. Then you can join the issue without the plaintiff's life being a distraction to the court or jury in considering the issue at hand.

This is what happens with the Book of Job. The issue of suffering disproportionate pain is best presented through the life of a blameless person. That blameless person has to show that he is still believing all the correct things up to the point of adjudication. Job 26 helps the author make that case.

> **Job 26:1-4, Mocking the Friends**
> **Job 26:5-14, God's Unsearchable Majesty.**

## Job 26:1-4, Mocking the Friends

> 1 Then Job answered:
> 2 "How you have helped one who has no power!
>     How you have assisted the arm that has no strength!
> 3 How you have counseled one who has no wisdom,
>     and given much good advice!
> 4 With whose help have you uttered words,
>     and whose spirit has come forth from you?

Though we can't hear Job's tone as he speaks his biting words in verses 2-4, they really are both a reprise of his words in 16:2, "miserable comforters are you all" and a further development of that thought. The scornful mockery comes through in the rolling crescendos of the NRSV, which is worth repeating:

"How you have helped him who has no power!
How you have assisted the arm that has no strength!
How you have counseled one who has no wisdom,
and given much advice!" (26:2-3).

The counselors are not only miserable; they are worthless. I think this tone carries over to Job 27, where Job mockingly repeats the words of the friends, perhaps over the words of Zophar, who is ready to deliver his third speech.

## Job 26:5-14, God's Unsearchable Majesty.

5 "The shades below tremble,
   the waters and their inhabitants.
6 Sheol is naked before God,
   and Abaddon has no covering.
7 He stretches out Zaphon over the void,
   and hangs the earth upon nothing.
8 He binds up the waters in his thick clouds,
   and the cloud is not torn open by them.
9 He covers the face of the full moon,
   and spreads over it his cloud.
10 He has described a circle on the face of the waters,
   at the boundary between light and darkness.
11 The pillars of heaven tremble,
   and are astounded at his rebuke.
12 By his power he stilled the Sea;
   by his understanding he struck down Rahab.
13 By his wind the heavens were made fair;

> his hand pierced the fleeing serpent.
> 14 These are indeed but the outskirts of his ways;
> and how small a whisper do we hear of him!
> But the thunder of his power who can understand?"

Job turns from his friends and delivers one of the more memorable soliloquies on the divine majesty in the Book of Job. It is breathtaking in scope as it tries to capture the amazing majesty of divine power. Job begins with trembling (v 5) which perhaps mirrors the emotion, or action, that has taken over his own heart and limbs. In this case it is "the shades below tremble," pointing to the shadowy abode of the dead and its quaking inhabitants. We would love to stop Job and ask for clarification, but he won't stop. He speaks of the regions beneath (v 6) and the vast heavens above (v 7). God has, as it were, hung the earth between these expansive realms, though the earth is hanging without a thread. No twenty-first century scientific description of the earth's location in space is any more eloquent.

The divine artistry continues. In fact, the verbs used to describe God's creative work are words we usually associate with artists. "They "cover" things or "spread out" their work (v 9). They "make circles/motions" (v 10) as they focus in on their subject. God has done that, though painting his drama on a larger canvas. But God is more than simply an artist. His mere presence makes pillars of heaven "tremble" (v 11). He shows his martial spirit and abilities by striking down Rahab (v 12), a mythological sea creature who received its first mention in in Job 9:13 as the victim of the divine anger. Make no mistake about it. Job believes in some kind of primordial battle activity of God with recalcitrant forces. "His hand pierced the fleeing serpent" (v 13).

As the creatures are awed by the display of the divine majesty, we are touched by the power of Job's description. Job tells us that this is just the beginning. In a felicitous phrase he adds, "These are indeed the outskirts of his ways" (v 14). You wonder what things would look like if Job actually described the *center* of the divine activity.

Job stops at this point. The universe is trembling. He is probably trembling. But we lose the point if we think that this is all that is at stake here. Job is really setting up God, or even laying a trap for God, in a rhetorically powerful way. Job is terrified, vulnerable, pleading. He is completely at the mercy of God. It will all be up to God now. God bears an enormous responsibility not just to Job but to all the readers who are wrestling with Job-like problems. How God handles this issue will give insight into whether the God who no doubt possesses all this power, and uses it so lavishly, is really a God who bends down and is concerned with the case of a lowly sufferer. We will get a surprising answer to that question… But first, a few more speeches.

# 38.

## Job 27, Job and Zophar Talking Over Each Other

JOB 27 PRESENTS A PROBLEM FOR ALL INTERPRETERS. THE BASIC problem is that the Third Cycle of speeches seems to break down in this chapter. The normal pattern of speaking: Job then Eliphaz; Job then Bildad; Job then Zophar, is seemingly abandoned in Job 27. In the Third Cycle we have Job and Eliphaz (Job 21-22); Job and Bildad (Job 23-25, though Bildad's second speech is only six verses); and Job and Job (Job 26-27). In addition, Job 27 begins with the unusual, "Job again picked up his discourse" (27:1). I will stick with the suggestion made earlier: that instead of having an incomplete cycle with Job somehow uttering words that don't really "fit" his theology in Job 27:13-23 (which is one reason why scholars for two centuries now have attributed those verses to Zophar), we have a complete Third Cycle, slightly shorter than the other two (seven chapters vs nine) where Job speaks his own words in 27:1-12 and then Zophar chimes in with *his* words in 27:13-23. But because the relations between friends have completely broken down at this point, and because Job knows their thoughts even before they utter them, Job is as it were "shouting" out Zophar's words *at the same time* Zophar is uttering them. But Job is talking louder. And he is sarcastic. Zophar is deadly serious. Zophar has, however, toned down his over-the-top rhetoric of Job 20 a bit, avoiding language like swords skewering the wicked, but the words of 27:13-23 are entirely consistent with his theology.

By looking at Job 27:13-23 in this way we solve both a theological and literary problem. *Theologically*, it really doesn't make sense to have Job say these lines with a straight face. He has spoken in an eloquent and heartfelt way both in Chapters 21 and 24 of the prosperity of the wicked and how they flourish in life, even though he nuances that a bit with a "some prosper/some die" approach in 24:18-25, but he never elsewhere fully adopts the confident orthodox theology of retribution of the friends. Thus, if he says the words of 27:13-23, he is saying them in a mocking tone. But he is shouting louder than Zophar; hence the author gives the impression it is Job speaking. Yet, it is Zophar's theology. By having Zophar speak here, we have a complete Third Cycle, giving the book a *literary* tidiness that it has in every other place. Of course, one may argue that the debate falls apart in the Third Cycle, and a disordered arrangement of speeches is an indication of it, but if you argue this way you still have to explain why Job is speaking 27:13-23.

Job will never abandon his belief in the all-powerful nature of God, or the justness of his cause, but his experience of suffering has convinced him that the simple doctrine of retribution as taught perhaps in the wisdom schools and other places is not true. He is not yet ready to develop a full-orbed doctrine of divine malevolence, but he could go that direction if pushed much harder. Right now he believes that God has anger-control issues and just needs a time-out until the anger passes. Then,

God will come to the divine senses, recognize the justness of Job's cause and explain what the heck God was thinking when He brought about the terrible distress that Job faced. That, at least, is Job's hope. One of the really painful things of the Book of Job, which most other people think is its singular glory, is how God presents Himself in Job 38-41. Rather than being an exemplary statement, it just confirms Job's worst fears of God. God simply doesn't have the divine emotions under control.

But I am once again getting far ahead of myself. The rest of this essay will briefly comment on Job 27, as follows:

> Job 27:1-6, Swearing on His Innocence
> Job 27:7-12, Vengeance on the Friends
> Job 27:13-23, The Fate of the Wicked

## Job 27:1-6, Swearing on His Innocence

> 1 Job again took up his discourse and said:
> 2 "As God lives, who has taken away my right,
>    and the Almighty, who has made my soul bitter,
> 3 as long as my breath is in me
>    and the spirit of God is in my nostrils,
> 4 my lips will not speak falsehood,
>    and my tongue will not utter deceit.
> 5 Far be it from me to say that you are right;
>    until I die I will not put away my integrity from me.
> 6 I hold fast my righteousness, and will not let it go;
>    my heart does not reproach me for any of my days.

Though verse 1 begins with "Job again took up his discourse," we really have no major break between Chapters 26 and 27. Job has just sung the divine vastness and greatness; now he will turn to his own oath in 27:2. There is something fitting about swearing such an oath after his hymn of Job 26 because the oath has a kind of expansiveness or vastness to it, a kind of "go-for-broke" character that seems to fit the recognition of the greatness of the God with whom Job is dealing. Job swears by every fiber of his being that he is right in this instance. He will not let his case go; in his own words, "My heart does not reproach me for any of my days" (v 6). As long as breath is in his nostrils he will speak the truth (v 4). But the great irony is that he swears by the God who has embittered him, who has taken away his right (v 2). He swears by the God who has destroyed him. He still would love to believe that this God will be of help to him to resolve the terrible mental and physical anguish which he suffers.

## Job 27:7-12, Vengeance on the Friends

> 7 "May my enemy be like the wicked,
>   and may my opponent be like the unrighteous.
> 8 For what is the hope of the godless when God cuts them off,
>   when God takes away their lives?
> 9 Will God hear their cry
>   when trouble comes upon them?
> 10 Will they take delight in the Almighty?
>   Will they call upon God at all times?
> 11 I will teach you concerning the hand of God;
>   that which is with the Almighty I will not conceal.
> 12 All of you have seen it yourselves;
>   why then have you become altogether vain?

The gloves are off. Once you have sworn by God against God, you fear nothing. So he then turns to the friends and spits out his disgust: "May my enemy be like the wicked" (v 7). At first we might not know who this "enemy" is, but the enemy morphs from a singular to a plural in verse 8, and we must see the "enemy" as Job's (former?) friends. They have liberally peppered their speeches with oblique and explicit references to Job's suffering as a result of his sin; now it is his turn to get back at them. God will cut them off. So, while he has their attention, he will become their teacher: "I will teach you concerning the hand of God" (v 11). Earlier Job had appealed to the friends using the same verb for "teach" (*yarah*) when he wanted them to "teach" him how he was in the wrong (6:24). Now he will do the teaching. But then Zophar begins to speak, and Job speaks over him. Job coats his words with a layer of sarcasm that shouts louder than Zophar's solemn intonation of the justice of God in judging the wicked.

## Job 27:13-23, The Fate of the Wicked

> 13 "This is the portion of the wicked with God,
>   and the heritage that oppressors receive from the Almighty:
> 14 If their children are multiplied, it is for the sword;
>   and their offspring have not enough to eat.
> 15 Those who survive them the pestilence buries,
>   and their widows make no lamentation.
> 16 Though they heap up silver like dust,
>   and pile up clothing like clay—
> 17 they may pile it up, but the just will wear it,
>   and the innocent will divide the silver.
> 18 They build their houses like nests,
>   like booths made by sentinels of the vineyard.
> 19 They go to bed with wealth, but will do so no more;
>   they open their eyes, and it is gone.
> 20 Terrors overtake them like a flood;
>   in the night a whirlwind carries them off.
> 21 The east wind lifts them up and they are gone;
>   it sweeps them out of their place.
> 22 It hurls at them without pity;
>   they flee from its power in headlong flight.
> 23 It claps its hands at them,
>   and hisses at them from its place."

We already have seen everything that these final eleven verses present. It is a rather standard catalogue of disasters awaiting the wicked. War, famine, disease, yawn. Terrors overtake them like a flood (v 20). Job can now say the words without any problem: "The east wind lifts them…" (v 21). The wicked are in for a world of hurt. Take that, you friends! Under your theology, you suffer. Under my theology, I laugh at you. You are the most miserable losers imaginable. Job is done with the friends. Done with his argument. Any semblance of orderly discussion has broken down. Emotions run high. We need a break—which is exactly what is coming in Job 28.

# 39.

## Job 28, Searching for Wisdom

THERE SEEMS TO BE A VIGOROUS DEBATE IN SOME SCHOLARLY QUARters as to why this chapter appears here. The tone, content, direction all seem inconsistent with what has gone before. As a result, some argue that because it interrupts the flow, that it doesn't relate to the debate, it ought to be moved or even excised. But to me its placement is not only brilliant but rather obvious. Speaking in the language of law (and Job is bringing a lawsuit), it makes procedural and substantive sense.

The procedural sense it makes is to give a pause, a break, in a proceeding where civility has broken down. The last straw, according to my interpretation, was Job's 'talking over' Zophar in Job 27, where the latter spoke the words deadly seriously while Job mocked his three companions. Complete communication breakdown. Timeout necessary.

Procedurally, then, Job 28 functions as a pause, a timeout, a breather in an intense and exhausting debate. It lends an air of mature reflection or of studied calm to a wild debate. From the perspective of the structure of the Book of Job, it is also brilliantly inserted. Job 14 and Job 28 come at 1/3 and 2/3 through the book. The former was also a poem of mature reflection and studied calm, the final words as Job launched the Second Cycle of speeches. We are given two "breaks" in the Book of Job, and they are evenly spaced.

But Job 28's placement also makes sense from a substantive perspective. That is, the actual idea discussed in the poem is exactly what everyone needs. One could argue that debate has come to an end because no one has demonstrated the kind of wisdom which shows itself in prudence, wise decisions, understanding and good judgment that is taught in that most orthodox of wisdom books—Proverbs. The participants need both a break and they need wisdom. This poem tells them, and us, both of these things.

Seen in this light, Job 28 functions perhaps like an intermission at the symphony. It both gives a break but it allows people to do some substantive talking if they desire. More than one business deal or personal relationship has developed in the 15-minute break, while for others it is the occasion to count the gray hairs in the head of the person ahead of you in the bathroom line.

Several outlines to the chapter are possible but, once you understand the preceding points, quibbling over which verse goes in which sub-section becomes relatively unimportant. My division is:

Job 28:1-11, The Diligent Search for Precious Metals
Job 28:12-19 But Where is Wisdom?
Job 28:20-28, God is the Source of Wisdom

## Job 28:1-11, The Diligent Search for Precious Metals

> 1 "Surely there is a mine for silver,
>    and a place for gold to be refined.

> 2 Iron is taken out of the earth,
>     and copper is smelted from ore.
> 3 Miners put an end to darkness,
>     and search out to the farthest bound
>     the ore in gloom and deep darkness.
> 4 They open shafts in a valley away from human habitation;
>     they are forgotten by travelers,
>     they sway suspended, remote from people.
> 5 As for the earth, out of it comes bread;
>     but underneath it is turned up as by fire.
> 6 Its stones are the place of sapphires,
>     and its dust contains gold.
> 7 That path no bird of prey knows,
>     and the falcon's eye has not seen it.
> 8 The proud wild animals have not trodden it;
>     the lion has not passed over it.
> 9 They put their hand to the flinty rock,
>     and overturn mountains by the roots.
> 10 They cut out channels in the rocks,
>     and their eyes see every precious thing.
> 11 The sources of the rivers they probe;
>     hidden things they bring to light.

One effective way to give an intellectual break is to change subjects completely. We go from the whirling east wind which sweeps the wicked away in 27:20-23 to the methodical but dangerous task of extracting precious metals from the earth in 28:1. Instead of wondering how the wicked will die, we are now in a remote, subterranean world where men of adventure put their lives on the line to find and take out silver, gold, iron and brass. Rather than darkness swallowing people, as in Job 3-27, miners actually bring light to the darkness by hewing out a shaft, or shining their flickering candles in the immense dark. Darkness is to be dispelled here rather than embraced as in several parts of Chapters 3-27.

The sense of danger and remoteness also is evident. After the shaft is broken open (v 4), people hang between the top and the bottom, "and they swing to and fro" (on ropes) or they "go to and fro" (from obscurity to society, v 4). We can see them searching, testing the walls, making sure their ropes are secure, with little comfort and fewer amenities. The place is so remote that no bird of prey has been there (v 7); the proud beasts that might rule the forest have not trodden this landscape (v 8).

And so the miner goes to work, cutting out channels and seeking out every precious thing (v 10). Diligence, danger, remoteness and the potential reward of the task are powerfully presented.

## Job 28:12-19 But Where is Wisdom?

> 12 "But where shall wisdom be found?
>   And where is the place of understanding?
> 13 Mortals do not know the way to it,
>   and it is not found in the land of the living.
> 14 The deep says, 'It is not in me,'
>   and the sea says, 'It is not with me.'
> 15 It cannot be gotten for gold,
>   and silver cannot be weighed out as its price.
> 16 It cannot be valued in the gold of Ophir,
>   in precious onyx or sapphire.
> 17 Gold and glass cannot equal it,
>   nor can it be exchanged for jewels of fine gold.
> 18 No mention shall be made of coral or of crystal;
>   the price of wisdom is above pearls.
> 19 The chrysolite of Ethiopia cannot compare with it,
>   nor can it be valued in pure gold.

Even though precious metals are in the remotest parts of the earth and can only be extracted with care, they can be found if humans exert tremendous energy to find them. Yet wisdom, a far more precious commodity, is seemingly harder to find. It escapes detection. The same question is posed once here and once in the next section: "But wisdom, where shall it be found?" (vv 12, 20). Its insistence hammers at us like the primitive jackhammers that must have penetrated the stony exterior of the mine. Where can we find wisdom? It is necessary because without wisdom no one can solve the knotty problems at hand.

Then, with a kind of sad eloquence that forever emblazons this poem on human hearts, we have humans knowing neither its location or value (v 13) and the deep and the sea saying, "It is not in me" (v 14). But that is both the nub and the rub of it. Wisdom is both *much more valuable* than precious metals and *much more inaccessible*. Our poem spends five verses (vv 15-19) talking about wisdom's incomparable value. Gold can't be compared with it, much less the striking topaz of Ethiopia or the shimmering coral of land and sea.

## Job 28:20-28, God is the Source of Wisdom

> 20 "Where then does wisdom come from?
>   And where is the place of understanding?
> 21 It is hidden from the eyes of all living,
>   and concealed from the birds of the air.
> 22 Abaddon and Death say,
>   'We have heard a rumor of it with our ears.'
> 23 God understands the way to it,
>   and he knows its place.
> 24 For he looks to the ends of the earth,
>   and sees everything under the heavens.
> 25 When he gave to the wind its weight,
>   and apportioned out the waters by measure;
> 26 when he made a decree for the rain,
>   and a way for the thunderbolt;
> 27 then he saw it and declared it;
>   he established it, and searched it out.

> 28 And he said to humankind,
> 'Truly, the fear of the Lord, that is wisdom;
>   and to depart from evil is understanding.'"

This section opens with the insistent question: "Whence does wisdom come?" It is followed by, "Where is the place of understanding?" (v 20). The only thing that any forces, human or divine, can say, is that "We have heard a rumor of it" (v 22).

We just saw that the central section of this poem closed with a statement of eloquent hopelessness. As a counter to that, this poem ends by telling us that the source of this valuable and inaccessible treasure is God. But just because that answer was predictable doesn't mean it is trite. In the statement that God is the source of wisdom is the clarity of a blue sky after days of unremitting rain. Yes, that is the source of wisdom. That is the place where understanding resides. The author employs four verbs in verse 27 to stress the solidity and divine origin of it: God "saw" it and "declared" it and "established" it and "searched it out." Certainly God will be the only source to resolve this problem.

Intermission is over. Everyone is refreshed. A hint at a possible resolution to the dilemma has been given. Now, we go back to Job and to his final speech.

# 40.

## Job 29, Job's Peroration

JOB 29-31 PRESENTS JOB'S FINAL SPEECH. IT FUNCTIONS AS HIS SUMmary statement and final declaration of innocence. But even more than that, this section brings us into the mind of Job as no other previous speech. The curtains are drawn back on his earlier life, and we see the man Job and why he could have been accorded the moniker of an "upright" and "blameless" man. In these chapters, however, we also get a kind of wistful and painful look at what Job really lost when the world came crashing down on him.

The first chapter of this three-chapter speech can be divided as follows:

Job 29:1-20, Longing for the Days of Old
Job 29:21-25, The Reaction of Those Helped by Job

## Job 29:1-20, Longing for the Days of Old

1 Job again took up his discourse and said:
2 "O that I were as in the months of old,
    as in the days when God watched over me;
3 when his lamp shone over my head,
    and by his light I walked through darkness;
4 when I was in my prime,
    when the friendship of God was upon my tent;
5 when the Almighty was still with me,
    when my children were around me;
6 when my steps were washed with milk,
    and the rock poured out for me streams of oil!
7 When I went out to the gate of the city,
    when I took my seat in the square,
8 the young men saw me and withdrew,
    and the aged rose up and stood;
9 the nobles refrained from talking,
    and laid their hands on their mouths;
10 the voices of princes were hushed,
    and their tongues stuck to the roof of their mouths.
11 When the ear heard, it commended me,
    and when the eye saw, it approved;
12 because I delivered the poor who cried,
    and the orphan who had no helper.
13 The blessing of the wretched came upon me,
    and I caused the widow's heart to sing for joy.
14 I put on righteousness, and it clothed me;
    my justice was like a robe and a turban.
15 I was eyes to the blind,
    and feet to the lame.
16 I was a father to the needy,
    and I championed the cause of the stranger.
17 I broke the fangs of the unrighteous,
    and made them drop their prey from their teeth.

> 18 Then I thought, 'I shall die in my nest,
>     and I shall multiply my days like the phoenix;
> 19 my roots spread out to the waters,
>     with the dew all night on my branches;
> 20 my glory was fresh with me,
>     and my bow ever new in my hand.'

The good old days. Yes, it is truly the case. For Job there actually were good old days, and the pain of the present is a stinging and brutal reminder of the glory of those days. That he brings up the stories of his past glories and honored position in society displays an incredible vulnerability which we haven't previously really seen from Job. We have seen him angry and grieved; we have seen him attacking the friends and declaring his innocence; we have seen him challenging God to appear to clarify the situation, but never do we see him speak of those simpler, more blessed days of his life and show them to us. The ornate vessel he once held, so to speak, is now nothing but jagged shards scattered around him. These verses bring us into the throbbingly painful, but gloriously described, memories of those days.

Verse 2 begins with a call from the depths of Job's being. Literally it is, "Who will give me like/as the months of old?" It is a question that we all know has only one possible answer to it, 'No one, Job, can restore your past glories,' even though the friends have glibly assured Job of future success.

This section may be further subdivided into the three things that Job remembers from his past: the pleasant memories of his family life; his prosperity; his honor among the people. The last one gets most of the attention, but the others deserve mention. Job longs first for the "days of his youth," which literally are the "days of his harvest" (v 4). Shakespeare, in another context, invented the phrase "salad days," and that might be appropriate here, though the emphasis seems to be on Job's earlier days of full maturity, rather than the more carefree days of youth or what we today call young adulthood.

Job is looking back on the days of his prime, perhaps not too long ago. They differed from today because the "converse/intimacy/counsel" (*sod*) of God was with him (v 4). The various possible translations for *sod* in verse 4 provoke the thought that what is most tellingly absent from Job's life now is intimacy—the intimacy that family brought. Most of us are made for both the silent and boisterous connections that come from the intimacy with one person or with a family. Most of us feel bereft if we once had those connections but they no longer exist. Job expresses his wistful longing for that time.

He also mentions the prosperity of that time, in only one verse, but it is a verse worth memorizing: "when my steps were washed with butter, and the rock poured me out rivers of oil" (v 6). We see the sleek and impressive wealth that adorned his home and his way.

But the most important movement of these verses is the description of the honor and recognition Job experienced in the former days. We can see him sitting at the gate (v 7); we descry the young men withdrawing and older men standing to greet him (v 8); we see people stopping their conversations because 'Job has arrived' (v 9).

It was not just a show, an elaborate pageant to give faux or insincere honors to the richest guy in the region. People shut up because Job had something to say (vv 10-20). The detailed catalogue in these verses of the judgments rendered and people helped has such an air of verisimilitude to it that we know a real person's life is being described. It stands in impressive contrast to the formulaic proclamations of the friends on the fate of the wicked, sprinkled like a literary sarin over the proceedings.

Job delivered the poor and those who had no help (v 12). He made the heart of the widow sing (v 12), an accomplishment that is all the more arresting when it is the post-disaster Job that is speaking, when no one is singing. He became like eyes to the blind, feet to the lame and father to the needy (vv 15-16). Justice was his cardinal principle (v 14). This was justice that served human need, that respected people of lowly status, that didn't hesitate to "break the jaws of the unrighteous" (v 16). Not only is this a powerful catalogue of Job's good acts in the past, but it serves to refute Eliphaz's petty allegations in 22:5-9.

As a result of this labor, Job entertained hopes. His fondest was that "I shall die with my nest" with "my root spread out to the waters." He hoped that his influence would be long-lasting and his final days would be spent surrounded by those he loved. It would be the crowning achievement of a life well-lived. He had every reason to believe that this would be his end.

## Job 29:21-25, The Reaction of Those Helped by Job

> 21 "They listened to me, and waited,
>    and kept silence for my counsel.
> 22 After I spoke they did not speak again,
>    and my word dropped upon them like dew.
> 23 They waited for me as for the rain;
>    they opened their mouths as for the spring rain.
> 24 I smiled on them when they had no confidence;
>    and the light of my countenance they did not extinguish.
> 25 I chose their way, and sat as chief,
>    and I lived like a king among his troops,
>    like one who comforts mourners."

We might have expected that our author would immediately go to something like 'but now everything is different.' He gets to that soon enough. But before getting there, he brings us into the reaction of those whom he served. Job's word was law. His sayings were respected. "After I spoke they did not speak again, and my word dropped upon them like the dew" (v 22). In saying that last phrase, he may have had in mind Moses' description of his inspired words in the fruitful and beautiful poem in Deut 32. Job 29:24 is hard to translate, but the chapter closes with a great summary of the preceding: "I lived like a king among his troops, like one who comforts mourners" (v 25).

Such is the power of memory, a memory that can create the past as if it were present and then, in the same moment, take away that past and bury it more deeply than the hidden precious metals of Job 28. Job faces the present, though the weight of the past is still on him.

# 41.

## Job 30, Dramatic Reversal

JOB HAD EVERY REASON TO BELIEVE THAT THE BLESSINGS THAT ATTENDED his earlier life would continue. He would continue to be faithful to God, caring for family, servants, goods and dispensing justice in the gate. God would be true to the divine end of the bargain: giving wealth, peace and long life to Job and his family.

But disaster happened. Job 30 is Job's reaction to that immediate change of fortune. It is natural to compare such a reaction to Job's first response to the disaster in Job 3. There are some similarities between the two chapters, but in Job 3 the emphasis is on the pure emotion of loss. There the poet emphasizes the desire to reverse time, or to escape from time, and the numbing awareness that this new reality would be his reality forever.

Job 30 allows a deeper look into the psychology of loss. So many ideas pour forth here, but the author has neatly divided them using the literary signal of *atah* or "but now" in verses 1, 9, 16. Job 29 described the "then" and Job 30 describes the "now."

Job 30 is, as one commentator has said, the most pathetic of Job's speeches, where pathetic means "arousing sadness or compassion."

We may conveniently divide it as follows:

Job 30:1-8, But Now They Make Fun of Me
Job 30:9-15, The Mocking Never Ends
Job 30:16-23, Job's Physical and Psychic Pain
Job 30:24-31, Utter Desolation

The major point of a few of the sections is caught most dramatically in one or very few verses. Quotation of those verses will illumine meaning.

## Job 30:1-8, But Now They Make Fun of Me

> 1 "But now they make sport of me,
>     those who are younger than I,
>     whose fathers I would have disdained
>     to set with the dogs of my flock.
> 2 What could I gain from the strength of their hands?
>     All their vigor is gone.
> 3 Through want and hard hunger
>     they gnaw the dry and desolate ground,
> 4 they pick mallow and the leaves of bushes,
>     and to warm themselves the roots of broom.
> 5 They are driven out from society;
>     people shout after them as after a thief.
> 6 In the gullies of wadis they must live,
>     in holes in the ground, and in the rocks.
> 7 Among the bushes they bray;
>     under the nettles they huddle together.
> 8 A senseless, disreputable brood,
>     they have been whipped out of the land.

"But now they make sport of me, those who are younger than

I, whose fathers I would have disdained to set with the dogs of my flock" (30:1). Job betrays both his utter reversal and his upper-class bias. He uses the example of how people whom he formerly wouldn't have noticed now hold him in contempt. Not only that, he says that the *sons* of thoroughly disreputable people are now mocking him. Even such sons would give honor to their disreputable fathers, whom Job would have ignored. But these *sons* don't even honor Job. The rest of the section is difficult to understand, but it seems to point to the realities of social life for the most disreputable people. "They are driven out from society; people shout after them as after a thief" (v 5). And, "In the gullies of wadis they must live, in holes in the ground, and in the rocks" (v 6).

## Job 30:9-15, The Mocking Never Ends

> 9 "And now they mock me in song;
>     I am a byword to them.
> 10 They abhor me, they keep aloof from me;
>     they do not hesitate to spit at the sight of me.
> 11 Because God has loosed my bowstring and humbled me,
>     they have cast off restraint in my presence.
> 12 On my right hand the rabble rise up;
>     they send me sprawling,
>     and build roads for my ruin.
> 13 They break up my path,
>     they promote my calamity;
>     no one restrains them.
> 14 As through a wide breach they come;
>     amid the crash they roll on.
> 15 Terrors are turned upon me;
>     my honor is pursued as by the wind,
>     and my prosperity has passed away like a cloud.

This section builds on the preceding by describing what these people of no reputation did to Job to humiliate him further. They even made up songs about Job (v 9).

'Look at Job, formerly rich; now he's not fit to live in a ditch.'

I just made that up. I'm sure their songs were much more eloquent. Verse 11 is difficult but yields a powerful picture. God has "opened/loosened" Job's "abundance/cord," and they have then "cast away" their "bridle." There seem to be two acts of "loosening" going on here. By loosening Job's cord or bowstring, he cannot any longer shoot his arrows; his power is gone. But this loosening is complemented with another—where the restraints or bridles of the disreputable are also loosed or released. Job is helpless while their mouths are just getting warmed up. The images now come at us furiously. They are like a rabble (v 12); they cast him away (v 12); they make his path difficult (v 13); they break through his defense lines (v 14); they turn terrors on Job (v 15). The result is that Job's prosperity "has passed away like a cloud" (v 15).

## Job 30:16-23, Job's Physical and Psychic Pain

> 16 "And now my soul is poured out within me;
>    days of affliction have taken hold of me.
> 17 The night racks my bones,
>    and the pain that gnaws me takes no rest.
> 18 With violence he seizes my garment;
>    he grasps me by the collar of my tunic.
> 19 He has cast me into the mire,
>    and I have become like dust and ashes.
> 20 I cry to you and you do not answer me;
>    I stand, and you merely look at me.
> 21 You have turned cruel to me;
>    with the might of your hand you persecute me.
> 22 You lift me up on the wind, you make me ride on it,
>    and you toss me about in the roar of the storm.
> 23 I know that you will bring me to death,
>    and to the house appointed for all living.

Until this point we have been *told* about Job's physical suffering, but we have rarely *heard* a description of it from his mouth. Here Job gives us some of the awful truth: "In the night my bones are pierced/racked; and the pain that gnaws me takes no rest" (v 18). In those words Job captures the distress of those who suffer unremitting pain. The combined sense of distress and sleeplessness gives a kind of weariness that makes questions of meaning or productivity fade away like a dying echo. Job makes it clear that God is responsible for this. He has been clear on this point for more than 20 chapters now; now he says, "He has cast me into the mire, and I have become like dust and ashes" (v 19). The worst thing in all of this is the sense of divine abandonment: "I cry to you and you do not answer me; I stand, and you merely look at me" (v 20). What conclusion is Job to draw other than, "You have turned cruel to me" (v 21)? Death is the certain end to his path (v 23).

## Job 30:24-31, Utter Desolation

> 24 "Surely one does not turn against the needy,
>   when in disaster they cry for help.
> 25 Did I not weep for those whose day was hard?
>   Was not my soul grieved for the poor?
> 26 But when I looked for good, evil came;
>   and when I waited for light, darkness came.
> 27 My inward parts are in turmoil, and are never still;
>   days of affliction come to meet me.
> 28 I go about in sunless gloom;
>   I stand up in the assembly and cry for help.
> 29 I am a brother of jackals,
>   and a companion of ostriches.
> 30 My skin turns black and falls from me,
>   and my bones burn with heat.
> 31 My lyre is turned to mourning,
>   and my pipe to the voice of those who weep."

Job's moral indignation knows no bounds. Surely in a situation like this, in the past, he would have rescued people. He tells us as much in Job 29. We are not helped by the obscurity of verse 24, widely recognized as one of the most obtuse of the entire book. But, we can say that Job wept for those who faced hardship; he grieved for the poor (v 26). But that wasn't what Job got in return. "When I looked for good, evil came; and when I waited for light, darkness came" (v 26). Turmoil, gloom, utter forlornness is his lot. He can't even associate with people: "I am a brother of jackals and a companion of ostriches" (v 29). His skin falls away; his bones burn. All music is now dirge music. *That* is Job's reality.

# 42.

## Job 31, Job's Serial Denials

This last chapter of Job's three-chapter peroration (29-31) presents a series of individual denials or protestations of Job's innocence. This chapter may be contrasted with what we may call the blanket denial of Job 23:10-12. In that passage Job just said, "My foot has held fast to his step...I have not turned aside" (23:11). Here, however, Job will focus on a number of particular allegations raised by Eliphaz in Job 22 as well as a few other possible bad acts he might have performed. In each case, the form is the same: 'If I have done XXX (bad thing), then let YYY (bad thing) happen to me.' Some have called this chapter Job "clearance oath," as if Job is "clearing" himself from all possible charges of malfeasance before he finally submits his case to God.

Two examples will show how this works in Job 31.

First, Eliphaz alleged in 22:6-7 that Job oppressed the poor by stripping the naked of their clothing and giving no water to the weary to drink. Job denies that charge specifically in 29:12

("because I delivered the poor who cried"), and he goes on further to say in 31:16 that *if* he had seen anyone perish for lack of clothing and did nothing about it, let his shoulder blade, supporting his right hand in oath, fall from its socket (31:22). The solemn duty to assist the poor is laid out as a legal requirement in Deut 15:7-11. Thus, Job has upheld the law and denies Eliphaz's charge by his oath.

Second, Eliphaz has alleged in 22:9 that "you have sent widows away empty-handed, and the arms of the orphans you have crushed." Job will deny those two charges in 29:12-13, "I delivered the poor who cried, and the orphan who had no helper," and "I caused the widow's heart to sing for joy." Then, attaching his solemn oath to this denial in 31:16, he says, "If I have caused the eyes of the widow to fail," and in 31:21, "If I have raised my hand against the orphan", then let his shoulder blade fall from its socket (31:22). The care for orphans and widows was likewise a legal requirement (Ex 22:22; Deut 10:18 and elsewhere). Job thus clears himself from this charge, too.

Job 31 isn't simply a complete catalogue of Job's good acts or a point-by-point refutation of Eliphaz's charges in Job 22. It presents an assorted series of denials of bad activity, denials that give him complete confidence that as he signs his complaint in verse 35 he will be vindicated.

With this lengthy introduction, we can proceed more quickly through the contents and argument of Job 31. It may be divided as follows:

**Job 31:1-4, No Escape from God's Searching Eyes**
**Job 31:5-34, A Series of Denials and an Oath**
**Job 31:35-37, Signing the Complaint**
**Job 31:38-40, One Last Denial**

This chapter is meant to be presented and read with utmost seriousness, but we can barely suppress a smile when we see verses 38-40. Job has just finished going through a list of about a dozen bad acts he hasn't performed (vv 5-34) and then puts his final signature on the complaint (vv 35-37). Then, as if an afterthought, he says, "Oh, but one more thing...." We are glad for the last words of the chapter, "The words of Job are ended" (31:40), because that means Job can't add another, 'Oh, just one more thing!'

## Job 31:1-4, No Escape from God's Searching Eyes

> 1 "I have made a covenant with my eyes;
>     how then could I look upon a virgin?
> 2 What would be my portion from God above,
>     and my heritage from the Almighty on high?
> 3 Does not calamity befall the unrighteous,
>     and disaster the workers of iniquity?
> 4 Does he not see my ways,
>     and number all my steps?

In this passage Job will deny looking lustfully at unmarried women, but his larger point is his awareness that nothing he does is hid from God. "Does he not see my ways, and number all my steps?" (v 4). When Jesus uttered a similar thought in the Matt 11:20 ("all your hairs are numbered"), he said so to allay the disciples' fears. If God so knows us, God will see to it that no harm befalls us. Yet with Job there is a twist to this idea. God not only knows all of Job's ways but isn't averse to playing 'Gotcha!' with him. Thus, when Job makes his oath in Job 31, he does so with the full knowledge that he is open before God, unable to hide anything. In fact, that becomes one of his points of complaint: None of his activity is hidden from God, but God is hidden from him. Not fair!!

## Job 31:5-34, A Series of Denials and an Oath

> 5 "If I have walked with falsehood,
>     and my foot has hurried to deceit—
> 6 let me be weighed in a just balance,

and let God know my integrity!—
7 if my step has turned aside from the way,
    and my heart has followed my eyes,
    and if any spot has clung to my hands;
8 then let me sow, and another eat;
    and let what grows for me be rooted out.
9 If my heart has been enticed by a woman,
    and I have lain in wait at my neighbor's door;
10 then let my wife grind for another,
    and let other men kneel over her.
11 For that would be a heinous crime;
    that would be a criminal offense;
12 for that would be a fire consuming down to Abaddon,
    and it would burn to the root all my harvest.
13 If I have rejected the cause of my male or female slaves,
    when they brought a complaint against me;
14 what then shall I do when God rises up?
    When he makes inquiry, what shall I answer him?
15 Did not he who made me in the womb make them?
    And did not one fashion us in the womb?
16 If I have withheld anything that the poor desired,
    or have caused the eyes of the widow to fail,
17 or have eaten my morsel alone,
    and the orphan has not eaten from it—
18 for from my youth I reared the orphan like a father,
    and from my mother's womb I guided the widow—
19 if I have seen anyone perish for lack of clothing,
    or a poor person without covering,
20 whose loins have not blessed me,
    and who was not warmed with the fleece of my sheep;
21 if I have raised my hand against the orphan,
    because I saw I had supporters at the gate;
22 then let my shoulder blade fall from my shoulder,
    and let my arm be broken from its socket.

23 For I was in terror of calamity from God,
   and I could not have faced his majesty.
24 If I have made gold my trust,
   or called fine gold my confidence;
25 if I have rejoiced because my wealth was great,
   or because my hand had gotten much;
26 if I have looked at the sun when it shone,
   or the moon moving in splendor,
27 and my heart has been secretly enticed,
   and my mouth has kissed my hand;
28 this also would be an iniquity to be punished by the judges,
   for I should have been false to God above.
29 If I have rejoiced at the ruin of those who hated me,
   or exulted when evil overtook them—
30 I have not let my mouth sin
   by asking for their lives with a curse—
31 if those of my tent ever said,
   'O that we might be sated with his flesh!'—
32 the stranger has not lodged in the street;
   I have opened my doors to the traveler—
33 if I have concealed my transgressions as others do,
   by hiding my iniquity in my bosom,
34 because I stood in great fear of the multitude,
   and the contempt of families terrified me,
   so that I kept silence, and did not go out of doors—

Some commentators go through each of Job's ten or eleven denials in these 30 verses, but I will spare you that. Job's denials of bad conduct both relate to general activity ("If my step has turned aside from the way," v 7) and to specific acts ("If I have rejected the cause of my male or female slaves," v 13). Each of these is solemnly denied, but it is the denial of orphan neglect that is most memorable. If he has done this—"then let my shoulder blade fall from my shoulder, and let my arm be broken from its socket" (v 22). We see in our mind's eye Job raising his right hand to swear to his innocence not just to the charge of mistreating orphans but to all the particulars he has raised. If he is false to his oath, he wants that raised arm to be snapped from the body right then and there. If he is false, he wants the whole world to know. But, the flip side is that if he is innocent of the charges of infidelity to God or humans, he wants to be justified. Big time. From God's mouth. Nothing less.

## Job 31:35-37, Signing the Complaint

> 35 "O that I had one to hear me!
>   (Here is my signature! Let the Almighty answer me!)
>   O that I had the indictment written by my adversary!
> 36 Surely I would carry it on my shoulder;
>   I would bind it on me like a crown;
> 37 I would give him an account of all my steps;
>   like a prince I would approach him.

Even though some translations, like the NRSV, put Job's signature in parentheses, there are few more dramatic acts in Scripture than this act. Not only does Job sign the complaint, but he wishes the adversary would actually write out the indictment against him so that he could wear it on his shoulder. He would wear it with pride, like a military figure might wear the plume from his defeated enemy's helmet on his own helmet as a sign of his victory. Job would carry that indictment with pride, approaching God like a prince, confidently striding into God's presence (v 38).

## Job 31:38-40, One Last Denial

> 38 "If my land has cried out against me,
>   and its furrows have wept together;

> 39 if I have eaten its yield without payment,
>   and caused the death of its owners;
> 40 let thorns grow instead of wheat,
>   and foul weeds instead of barley.
> The words of Job are ended."

Job's confidence is at its peak. He has thoroughly searched his heart. "The words of Job are ended" (40). There really is nothing more for him to say.

# 43.

## An Interlude at the End of Job's Words

As readers we need to take a deep breath at this point to assess where we are and where we still have to go in this marvelous book. The friends have shown themselves to be unhelpful, God is silent and Job isn't backing down. Let's consider each in turn.

First, the friends. They might have been at their most effective when they wordlessly sat with Job on the ash heap in Chapter 2. But as soon as Job opened the door to conversation by his plaintive words of Chapter 3, the friends eagerly followed suit. Eliphaz tried to show some sympathy with Job by pointing out that the suffering Job was experiencing could best be interpreted as the divine discipline, rather than punishment for sin (5:17ff). Yet Job didn't take the bait, and the friends soon descended into various levels of innuendo as well as explicit affirmation that Job was suffering because of his bad deeds. They still held out hope for better days for Job, but that hope had disappeared by the time of the final cycle of speeches. We make a mistake, however, if we just paint the friends in a negative light; Job has contributed mightily to his alienation from them by calling them miserable counselors and by treating them dismissively. In the end, all the friends can do is to recite the tested truths of the wisdom tradition. Their advice is very similar to the "trust God" approach taken by many today to comfort a friend in affliction. But it really is "trust God" with an edge. As their patience runs thin with Job, the friends strongly imply that God's patience, also, has a limit.

God, for His part, is silent. After playing a central role with the Satan in Job 1-2, God drops out. Is God "secretly" working through the conversations of the friends, directing it in the direction of the sovereign divine will? Not a hint of it. Later on, in Job 42, God will make the somewhat remarkable statement, to be clarified below, that the friends "have not spoken of me what is right, as my servant Job has done" (42:7, 8). Thus, God is "all ears" as the conversation unfolds, but God doesn't intervene. After Job finishes his peroration, the longest appearance of any one individual in the entire Book of Job will happen (Elihu, with his four speeches in Job 32-37). Still God doesn't speak. The theological question that God's silence provokes is whether God can be silent *too long and whether this silence can actually do damage—to God.* I have argued elsewhere in my commentary on Genesis that God might have acted *too soon* in bringing the Great Flood of Gen 6. Maybe the Book of Job is probing themes that make us all uncomfortable—that God, too, is trying to come to grips with the results of His actions, struggling like the rest of us, and perhaps not struggling that successfully. The only problem is that the results of the divine work are more evident than that of humans. God paints on a much larger canvas than we do.

Job, unsurprisingly, is the most engaging character of the book so far. One way to look at the Book of Job, from the perspective of law, is to see it as an elaborate hypothetical. Hypotheticals are developed by law professors (and I did so as a law professor) in order to test whether students understand underlying legal principles. A hypothetical is often a "worst-case" scenario, laid out for students so that they can evaluate every aspect of this "worst" case and call each aspect by its proper legal name. Thus, a professor would not just ask a student to analyze a case of simple burglary, but perhaps posit that the burglar had parked his car in a forbidden zone, cut across a neighbor's property, tripped and hurt himself badly in an unmarked hole dug by the neighbor next to the city-owned sidewalk, then scaled an unstable fence that had been scheduled for demolition which he broke in the process of getting to the target house. Before entering the property, he was confronted by an unleashed dog that he shot and killed. Once inside the house he not just steals things....you can see where this is going. Paint a situation as bad or complex as it can be and see if the students can tease out all the legal things (or, illegal things) going on.

The same is true here. Job's is the "worst-case" scenario, a kind of 'How would you handle *this* case, all you eager and smart students?' Job is righteous, blameless, loving towards his family, dealing justly with all people in his life, and he then unexpectedly faces the most unimaginable loss.

He tries to figure out what has happened, but he can't. He interprets his loss, correctly, as the result of some kind of divine permission or direct divine action. He would like to get clarification from God as to why God has allowed these bad things to happen to him. He searches his behavior and can find nothing that would deserve this kind of devastating loss. It doesn't occur to Job that stuff this bad 'just happens.' So, he has to seek an explanation of his loss from the only source that knows: God.

But God isn't telling. God is silent, AWOL, unapproachable. This adds to Job's frustration. He imagines that God is just having an extremely bad, horrible, no good day, a day that is drawing out longer and longer as the silence becomes more deafening.

Yet, Job isn't without resources. Though he spends the First Cycle and a good bit of the Second Cycle in anger and grief, Job is also resourceful. He posits the existence in Job 19 of a Redeemer or Vindicator, one who is not God but will stand and work for Job to save him from this mess. There just has to be a Redeemer; the nature of God requires it.

Armed with the twofold assurance of his innocence and the existence of a Redeemer on his side, Job lays his case before God. He knows that he will be vindicated. This is a slam-dunk case. He has tested it from every angle. No possible leaks in this structure. And he waits. And waits. The major question, to which we don't know the answer, is whether Job is thinking of leaving the God who has blessed him, and who now has brought this terrible evil on him. I think Job is more than toying with the idea. Though one might say that Job has nowhere else to turn, he obviously does—he can turn to his Redeemer.

One thing, however, is missing. That would be an interpretation of his distress or a satisfactory way of explaining to himself what has happened to him. It isn't ultimately satisfactory just to say that God has "torn me in His wrath and hated me" (see 16:9). He needs a gentler, more convincing explanation. That, I will argue, is the function of the speeches of Elihu in Job 32-37. Elihu will give Job all he needs to make a clean break from God—if he so chooses. To these mostly neglected, and often derided, speeches we now turn.

# 44.

## Job 32-37, Elihu's Speeches, An Introduction

ELIHU WILL NOW SPEAK. HE RECEIVES THE FULLEST INTRODUCTION OF any of the speakers: he is, drum roll, "Elihu son of Barachel the Buzite, of the family of Ram" (32:2). The others are just "Eliphaz the Temanite," "Bildad the Shuhite," or "Zophar the Naamathite." The Bible mentions a Buz in Gen 22:21, but this possible connection soon disappears when we realize we know nothing more than this name in two places.

The narrative assumes that Elihu has been present throughout the discussion because he quotes the friends' and Job's words when making his points. His speeches exceed in length by 50 verses the most voluble of Job's other friends (Eliphaz).

There is no scholarly agreement as to the purpose, or even value, of Elihu's speeches for the Book of Job. A majority of scholars, in my judgment, consider them relatively unimportant. The most that many will say is that they provide a human response to the dilemma (32-37) in preparation for the divine response (38-41). The implication of this approach is that the human response clouds the issue further; it is only God's resoundingly clear intervention in Job 38-41 that really saves the day. All attention, thus, is really directed to the divine speeches, with Elihu's speeches seen as nothing more than a fumbling and rather ineffective warm-up act.

Elihu's opening words in this chapter give us reason to support this perspective. He is young and inexperienced. He claims to have wisdom but by the end of Job 32 (22 verses) he hasn't expressed one idea. He just tells us that he is "full of words" (v 18), one of the great understatements of Scripture. He seems like a baseball pitcher whose wind-up to throw the ball is so convoluted and twisting that he falls off the mound before even delivering the pitch. Everyone laughs.

I think the author's method of portraying Elihu in Job 32, as a pompous buffoon who takes himself too seriously, is meant to lull us into subtly ignoring anything he says once he actually gets around to saying it. Yet my approach is that if we actually listen to Elihu, especially as he gets deeper into his speeches in Job 36, we hear him providing Job an explanation of his suffering that is not only clear but actually helpful. My approach, further, is that Elihu's words, combined with Job's own development of the Redeemer idea (19:25), give Job all that he needs to turn the tables on God so that it is God, rather than Job, that has to plead HIS case in Job 38-41. Whether God does so successfully will be explored later in these essays.

If the Book of Job is potentially subversive of traditional faith (by introducing a Redeemer, by challenging God so fearlessly), the speeches of Elihu will subvert the wisdom tradition. They will show that, as Elihu says, it is not age but spirit/Spirit that gives a person wisdom (32:8). Be ready for subversion, then, as we are tempted to guffaw at the hapless pitcher who has just fallen off the mound.

# 45.

## Job 32, Elihu Winds Up ...

THE CHAPTER MAY BE OUTLINED AS FOLLOWS:

Job 32:1-5, Introducing Elihu
Job 32:6-10, Caution At First, then Throwing Off Restraints
Job 32:11-15, The Hopelessness of the Friends
Job 32:16-22, Let Me Answer

## Job 32:1-5, Introducing Elihu

> 1 "So these three men ceased to answer Job, because he was righteous in his own eyes. 2 Then Elihu son of Barachel the Buzite, of the family of Ram, became angry. He was angry at Job because he justified himself rather than God; 3 he was angry also at Job's three friends because they had found no answer, though they had declared Job to be in the wrong. 4 Now Elihu had waited

> to speak to Job, because they were older than he. 5 But when Elihu saw that there was no answer in the mouths of these three men, he became angry.

Elihu's appearance is unexpected. Job has just finished presenting his case. We think that the only one who can adequately deal with Job's questions and objections is God. We have been waiting around for God to speak since Job 3. We naturally expect God to speak now. But instead of that, we have another one who enters, who not only hasn't been introduced previously but who isn't mentioned at the end when God wants the friends to "make up" with each other (42:8-10). Elihu appears, seems to fumble around at first, speaks more than 100 verses, and then disappears. For an author such as ours who treasures words so deeply, we have to wonder whether something is amiss here.

But at first there is no hint of anything special. We are told that the friends stop speaking because Job "was righteous in his own eyes" (v 1). In a word, the conversation has reached an impasse. Then Elihu appears. Who is he? He is introduced, but we have no more knowledge of him after the introduction than before. All we know, because it is mentioned four times in five verses (vv 2, 2, 3, 5), is that Elihu is angry. He is angry at both sides in the conversation: at Job because he considered himself, rather than God, to be in the right; at the friends because they really had no convincing argument as to why Job was in the wrong, even though they told him so. Elihu patiently waited for the elders to speak. But there was no light. So he speaks.

Might we be on the right track to see him as the "umpire" for whom Job longed in 9:33? Elihu will "lay his hands" on both parties, but the two parties he stands between are Job and the friends and not, as Job longs for in 9:33, Job and God. So he remains an enigmatic figure. He is a young man, an angry young man, and now he will weigh in.

## Job 32:6-10, Caution at First, then Throwing Off Restraints

> 6 Elihu son of Barachel the Buzite answered:
> "I am young in years,
>     and you are aged;
>     therefore I was timid and afraid
>     to declare my opinion to you.
> 7 I said, 'Let days speak,
>     and many years teach wisdom.'
> 8 But truly it is the spirit in a mortal,
>     the breath of the Almighty, that makes for understanding.
> 9 It is not the old that are wise,
>     nor the aged that understand what is right.
> 10 Therefore I say, 'Listen to me;
>     let me also declare my opinion.'

Elihu begins with a strikingly elegant and clear introduction. He is young (he chooses the relatively rare word *tsair*, which appeared in 30:1 on Job's lips to describe young mockers—though Elihu will present himself as a young insight-giver), and so has, in good wisdom tradition fashion, deferred to his elders. These elders are described as *yashish* ("old"), a word only appearing in Job. Earlier Job himself had admitted that wisdom is with the *yashish* (12:12). Thus, when Elihu first deferred to the *yashishim*, he was doing what was expected of him.

But now come the subversive words. After seeing the inconclusive nature of the debate, Elihu asserts that it not "great people" or the "bigger" (*rabim*) that are necessarily wise, nor the "old" (*zaqen*) who understand justice (v 9). Rather, it is the spirit (*ruach*) of a person, the breath (*neshamah*) of the Almighty that makes the difference. I pause on *neshamah* because it only appears 23x in the Bible, but four of them are on Elihu's lips in his speeches.

God breathed into humans the *neshamah* of life (Gen 2:7); Elihu believes strongly that this special breath is in him.

If breath rather than age is the determining factor in possession of wisdom, then the tradition is potentially upended. Spirit-filled people of all ages and descriptions can show up and proclaim their special relationship to God and the insight that uniquely flows into and out of them. This is potentially dangerous for the wisdom tradition, a tradition based on slow accumulation of knowledge, of insight gained by long and distilled experience, of communally-developed rather than individually-revealed insight. Elihu thus can boldly say, "Listen to me; let me also declare my opinion" (v 10).

## Job 32:11-15, The Hopelessness of the Friends

> 11 "See, I waited for your words,
>     I listened for your wise sayings,
>         while you searched out what to say.
> 12 I gave you my attention,
>     but there was in fact no one that confuted Job,
>         no one among you that answered his words.
> 13 Yet do not say, 'We have found wisdom;
>     God may vanquish him, not a human.'
> 14 He has not directed his words against me,
>     and I will not answer him with your speeches.
> 15 They are dismayed, they answer no more;
>     they have not a word to say.

We are now ready for Elihu to deliver the wisdom from the spirit that resides in him. But, not so fast. Elihu is just getting warmed up. He first addresses the friends. The words have a startlingly intimacy to them, as if Elihu could discern the twitches in the friends' faces as they "searched out" words to say to Job (v 11). The verb *chaqar* ("to investigate/search out") is especially beloved of Job (6 of 27 biblical appearances are in Job) since everyone, it seems, is trying to get to the bottom of things in this book. But Elihu is close enough to see the friends "searching" for words. He paid close attention to them, but none could confute Job (v 12). Verses 13-14 are difficult to understand. I suggest the close linkage of verse 13 with the preceding. Thus, we would then have: 'None (of the friends could confute Job); thus, they could not say, 'We have found wisdom and God need not vanquish/pursue him" (vv 12-13). But since Job's words weren't directed at Elihu, he doesn't have to be confined to the friends' reasoning or words to address Job (v 14).

## Job 32:16-22, Let Me Answer

> 16 "And am I to wait, because they do not speak,
>   because they stand there, and answer no more?
> 17 I also will give my answer;
>   I also will declare my opinion.
> 18 For I am full of words;
>   the spirit within me constrains me.
> 19 My heart is indeed like wine that has no vent;
>   like new wineskins, it is ready to burst.
> 20 I must speak, so that I may find relief;
>   I must open my lips and answer.
> 21 I will not show partiality to any person
>   or use flattery toward anyone.
> 22 For I do not know how to flatter—
>   or my Maker would soon put an end to me!"

Elihu is getting ready to speak. We are still waiting... We almost want to double over with laughter when he asks, "Am I to wait, because they do not speak?" (v 16), because *we* have been waiting quite a long time for *him* to start speaking. He is like a concert pianist who tells the audience,

> 'I am now placing my fingers near the keyboard. Any second now I will begin to play. The most mellifluous melodies will

flow from my fingers. Be ready for my playing. Don't miss anything. I am SO READY to play.'

By this time the audience is shifting uncomfortably in their chairs; some whispering and grumbling can be heard. People stream for the exits.

Elihu continues to stall. "For I am full of words; the spirit within constrains me" (v 18). We are much more sympathetic when Jeremiah moans about the constraint of God's spirit within in Jeremiah 20:9. We are seriously beginning to wonder what kind of spirit resides within Elihu. He continues with his introduction as he now uses an image of wine constrained in skins that threatens to burst the wineskin because it has no opening, no vent (v 19). We now become fascinated by the show Elihu is putting on. We can imagine him like a huge balloon ready to burst. We wonder if he will actually burst before he says anything of value. Maybe we would rather see *that* than listen to him.

But then, he changes course and the audience stops laughing. "I will not show partiality to any person" (v 21). No flattery to either side. He doesn't know how to flatter (v 22), which actually is rather rare in a young person who wants to get ahead in life. Maybe, we think, there is something in him. We are a bit bewildered but allured. He will continue to speak seven more verses before actually getting to his point. But the entertainment has been worth it.

# 46.

## Thinking About Elihu

ALTHOUGH WE CAN BARELY SUPPRESS A SMILE AS WE SEE ELIHU 'warming up' in Job 32, we understand him best if we see him concerned with *big ideas*. At first, he takes an inordinate amount of time settling in to what he wants to say: a full 25 verses (out of a total of 160 he utters) are taken up with a preparatory verbal display (32:6-33:7). But then, after laying out the essence of Job's case (33:8-11), he speaks of:

1.  The Ways God Speaks to Mortals (33:14-33);

2.  The Justice of God (34)

3.  The Insignificance of Humans (35:1-9)

4.  God as Teacher with a Special Message for Job (35:10-36:24)

5.  God as the Glorious Creator of all things; Announcing God's Presence (36:25-37:24)

If we stop laughing at Elihu long enough to listen to him, we will see him as harshly judgmental at first (Points 1-3), mostly because he "overreads" a few of Job's words, but then surprisingly insightful in Point 4. Rather than simply arguing that God is either the judge of the wicked (which all three friends have done) or the one bringing discipline through suffering (as Eliphaz has done), Elihu will be more concerned with describing God as a teacher who uses Job's suffering as a means of trying to instruct Job. Will Job get the message? And, most crucial for our understanding of the Book of Job, what will be Job's most likely reaction if and when he understands Elihu's message?

# 47.

## Job 33, Elihu Continues

BEFORE WE CAN EVEN GET TO THAT QUESTION, HOWEVER, WE NEED TO examine how Elihu moves from his elaborate introduction in Chapter 32 to his parsing of and response to Job's argument earlier in the book. We may profitably divide this chapter as follows:

Job 33:1-7, Elihu's Passionate Prolixity

Job 33:8-11, Job's Claims, According to Elihu
Job 33:12-18, God Speaks Through Dreams

Job 33:19-28, God Speaks Through Pain

Job 33:29-33, Listen Up, Job, I'm Just Getting Started!

## Job 33:1-7, Elihu's Passionate Prolixity

> 1 "But now, hear my speech, O Job,
>    and listen to all my words.
> 2 See, I open my mouth;
>    the tongue in my mouth speaks.
> 3 My words declare the uprightness of my heart,
>    and what my lips know they speak sincerely.
> 4 The spirit of God has made me,
>    and the breath of the Almighty gives me life.
> 5 Answer me, if you can;
>    set your words in order before me; take your stand.
> 6 See, before God I am as you are;
>    I too was formed from a piece of clay.
> 7 No fear of me need terrify you;
>    my pressure will not be heavy on you.

Elihu continues with his elaborate self-introduction; his words in this subsection can further be divided into three claims: his *sincerity* (vv 1-3); the indwelling of God's *spirit* in him (v 4); and his commitment to open and *non-terrorizing conversation* (vv 6-7). With respect to sincerity, Elihu has previously mentioned his impartiality and unwillingness to flatter anyone (32:21). The appeal to sincerity here continues that theme. He uses the word *yosher* to describe his sincerity; God had used the adjectival form of that word (*yashar*) to describe Job's uprightness (1:8; 2:3). He once again turns the wisdom tradition on its head when he emphasizes that it is the indwelling divine spirit, rather than long association with a teaching tradition, that inspires him (v 4). Finally, relating to the third theme—a non-terrorizing conversation—we might tend to see the reference in verse 7 as somewhat irrelevant until we realize that removal of the divine terror was precisely the thing that Job requested in 13:21. Job has prepared his case (13:18). He was ready to appear before God. He wanted his case considered dispassionately so that "dread of you (God) doesn't terrify me (Job)," 13:21. Elihu wants to allay Job's fears.

## Job 33:8-11, Job's Claims, According to Elihu

> 8 "Surely, you have spoken in my hearing,
>    and I have heard the sound of your words.
> 9 You say, 'I am clean, without transgression;
>    I am pure, and there is no iniquity in me.
> 10 Look, he finds occasions against me,
>    he counts me as his enemy;
> 11 he puts my feet in the stocks,
>    and watches all my paths.'

Just because Elihu pledges not to terrify Job doesn't mean that he will become Job's patsy. In these verses he lays out what he believes is the essence of Job's case. Then, in the next two chapters, Elihu will firmly, and some might say a bit viciously, deal with Job's case. But first to Job's case. Elihu says that Job makes two types of claims: first, that Job is pure (v 9); and second, that God treats Job as an enemy (vv 10-11).

One could go through the Book of Job in quite some detail to evaluate whether Elihu's summary of Job's case is absolutely fair, somewhat fair or somewhat inaccurate. Scholars don't agree. Most would claim that Elihu's summary is 'in the ballpark' or 'not a bad summary.' I would agree. In fact, in verse 11 he actually quotes Job's earlier words in 13:24. What is fascinating is that Elihu introduces three either new or somewhat rare words to capture Job's first point. Job, according to Elihu, claims he is *zak, beli pesha,* and *chaph* in verse 9. He then adds a common word (*lo avon,* "no guilt") to finish it off. Literally we have "pure, no sin, clean, no guilt." I think Elihu possibly overstates Job's case slightly, and that this overstatement will lead to Elihu's inadvisedly harsh words in Job 34-35. Job isn't claiming sinlessness; he is claiming that he is the recipient of punishment disproportionate to his sin. Elihu's second point is right on target: Job has said that God is his adversary or enemy. Job has explicitly asked, "Why do you hide your face and consider yourself my enemy?" (13:24).

Elihu will not deal with these claims right away other than to say, in verse 12, "God is greater than any mortal." That really isn't the point at issue, but Elihu has another item on his agenda before he returns to Job's putative righteousness and God's being his enemy...

## Job 33:12-18, God Speaks Through Dreams

> 12 "But in this you are not right. I will answer you:
>   God is greater than any mortal.
> 13 Why do you contend against him,
>   saying, 'He will answer none of my words'?
> 14 For God speaks in one way,
>   and in two, though people do not perceive it.
> 15 In a dream, in a vision of the night,
>   when deep sleep falls on mortals,
>   while they slumber on their beds,
> 16 then he opens their ears,
>   and terrifies them with warnings,
> 17 that he may turn them aside from their deeds,
>   and keep them from pride,
> 18 to spare their souls from the Pit,
>   their lives from traversing the River.

Though Elihu has summarized Job's case fairly well, he is interested to move on to something that Job often mentions—the divine silence. Job believes that God is nowhere to be found and that God doesn't want to talk with him. In this and the next sub-sections, Elihu points to the fact that God has unexpected ways of communicating to people. Using typical Hebrew poetic parallelism, he says, "For God speaks in one way; yes in two, even though humans don't perceive it" (v 14). One way God speaks is through dreams or visions (v 15). Elihu's language borders on the mysterious. God speaks at this time "when deepest darkness (*tardemah*) falls on people" (v 15). Eliphaz had used the identical phrase in 4:13. Dreams "uncover" human ears (v 16), turning them from their pride (v 17). Job had claimed that God terrified him in his night visions. Elihu may be suggesting that Job is drawing the wrong conclusions from those dreams...

## Job 33:19-28, God Speaks Through Pain

> 19 "They are also chastened with pain upon their beds,
>     and with continual strife in their bones,
> 20 so that their lives loathe bread,
>     and their appetites dainty food.
> 21 Their flesh is so wasted away that it cannot be seen;
>     and their bones, once invisible, now stick out.
> 22 Their souls draw near the Pit,
>     and their lives to those who bring death.
> 23 Then, if there should be for one of them an angel,
>     a mediator, one of a thousand,
>     one who declares a person upright,
> 24 and he is gracious to that person, and says,
>     'Deliver him from going down into the Pit;
>     I have found a ransom;
> 25 let his flesh become fresh with youth;
>     let him return to the days of his youthful vigor';
> 26 then he prays to God, and is accepted by him,
>     he comes into his presence with joy,
>     and God repays him for his righteousness.
> 27 That person sings to others and says,
>     'I sinned, and perverted what was right,
>     and it was not paid back to me.
> 28 He has redeemed my soul from going down to the Pit,
>     and my life shall see the light.'

Elihu continues to address Job's underlying argument that

*Job 33, Elihu Continues*

God has been silent. Perhaps that is why when Elihu asks Job at the end of the chapter if he has anything to say (v 32), Job is silent. None of his other friends had been able to shut him up. Job finally realizes that this young man is someone to be reckoned with, someone who actually has something to say to his condition. He had better listen.

The second means by which God speaks to people is through pain or, more precisely, through a "bed of pain" (v 19). The phrase "bed of pain" has a kind of macabre euphony to it: *makob al mishkab*. Rather than just saying this general point, he speaks to Job's specific condition: "All his bones grow stiff" (v 19); "he abhors bread and good food" (v 20). Perhaps even looking directly at Job he says, "His flesh is consumed away...his bones corrode to unsightliness" (v 21). Elihu is suggesting something eerily powerful here, that God might actually be speaking in the midst of Job's racking pains and through the food that repels him.

Elihu's suggestive thinking continues. He posits the existence of some kind of figure, an angel, intercessor, interpreter (v 23) that might meet such a suffering person in his pain. Alert readers might immediately think of 9:33 or 16:19. Is Elihu trying to pick up on Job's earlier longings and respond to them through a figure who will help interpret his pain to him? But we see that Elihu uses different words to describe this person, again a combination of two "m's": *malak, melits,* and we see that his agenda is quite different than Job's in those other passages. Yet, Elihu suggests that pain on the bed may be the means for God to communicate with a person through an interpreter or intercessor. The intercessor will be gracious to the sufferer and draw him out of the pit (vv 23-24). The intercessor or interpreter then prays to God and restores the person to righteousness (v 26). Thus, pain is the second means that God sometimes uses to redeem a person from the pit.

## Job 33:29-33, Listen Up, Job, I'm Just Getting Started!

> 29 "God indeed does all these things,
>     twice, three times, with mortals,
> 30 to bring back their souls from the Pit,
>     so that they may see the light of life.
> 31 Pay heed, Job, listen to me;
>     be silent, and I will speak.
> 32 If you have anything to say, answer me;
>     speak, for I desire to justify you.
> 33 If not, listen to me;
>     be silent, and I will teach you wisdom."

Elihu speaks with a kind of confidence and clarity that belies his years. He is confident that God does this (speaking through dreams or through pain) twice or even three times in order to redeem a person's soul from the pit (*shachath*). *Shachath* is the same word that Job used in one of his most vivid passages to describe the place where God would plunge him (9:31). Now Elihu is saying that God speaks to people in pain to redeem them perhaps even from that same pit into which Job thinks he has been plunged.

No wonder Job doesn't pick up on Elihu's invitation in verse 32 to speak. Elihu's words are to "justify" Job (v 32), which probably means that his words are to bring Job back into a good and right relationship with God. Elihu is really on a roll. Job is silent. Elihu concludes, "If not, then I will teach you wisdom" (v 33). The verb "to teach" here is the rare *alaph*, a verb confined to the wisdom tradition and suggesting a kind of formalized and specialized teaching that only wisdom can provide. After Elihu's inauspicious beginning, he is now acquitting himself quite well.

# 48.

## The Background to Job 34

WE RECALL FROM 33:9-12 THAT ELIHU SUMMED UP JOB'S CURRENT situation and claims against God under two heads: a) Job is pure/righteous; and b) God considers Job an enemy. But then, instead of dealing immediately with these issues, Elihu took a bit of an argumentative detour. Because Job had *also* argued here and there that God was hiding Himself and not speaking to Job, Elihu dealt first with that issue. Elihu's twofold answer to that issue, developed in the rest of Job 33, was that God indeed does speak to humans: through a dream of the night and through pain on the bed. Elihu's point is that God has been speaking to you all along, Job! There may even be some kind of angelic interpreter that communicates the divine will to the sufferer, who then aids the sufferer to pray and be restored to God. That was Elihu's approach in Job 33. God still speaks to humans. Not a bad point.

But now in Job 34, he will return to one of the major points of Job's complaint which Elihu summarized in 33:8-12. Elihu will address Job's claim to being righteous or pure. As I mentioned above, Elihu turns rather vicious here and in Job 35. My explanation for that, especially after he has characterized himself as impartial at the end of Job 32, is that he has slightly mischaracterized Job's argument, and the mischaracterization gets Elihu's dander up. Instead of hearing Job say, 'How have I sinned *in this instance?*' Elihu hears Job saying, 'How have I sinned *at all?*'

This slight difference in wording imports a world of difference in meaning. By hearing Job making a plea for his complete innocence, Elihu perceives Job as a rather rash, untutored, morally confused person. To such a person one must bring both condemnation and instruction. That is what Elihu tries to do in so vigorously in the next few chapters. In Job 34-35 Elihu speaks harshly and even in condemnatory language, but by the end of Job 35 (and most of Job 36), he has softened his tone and speaks in a more inviting and conciliatory manner.

We have to remember that we are witnessing an argument here, and so before looking at Elihu's words in Job 34, we should briefly reflect on the nature of argument and the characterization of one's opponent's position. Most people who argue or debate say that they characterize their opponent's position fairly, before attacking it, but few really do. When we characterize another's argument, we try to juggle two difficult things in our mind: accurate statement of his/her position and figuring out the way to respond to it. It is a complex intellectual tightrope to walk.

The best way to characterize another's position is to quote them, but even this is fraught with difficulties. The opponent may say the quotation is taken out of context, or that it has to be put in connection with other comments softening or further explaining his or her position. Because of this, accurate characterization of another's position, without first garnering their support for your characterization, is very difficult.

Instead, what opponents do is set up a 'straw-man,' a phrase going back in English to 1594 and defined at that time as a sort of "scarecrow" set up to "make them afraide." The OED further tells us that the meaning of 'straw-man' had morphed by the end of the 19th century to be something that could be "easily enough knocked over." So, even though Elihu seems to try to characterize Job's position accurately, he really will be setting up a straw-man, something that can be "easily enough knocked over." We never learn if Elihu's slight mischaracterization of Job is because Elihu innocently 'misheard' Job, because Job was not fully clear in stating his position or because there was a genuine attempt to manipulate Job's words by Elihu.

But that is the nature of human communication. 'You said XX.' 'No I didn't.' Or, 'Yes, I did but I said it tongue-in-cheek.' Or 'You were so caught up in your own thoughts that you couldn't hear me.' The permutations of how misunderstandings arise are nearly endless. We have one here, too. It isn't a huge one in words, but Elihu has *heard* Job say he is blameless, while Job has *wanted* or *intended* to say that he is blameless in this instance. Now we are ready to hear Elihu respond to all this.

# 49.

## Job 34, Elihu's Lack of Sympathy for Job

BECAUSE OF WHAT I SAID IN THE PREVIOUS ESSAY, WE SHOULDN'T BE too upset if Elihu not only doesn't quote Job precisely, but also slightly distorts Job's arguments. This is often what happens in an argument...

We may divide this chapter as follows:

Job 34:1-9, Characterization and Condemnation of Job's Words
Job 34:10-15, God Won't Act Wickedly

Job 34:16-30, It's Inconceivable that God Could Be Unjust
Job 34:31-37, Job Speaks without Knowledge

## Job 34:1-9, Characterization and Condemnation of Job's Words

| 1 Then Elihu continued and said:

> 2 "Hear my words, you wise men,
>     and give ear to me, you who know;
> 3 for the ear tests words
>     as the palate tastes food.
> 4 Let us choose what is right;
>     let us determine among ourselves what is good.
> 5 For Job has said, 'I am innocent,
>     and God has taken away my right;
> 6 in spite of being right I am counted a liar;
>     my wound is incurable, though I am without transgression.'
> 7 Who is there like Job,
>     who drinks up scoffing like water,
> 8 who goes in company with evildoers
>     and walks with the wicked?
> 9 For he has said, 'It profits one nothing
>     to take delight in God.'

Elihu here addresses either the friends or a larger crowd that has gathered. Elihu begins by uttering both a formulaic statement (v 2) and a proverb (v 3). He wants the reader to hear him as a representative of the wisdom tradition, even though he has already upended the central principle of that tradition by claiming it is the spirit in a person that allows wise speech, rather than any long process of reflection on experience.

But then he turns to Job's leading point, which he had previously mentioned in 33:9. "Job has said, 'I am righteous/innocent (*tsadiq*), and God has taken away my right'" (34:5). Note that Elihu has slightly changed Job's words from 33:9, but has he changed the meaning? In 33:9 he used four phrases or words to capture Job's argument: Job claimed he was *zak* ("pure") and *beli pasha* ("without transgression") and *chaph* ("innocent") with *lo avon* ("no iniquity"). We see both the delightful and potentially confusing nature of language as we compare the two passages.

Almost everyone would agree that Elihu's slight verbal alteration of Job's complaint in 34:5 isn't inconsistent with his characterization of Job's claim in 33:9. That *both* are built on an incorrect foundation (Job never claims sinlessness) is never broached. Elihu is now ready to deal with the issue of Job's apparent claim to righteousness (*tsadiq*).

[For word lovers, note that the way *God* describes Job in 1:8 and 2:3 is *tam* and *yashar*, blameless and upright. Thus, when we add these to the catalogue of words describing Job, we now have at least seven or eight words floating around to capture Job's moral condition. All of them may mean pretty much the same thing. Words are both among the biggest joys and largest impediments in life].

But now Elihu pounces. We rightly characterize Elihu's reaction in verses 7-9 as an abhorrence of Job's putative claim to blamelessness and righteousness. This claim of Job to sinlessness (in Elihu's mind) is nothing more than evidence that Job "drinks up scoffing like water" (v 7) and that he "walks with the wicked" (v 8). Such depraved and misguided thinking can only come from a mind which says, "It profits one nothing to take delight in God" (v 9). It is hard to separate one's disgust with a position and disgust with a person. Elihu seems to have a large share of both in this instance.

## Job 34:10-15, God Won't Act Wickedly

> 10 "Therefore, hear me, you who have sense,
>     far be it from God that he should do wickedness,
>     and from the Almighty that he should do wrong.
> 11 For according to their deeds he will repay them,
>     and according to their ways he will make it befall them.
> 12 Of a truth, God will not do wickedly,
>     and the Almighty will not pervert justice.
> 13 Who gave him charge over the earth
>     and who laid on him the whole world?
> 14 If he should take back his spirit to himself,

> and gather to himself his breath,
> 15 all flesh would perish together,
> > and all mortals return to dust.

Job's apparent claim to sinlessness has made Elihu mad. It is equivalent to Job's accusing God of acting wickedly because God would then have visited terrible calamity on an innocent party (v 10). In these verses Elihu vigorously defends God against such a claim. "Far be it from God that he should do wickedness" (v 10). And, "Of a truth, God will not do wickedly, and the Almighty will not pervert justice" (v 12). Elihu wants to emphasize, because Job seems to have forgotten it, that God is in charge of the world. "If God should take back spirit to himself …all flesh would perish together and all mortals return to dust" (vv 14-15). Verse 15 is a masterstroke of eloquent poetic parallelism, with verbs as the first and last words acting like what scholars call an *inclusio,* an 'envelope' type of structure that includes or covers intervening material. Literally we have "Perish all flesh together; and humans onto the dust shall return." Very effective.

## Job 34:16-30, It's Inconceivable that God Could Be Unjust

> 16 "If you have understanding, hear this;
> > listen to what I say.
> 17 Shall one who hates justice govern?
> > Will you condemn one who is righteous and mighty,
> 18 who says to a king, 'You scoundrel!'
> > and to princes, 'You wicked men!';
> 19 who shows no partiality to nobles,
> > nor regards the rich more than the poor,
> > for they are all the work of his hands?
> 20 In a moment they die;
> > at midnight the people are shaken and pass away,

> and the mighty are taken away by no human hand.
> 21 For his eyes are upon the ways of mortals,
>     and he sees all their steps.
> 22 There is no gloom or deep darkness
>     where evildoers may hide themselves.
> 23 For he has not appointed a time for anyone
>     to go before God in judgment.
> 24 He shatters the mighty without investigation,
>     and sets others in their place.
> 25 Thus, knowing their works,
>     he overturns them in the night, and they are crushed.
> 26 He strikes them for their wickedness
>     while others look on,
> 27 because they turned aside from following him,
>     and had no regard for any of his ways,
> 28 so that they caused the cry of the poor to come to him,
>     and he heard the cry of the afflicted—
> 29 When he is quiet, who can condemn?
>     When he hides his face, who can behold him,
>     whether it be a nation or an individual?—
> 30 so that the godless should not reign,
>     or those who ensnare the people.

Though Elihu can be perceived here as attacking Job, he also takes it as his role to defend God. Apologists for traditional religion often confuse themselves a bit because they think they are aiding God by defending God, as if a child with a flimsy sword made out of aluminum foil wrapped around cardboard can forestall the advance of an army of unbelievers and wicked people. Yet, Elihu will speak for God. His major point in the somewhat confusing opening verses of this section is that it is inconceivable that one who "hates justice" should govern (v 17).

Note that Elihu has further slightly twisted Job's thoughts.

Job has said that God has attacked him unmercifully and without reason *in this instance*. Elihu has 'heard' Job saying that he is sinless and God is in the wrong. Elihu has extrapolated from that the idea that God must, in Job's mind, be an evildoer and one who hates justice. Ergo, Elihu's question, "Shall one who hates justice govern?" (v 17).

Rather than hating justice, God knows exactly what He is doing. God will show no partiality to kings or nobles. "In a moment they die; at midnight the people are shaken and pass away, and the mighty are taken away by no human hand" (v 20). God sees what mortals are up to. Though Job might think he is sinking into a land of darkness, invisible even to God, Elihu assures Job that "there is no gloom or deep darkness where evildoers may hide themselves" (v 22). God is the judge who has appointed a time where all will face judgment. God can overturn people in the night, and they are crushed (v 25). Then, perhaps getting carried away by his flowing eloquence, Elihu concludes this section with a direct jab at Job. "When he (God) is silent, who can condemn?" (v 29). Though he never characterizes Job's position as full of presumption, Elihu believes that Job is being presumptuous, even though he doesn't use the word. God is in control; God knows what He is doing; God can be silent and withdrawn if He desires, but God definitely doesn't do injustice.

## Job 34:31-37, Job Speaks without Knowledge

> 31 "For has anyone said to God,
>    'I have endured punishment; I will not offend any more;
> 32 teach me what I do not see;
>    if I have done iniquity, I will do it no more'?
> 33 Will he then pay back to suit you,
>    because you reject it?
>    For you must choose, and not I;
>    therefore declare what you know.

> 34 Those who have sense will say to me,
>     and the wise who hear me will say,
> 35 'Job speaks without knowledge,
>     his words are without insight.'
> 36 Would that Job were tried to the limit,
>     because his answers are those of the wicked.
> 37 For he adds rebellion to his sin;
>     he claps his hands among us,
>     and multiplies his words against God."

Though the first few verses of this section aren't clear, Elihu concludes with ringing clarity. "Job speaks without knowledge, and his words are without insight" (v 35). Verse 35 literally drips with language of the wisdom tradition. The goal of education in wisdom is that a person might have knowledge (*daath*) and prudence (*sakal*) to face the multiform confusions of life. In verse 35 Job is portrayed as a person who is *without daath*, and whose words are spoken *without sakal*.

Elihu finishes this, his second, speech with words of raw and unfiltered vehemence. The first half of verse 36 is literally, "I wish/Oh that Job were tested to the utmost," where the word I rendered "utmost" (*natsach*) often is rendered "forever." When the Psalmist wants to declare eternal pleasures in the divine presence, he says, "in your right hand are pleasures for ever" (*natsach*, 16:11). We wonder if Elihu is really, at this point, consigning Job to some kind of hell. To make things even worse, from Elihu's perspective, Job is adding rebellion to all of this (v 37) and multiplying words against God. We wonder if the conversation will break down here with Elihu, as it has with Job's three friends.

# 50.

# Job 35, Elihu Continues Condemning Job

E LIHU IS AT HIS BEST WHEN HE SUGGESTS WAYS THAT GOD SPEAKS TO or instructs people. He isn't nearly as effective when he condemns Job or argues for the justice of God. The language and thoughts in 33:14-33 and, as we will see in the next essay, in 36:1-22 are exquisite and suggestive; the thought of Chapters 34 and 35 is more pedestrian and tangled. In this passage Elihu resurrects an argument discarded by Eliphaz in Job 22 before turning to brief mention of Job's pride and verbal vanity. Yet, we see the glint of eloquence begin again in 35:10-11, where Elihu speaks of God as the divine teacher. The way out of the morass for Job, more explicitly laid out in Job 36, will be for Job not to keep complaining of his circumstances but to seek out what God is trying to tell or teach him through them.

This short chapter may be profitably divided into two sections:

**Job 35:1-8, Job's Continuing Futility**
**Job 35:9-16, Job's Empty Words and God's Strength in the Night**

## Job 35:1-8, Job's Continuing Futility

> 1 Elihu continued and said:
> 2 "Do you think this to be just?
>     You say, 'I am in the right before God.'
> 3 If you ask, 'What advantage have I?
>     How am I better off than if I had sinned?'
> 4 I will answer you
>     and your friends with you.
> 5 Look at the heavens and see;
>     observe the clouds, which are higher than you.
> 6 If you have sinned, what do you accomplish against him?
>     And if your transgressions are multiplied, what do you do to him?
> 7 If you are righteous, what do you give to him;
>     or what does he receive from your hand?
> 8 Your wickedness affects others like you,
>     and your righteousness, other human beings.

Though his argument doesn't flow smoothly here, Elihu seems to be making four points that aren't that closely connected to each other. First, he suggests that Job is really saying that he is more righteous than God (v 2). Second, he accuses Job of arguing that there really isn't any advantage in righteous living, nor any disadvantage in unjust conduct (v 3). Third, he raises the issue that God is unaffected either by Job's righteousness or sinfulness (vv 5-7). Finally, he says that Job's bad deeds only hurt those around him and not God (v 8).

None of these points is earth-shattering or well-developed. The first issue arises when one translates the Hebrew word *min* in verse 2 as a comparative ("more than") rather than a simple preposition ("from"). *Min* may have either meaning in different contexts, and many translations render the question in verse 2, "Do you think it is right to say, 'I am righteous before (literally, "from") God?'" rather than, my choice, "Do you think it is right to say, 'I am more righteous than God?'" The latter is more shocking and more in the spirit of Elihu's attack against Job here. Though Job has never explicitly compared his righteousness to God's, his accusatory tone in 19:6, where he says that God has put him in the wrong/subverted his cause might have been taken by Elihu to suggest Job is accusing God of a moral deficiency that he, Job, doesn't have.

The second issue—it is of no advantage to serve God—really has to do with God's moral indifference. Elihu infers from Job's argument that because God has let the wicked roam freely and oppress others that God must be morally indifferent. Hence, Job, too, is indifferent to righteous or unrighteous living. Elihu doesn't pursue this argument at all. His third point, developed over three verses, is an argument that Eliphaz had tried in 22:3 but had quickly abandoned: that Job claims God is unaffected or unmoved by human conduct. But this kind of argument is tricky for those who want to argue for the glory and sovereignty of God. Usually those who argue for these doctrines (and Elihu and his friends would so do), want to paint God as a lofty God, far removed from the squabbles and pettiness of human life. This is perilously close to suggesting that a part of God's glory may be His being unaffected by anything that happens on earth—precisely the point that Elihu has accused Job of making. Perhaps that is why the argument was dropped quickly by Eliphaz—too close to home. Instead, Elihu retreats meekly to the fourth point, a non-starter.

## Job 35:9-16, Job's Empty Words and God's Strength in the Night

> 9 "Because of the multitude of oppressions people cry out;
> they call for help because of the arm of the mighty.
> 10 But no one says, 'Where is God my Maker,
> who gives strength in the night,
> 11 who teaches us more than the animals of the earth,

> and makes us wiser than the birds of the air?'
> 12 There they cry out, but he does not answer,
> because of the pride of evildoers.
> 13 Surely God does not hear an empty cry,
> nor does the Almighty regard it.
> 14 How much less when you say that you do not see him,
> that the case is before him, and you are waiting for him!
> 15 And now, because his anger does not punish,
> and he does not greatly heed transgression,
> 16 Job opens his mouth in empty talk,
> he multiplies words without knowledge."

Though Elihu continues the barrage against Job here, he hints at the direction he will take in Job 36, a chapter much more winsome and conciliatory than Job 34 or Job 35. His argument is as follows: Oppression is rife in the world and, because of oppression, people call out to God (v 9). They cry out but receive no answer. They receive no answer because of their arrogance (v 12). These cries are "empty cries" (v 13). Instead, in a theme developed in Job 36, they should have *asked* rather than *cried out*. They should have asked, "Where is God my maker, who gives strength in the night?" (v 10). They didn't see God as a teacher (v 11) who wants to interpret their pain to them.

Instead, they rail against God in their distress. Their screaming against God actually prevents them from hearing what God is trying to say. Now Elihu not so subtly applies this general human response to distress and oppression to Job's case. If God doesn't hear the empty cry, "How much less than when you say that you do not see him, that the case is before him, and you are waiting for him!" (v 14). Job has said *all* of those things. He had prepared his case (13:18); God is frighteningly elusive (23:9ff); Job so desires to find God (the entirety of Job 23).

After several unsuccessful arguments, Elihu finally is developing a theory or approach to Job's case that will yield insight.

Job is a sufferer. Many people suffer. In their suffering they cry out about being oppressed. They whinge and mope. They weep and wail. But this kind of talking and complaining (and we can imagine Elihu looking directly at Job when he is saying this) is empty. Job multiplies words without knowledge (v 16). He doesn't know what he is saying.

Instead of this kind of response, the divinely-approved manner of responding to terrible tragedy in personal life is to ask (vv 10-11), "Where is God my Maker, who gives strength in the night, who teaches us more than animals of the earth, and makes us wise than the birds of the air?" In other words, the more helpful way for Job to have dealt with this tragedy would have been for him to approach God and say, 'What are you trying to teach me, God?'

Though many of Elihu's words (especially v 15) aren't fully clear, the blinding clarity of the question in verses 10-11 is the linchpin of his argument. Job's words are empty not because, as the three friends might argue, Job has denied the truth of one of their pet doctrines (the inevitable punishment of the wicked) but because he is screaming rather than listening. That is why Job 36 begins with Elihu's asking Job to gather round and listen.

What has been a highly-charged screaming match will now become a quiet listening session. We can hardly wait...

# 51.

## Job 36:1-21, Introduction

I WILL TIP MY HAND OUT THE OUTSET OF THIS ESSAY. I SEE ELIHU'S words in 36:15-17 as the most important words in the more than 160 verses he utters in Job 32-37. These words not only provide an alternative way for Job to understand his distress but they give Job a way to exit the vicious cycle of anger, grief, accusation, self-defense and recrimination that characterized the Three Cycles of speeches of Job and the friends in Job 3-27. In addition, they point out the likely result if Job persists in his path of defiance and his quest for legal redress.

In a word, Elihu will encourage Job to see God not as judging him or as clobbering him without reason but as trying to speak to him, trying to teach him *in and through* his distress. The lesson God wants to teach, according to Elihu, is that God would like to lead Job *to freedom* or to the broad spaces of life (*rachab*) through the distress. Yet, according to Elihu, Job isn't ready to receive that message because he is enmeshed in a lawsuit rather than a listening session.

The key, then, to Elihu's speech in Job 36 is to understand that he presents God not simply as the judge of all the earth or the glorious creator of the universe, but as the one who gently lures or woos Job through instruction. Elihu has already adumbrated this theme in 33:14-33, where he presented God as speaking to humans in two ways: through dreams in the night or through pain on the bed. The point of a dream, for God, is not the dream itself but the divine message through the dream. The point of the pain on the bed, for God, is not the torment itself but a message God is trying to get across through it.

Elihu had also suggested the theme of God as speaker or teacher in 35:11-12. Thinking of Job's situation, Elihu says that people cry out in their oppression but they don't say, "Where is God my Maker...who *teaches* us more than the animals...?" If people would begin to see God as a teacher rather than a harsh judge, they might understand their situation more clearly. Finally, when Elihu finishes his crucial words of Job 36, he concludes by saying, "See, God is exalted in his power; who is a *teacher* like him?" (36:22). Ultimately, for Elihu, Job has been saying all along, 'I *will be heard*,' but he has never really said, 'Let *me* listen.' Had Job been ready to listen to God's alluring words of instruction, he would have realized there was a way out of his morass.

# 52.

## Job 36:1-21, Breakthrough!

The points mentioned by Elihu at the end of the previous essay are indeed profound and dramatic. We have to listen closely to Elihu to see how he develops them. Let's unpack Elihu's argument in these verses as follows:

Job 36:1-4, Listen up, Job!

Job 36:5-12, God and the Kings

Job 36:13-14, A Brief Interlude on the Godless
Job 36:15-21, Interpreting Job's Distress

## Job 36:1-4, Listen up, Job!

> 1 Elihu continued and said:
> 2 "Bear with me a little, and I will show you,

> for I have yet something to say on God's behalf.
> 3 I will bring my knowledge from far away,
>   and ascribe righteousness to my Maker.
> 4 For truly my words are not false;
>   one who is perfect in knowledge is with you.

Elihu begins in an inordinately complex way to ask Job to listen. Literally we have, "Gather (or suffer/bear) to me a bit and I will tell you, because again for God (are) the words." Or, more simply, "Listen to me, because I am speaking God's words" (v 2). Each of the three Hebrew words rendered "gather," "a bit" and "tell" appears fewer than ten times in the Bible; the word for "words" appears more than 35x but more than 90% of them are in the Book of Job. Perhaps Elihu wants to catch Job's attention by unusual words. He will bring knowledge from God. His words aren't false. Then, in words that might be seen as arrogant but no doubt reflect his belief that the spirit of God is in him, Elihu says, "One complete in knowledge is with you" (many translations have "one perfect in knowledge"). He doesn't want Job to miss his message.

## Job 36:5-12, God and the Kings

> 5 "Surely God is mighty and does not despise any;
>   he is mighty in strength of understanding.
> 6 He does not keep the wicked alive,
>   but gives the afflicted their right.
> 7 He does not withdraw his eyes from the righteous,
>   but with kings on the throne
>   he sets them forever, and they are exalted.
> 8 And if they are bound in fetters
>   and caught in the cords of affliction,
> 9 then he declares to them their work
>   and their transgressions, that they are behaving arrogantly.
> 10 He opens their ears to instruction,

> and commands that they return from iniquity.
> 11 If they listen, and serve him,
>    they complete their days in prosperity,
>    and their years in pleasantness.
> 12 But if they do not listen, they shall perish by the sword,
>    and die without knowledge.

Perhaps in order to test Job, to see if he really is listening, Elihu won't first speak directly to Job's issues. But the principle he develops in these verses will be the principle he will apply to Job's distress in 36:15-18. Elihu begins with a few commonly-accepted principles, to wit: God is mighty; God doesn't keep the wicked alive but gives justice to the oppressed (vv 5-6). But then he turns to his major point of the section. He begins by saying God has put kings on their thrones (v 7). If the kings are bound in fetters or seized in the knots of affliction, and then God tells the kings the reason for their bondage (i.e., they have acted defiantly/arrogantly, v 9), God will open their ear to *instruction/discipline* and tell them to turn from their sin (v 10). That is, God will use the affliction even of kings as a teaching tool to declare to them their own arrogance or false sense of self-importance.

Elihu continues this most important thought. If the kings actually listen and serve God, then they will finish their days with good and with pleasures (v 11). But, if they don't listen, they will perish with the sword and die without knowledge (v 12). Elihu has laid out all the principles he will apply to Job in just a few verses: Distress comes to kings; the distress is really the message of God to the kings to temper their arrogance; if the kings see it that way, they will receive long life and blessing; if the kings don't heed God's message, they will perish. Life, then, is about being in the correct frame of mind to hear the message that God is trying to communicate. *This* is a significant point for Elihu.

## Job 36:13-14, A Brief Interlude on the Godless

> 13 "The godless in heart cherish anger;
> they do not cry for help when he binds them.
> 14 They die in their youth,
> and their life ends in shame.

Elihu definitely won't let his point in verses 5-12 drop, but before applying it to Job's case, he takes a brief, and somewhat irrelevant, detour on the godless. They, like the unhearing kings, don't cry for help when "he binds them" (v 13); they die in their youth (v 14).

## Job 36:15-21, Interpreting Job's Distress

> 15 "He delivers the afflicted by their affliction,
> and opens their ear by adversity.
> 16 He also allured you out of distress
> into a broad place where there was no constraint,
> and what was set on your table was full of fatness.
> 17 But you are obsessed with the case of the wicked;
> judgment and justice seize you.
> 18 Beware that wrath does not entice you into scoffing,
> and do not let the greatness of the ransom turn you aside.
> 19 Will your cry avail to keep you from distress,
> or will all the force of your strength?
> 20 Do not long for the night,
> when peoples are cut off in their place.
> 21 Beware! Do not turn to iniquity;
> because of that you have been tried by affliction.

The first three verses of this section lay out Elihu's interpretation of Job's situation with clarity and force. They build on the theme he has been developing since Chapter 33, that God is a teacher who wants to get a message across to people. That message can be summarized in four principles:

1) God uses pain as a means to draw the afflicted out of their affliction. More precisely, God "opens the ears" through affliction (v 15). Affliction, therefore, is a means of communication God uses to get the sufferer's attention and eventually lead them out of their suffering.

2) Then, applying this principle to Job's situation, Elihu says that God has "stirred" or "lured" or "enticed" (verb is *suth*) you from your distress into a broad place (*rachab*) where there is no more distress (v 16). But Elihu doesn't stop there. Using language reminiscent of that most famous Psalm (23), he says what "rests" on his "table" is "full of fatness" (v 16). Some interpreters read this verse as pointing to a future state for Job—that God *will* lure him out of his distress, but the verb is best translated as a past or present tense. In the latter it would be, "God is wooing you/enticing you..." Elihu's dramatic interpretation of Job's distress as God's allurement or enticing to comfort and prosperity is thus deeply rooted in the hopes of the Hebrew people—for a prepared table and overflowing cup.

3) But Job currently isn't able to hear this teaching or instruction of God because he is "full of justice and judgment" (v 17). Another translation has "you are obsessed with justice and judgment." Note what Elihu is doing here. He is chiding Job but not in the same manner as the friends. Rather than clobbering Job by warning of a dire fate when the sword of judgment will be thrust through his exposed abdomen, Elihu points to the reason *why* he believes Job can't hear God's gentle allurement. Job is focused on his legal case and on winning the case. This has an immediate ring of truth to it for two reasons. First, from the text itself. Job has said, "I have indeed prepared my case; I know I shall be vindicated" (13:18). Job has been cultivating and nurturing his case like a parent a vulnerable child. He has put together an airtight explanation of everything. He loves his case. But Elihu is telling

Job that his focus on or even obsession with his case is hindering his ability to hear God.

Second, the point has a ring of truth because that is the way lawsuits function. Those who have invested a lot in making their legal case work for them can often become blind regarding other ways to solve the problem before them. They have already imagined the appearances in court, the recognition by judge or jury of the justness of their claims, their complete vindication before their peers. When all of this passes through the plaintiff's mind, it is very difficult to think of other ways short of litigation to resolve the problem. Elihu has spotted that and pointed it out to Job. Can Job hear him?

4) Elihu then moves to a more subtle psychological point in verse 18, difficult to translate, but my reading is that he is trying to show Job the effects of continuing to cling to his lawsuit. Beware lest wrath (which Job has because of his lawsuit) will lure you (using the verb *suth*, the same verb used two verses earlier to talk about God's "wooing" or "luring" Job into a broad place) to mockery (again, a difficult word). Then, in the final difficult words, it may be "that a great ransom would not help you." That is, Job is in a situation where he will either be lured away by wrath or by God's gentle instruction. If he hearkens to the former, there will be trouble. If he listens to the latter, there will be the broad spaces and the fatness.

Elihu then closes this section by repeating a few thoughts he has earlier mentioned, but his significant closing word, which I think is better put in the next section, is that God is a teacher. "Behold, God is set on high in his power. Who is like him as a teacher?" (v 22). Rather than hearing the words describing God's power as a prelude to divine judgment on Job, Job ought to hear them as a description of God as a teacher. Can Job put aside his anger and his legal case long enough to get the lesson?

# 53.

## Job 36:22-37:24, Elihu's Peroration

ELIHU'S FINISHES HIS LONG, SOMETIMES LABORED AND SOMETIMES brilliant, speeches with this extensive hymn on the greatness of God. With tongue only slightly in cheek, one might argue that the middle section of Elihu's speeches on God as judge and God as teacher (33:8-36:21) are sandwiched by two lengthy speeches on Elihu's (32:1-33:7) and God's (36:22-37:24) greatness. By 36:21 Elihu has said all that he needs to say about a potential resolution of our dilemma. The resolution: Job ought to realize that God is trying to get his attention through suffering, that God is trying to teach Job about freedom, and that in return Job should (like the "good" kings in 36:5-12), listen, confess and then serve God. Once Elihu has made this case, he can step back in this passage and proclaim the greatness of the God they all serve. Such a proclamation really is a magnificent way not only to end his speeches but also to prepare the way for God's entry in Job 38. This final section of Elihu's speech thus has a twofold function: to provide an impressive paean on the greatness of God and the comparative insignificance of humans as well as to provide the warm-up act for God, who is waiting to enter at stage left.

Elihu's peroration can be divided as follows:

Job 36:22-33, The Greatness of God

Job 37:1-13, My Heart Trembles at God's Greatness
Job 37:14-24, Job's Ignorance

## Job 36:22-33, The Greatness of God

> 22 "See, God is exalted in his power;
>     who is a teacher like him?
> 23 Who has prescribed for him his way,
>     or who can say, 'You have done wrong'?
> 24 Remember to extol his work,
>     of which mortals have sung.
> 25 All people have looked on it;
>     everyone watches it from far away.
> 26 Surely God is great, and we do not know him;
>     the number of his years is unsearchable.
> 27 For he draws up the drops of water;
>     he distills his mist in rain,
> 28 which the skies pour down
>     and drop upon mortals abundantly.
> 29 Can anyone understand the spreading of the clouds,
>     the thunderings of his pavilion?
> 30 See, he scatters his lightning around him
>     and covers the roots of the sea.
> 31 For by these he governs peoples;
>     he gives food in abundance.
> 32 He covers his hands with the lightning,
>     and commands it to strike the mark.
> 33 Its crashing tells about him;

| he is jealous with anger against iniquity.

The final section of Elihu's speech shows us that he has not engaged with Job simply to try to provide an explanation for Job's distress. He is playing for bigger stakes; those stakes are to reorient Job's thinking towards God. Rather than carping and complaining, focusing all attention on his own distress, Job ought to redirect his mind and submission towards the God that stands behind all of this. The reorientation of Job's mind starts with an exhortation to extol God (vv 24-25), continues with a statement of God's greatness (v 26), and then ends with recognizing the specific acts of God's mysterious preservation of the world (vv 27-33).

Elihu uses a strikingly rare adjective to declare God's greatness (*saggi*, v 26). It appears only here and in Job 37:23, the end of Elihu's speech. Its equally rare verb form, *saga* (to "be great" or to "make great") is used near the beginning of this speech in 36:24. It is almost as if Elihu is coining a new word to catch Job's attention to describe God's greatness, sort of like if we invented the word 'stupendiosity' to describe something 'hugeorific.' But Elihu won't just declare that greatness; he will describe it through specific meteorological phenomena. God brings the rain, eloquently and somewhat vividly described as "drawing up" the drops of water which then become refined/purified/distilled as rain from its mist (v 27). The only other biblical appearance of the word for "mist" in verse 27 (*ed*) is in the creation story of Gen 2; perhaps by using the word *ed* here Elihu is suggesting something about the rather mysterious and potent power of God in creation and in his day. This power is not only in the rain but also the provision of food (v 31) and the brilliant flashes of lightning (v 33). All of this ought to lead Job to extol (*sagga*) God's work (v 24).

## Job 37:1-13, My Heart Trembles at God's Greatness

> 1 "At this also my heart trembles,
>   and leaps out of its place.
> 2 Listen, listen to the thunder of his voice
>   and the rumbling that comes from his mouth.
> 3 Under the whole heaven he lets it loose,
>   and his lightning to the corners of the earth.
> 4 After it his voice roars;
>   he thunders with his majestic voice
>   and he does not restrain the lightnings when his
>     voice is heard.
> 5 God thunders wondrously with his voice;
>   he does great things that we cannot comprehend.
> 6 For to the snow he says, 'Fall on the earth';
>   and the shower of rain, his heavy shower of rain,
> 7 serves as a sign on everyone's hand,
>   so that all whom he has made may know it.
> 8 Then the animals go into their lairs
>   and remain in their dens.
> 9 From its chamber comes the whirlwind,
>   and cold from the scattering winds.
> 10 By the breath of God ice is given,
>   and the broad waters are frozen fast.
> 11 He loads the thick cloud with moisture;
>   the clouds scatter his lightning.
> 12 They turn round and round by his guidance,
>   to accomplish all that he commands them
>   on the face of the habitable world.
> 13 Whether for correction, or for his land,
>   or for love, he causes it to happen.

These meteorological signs lead to a trembling heart (v 1). The language of verse 1 is vivid, "because of this my heart trembles and leaps/jumps in its place." But then Elihu subtly brings in an allied concept flowing from the divine greatness, a concept that will underlie God's self-description in Job 38-41, and that is the divine *incomprehensibility*. All this loading of clouds with moisture, thundering from the heavens, sending the snow and rain in their seasons are part of a complex picture of natural phenomena that we "cannot comprehend" (v 5). The best we might be able to do is describe their effects. But the point will eventually be that since there is so much about God's ways we *don't* understand, why not trust God for them? We see God's greatness in the regulation of nature to provide the necessities of life. Why not swallow our pride and accept God's control over things we can't understand? Elihu doesn't specifically make each of those points, but that is the spirit underlying his argument here and especially God's argument in Job 38-41. Everything works in the world to accomplish what God commands them to do (v 12). But then, with a bracing note of realism, Elihu closes this section with the variety of ways that God guides the world: "for correction, or for his land, or for love, he causes it to happen" (v 13). The translation of the middle part of this verse is disputed, but the general meaning is clear: God is not only great and incomprehensible, but these attributes are used for the good of the creation.

## Job 37:14-24, Job's Ignorance

> 14 "Hear this, O Job;
>   stop and consider the wondrous works of God.
> 15 Do you know how God lays his command upon them,
>   and causes the lightning of his cloud to shine?
> 16 Do you know the balancings of the clouds,
>   the wondrous works of the one whose knowledge is perfect,
> 17 you whose garments are hot
>   when the earth is still because of the south wind?

> 18 Can you, like him, spread out the skies,
>    hard as a molten mirror?
> 19 Teach us what we shall say to him;
>    we cannot draw up our case because of darkness.
> 20 Should he be told that I want to speak?
>    Did anyone ever wish to be swallowed up?
> 21 Now, no one can look on the light
>    when it is bright in the skies,
>    when the wind has passed and cleared them.
> 22 Out of the north comes golden splendor;
>    around God is awesome majesty.
> 23 The Almighty—we cannot find him;
>    he is great in power and justice,
>    and abundant righteousness he will not violate.
> 24 Therefore mortals fear him;
>    he does not regard any who are wise in their own conceit."

Elihu begins a process in the final verses of Chapter 37 which God will continue in Chapter 38—asking Job about all these things. We can't hear Elihu's tone of voice, of course, but there appears to be not simply a tone of earnest questioning but also of accusation or even slight mockery of Job. "Can you, like him, spread out the skies, hard as a molten mirror?" (v 18). Of course, the answer is "No." Oh and, "Do you know how God makes things work so that the lightning shines?" (v 19). Of course not. *We* don't even understand the question in verse 16, that has something to do with how God arranged the clouds. But obviously Job doesn't know the answer to that one, either. Then, subtly turning us back to the role of God as the only reliable teacher in this instance, Elihu gives a slight dig: "Teach us (literally, "Cause us to know") what we should say to him/it" (v 19). I think Elihu is asking Job to provide answers to all these knotty questions. Of course, Job can't.

Thus, Elihu is done. All he can point to is the fact that God

is coming: "Out of the north comes golden splendor; around God is awesome majesty" (v 22). Though they might not be able to find the Almighty (v 23), it looks like God has finally found all of them (v 23). God is ready to speak. A hush falls…

# 54.

# With Job at the End of Job 37

THE PURPOSE OF THIS ESSAY IS TO TRY TO PRESENT WHERE THE ARGUment is, and especially where Job might be psychologically and spiritually, at the end of Job 37. There are still a few acts to go in this great drama, but I think that most of the issues have been laid out and discussed with sufficient clarity. Let's begin with Job *before* Elihu enters, then Elihu's contribution and conclude with Job *after* Elihu speaks. Since the last point is never explicitly mentioned (because God just begins the divine speech in Job 38), we have to draw reasonable inferences from the argument. The point that I will argue in this essay is that at the end of Chapter 37 the tables have been turned and all the pressure is now on God to perform well in Job 38-41. Elihu has subtly changed the terms of the argument so that while apparently declaring God's ability to do anything God wants, he has perhaps unwittingly boxed God into an undesirable corner. Here goes.

First, consider Job's case before meeting Elihu. Job suffered terribly and wanted an explanation for his suffering. He realized quickly that the friends were not going to provide a satisfactory one. In Job's mind they were too concerned with protecting their own flimsy intellectual position than in dealing with Job's distress. "You see my distress and you are afraid" is how Job characterized them (6:21). As a result, Job meticulously put his case together against God and sought an audience with God. But his search was unavailing. God was not to be found. Job said sadly, "If I go forward, he is not there; or backward, I cannot perceive him" (23:8). God, he feels, owes him an explanation for the terrible distress Job believes that God has permitted or caused to come up on him. Because God has been silent so long, Job considers other sources of help. There is no mediator (9:33) but he will have a witness in heaven (16:19). By 19:25, however, this witness has matured into a Redeemer, separate from God, who will do what redeemers have always done, and that is save people, in this case Job. So even before Elihu begins to speak Job's confidence is rather high: he has put together an air-tight case, and he has a Redeemer who will not just defend him but will save him.

Second, consider how Elihu's speeches change things. Elihu enters after the friends show their ineffectiveness in argument. Though it takes Elihu quite a while to get warmed up, he eventually begins to laser in on Job's issues. The quality and helpfulness of his speeches differs of course, but he is most on point when he reframes the issue and sees things *not* in terms of a legal case Job is bringing, but in terms of a *teaching and listening session* that God has initiated through Job's suffering. For Elihu, God is gently trying to use Jobs distress to lure Job out of his distress (36:16). What that means is that God will use the instrumentality of great pain to teach Job vital life lessons. In this case that vital life lesson is that God is leading Job to freedom and is presenting a richly-laden table as a sign of that freedom (36:16). But instead of listening to God's alluring words through suffering, Job has turned everything into a lawsuit (36:17). Once you 'sue' God you no longer can 'hear' God. God is the great teacher who is trying to get through to you, Job. Why don't you listen? Why don't you recognize God's mysterious glory? Rather than fighting, you should humbly submit yourself to God.

Finally, consider Job's response to Elihu. Job's response to Elihu's words is never given, but we can say the following. Elihu has, to his credit, actually 'softened Job up' a bit. We will see it in Job's reaction in the middle of the divine speeches in Job 40. But Elihu's take on Job's distress is so unique and insightful that Job no doubt felt two things: the continuing rightness of his earlier position but also the need to think about what Elihu had said. Was God indeed leading him to freedom through this suffering?

But ultimately Elihu's argument, effective as it is, will boomerang back on himself and force God into acting a certain way in the divine speeches. That is, Elihu has argued that God was trying to get Job's attention by teaching him through suffering. God is luring Job into a broad place. If I were Job, I would then say, 'OK, if and when God really appears (and that appearance, though unknown to Job, is actually imminent), you have led me to expect a gentle divine teacher, one who will perhaps not provide a full explanation of my suffering but will at least show a deep understanding of my situation.' That, of course, is what great teachers do. They tailor lessons to the capabilities of hearers.

We see now how Elihu has constrained God, even though his argument is that God is basically free to do anything the divine wants. By portraying God as a teacher who allures, Elihu has led Job to *expect* God to appear as that alluring teacher.

So, I believe that as Elihu's last words fade, and before God starts speaking, Job is thinking as follows: 'I have my Redeemer, but didn't have an explanation for my suffering. Elihu has provided a helpful way to look at it—as a means for me to reach freedom. If only God would appear, I will expect a sympathetic teacher, one who might help clarify some of Elihu's unclear words about the lessons that I ought to learn through suffering.' Though Job never says it, I think that he has been so affected by all of this that if God seems indifferent or unhelpful when God appears (and if God appears), Job has an exit strategy, an exit from God. He will have a Redeemer and he will have his explanation. And, he will be on his own...

Thus, God, whom most feel is *never* on the hot seat, is now

on the hot seat. His faithful servant Elihu has spoken *for God* for several chapters. God can disavow what Elihu has said, but God never does this. Thus, Job's reasonable expectation is that God will appear as a gentle and alluring teacher. But what happens if God appears in the form Job most fears—the God who has frightened him in dreams and who "terrifies" Job "by his presence" (23:15)? At this point it could go either way for Job. If God treats him 'respectfully' by being the alluring teacher, Job will have good reason willingly to re-embrace faith. But if God appears and doesn't seem to show much regard for Job, then all bets are off, and Job may find his freedom in other ways. Let's hear God and see how it unfolds, but first let's state the problem and then try to understand the divine strategy in Job 38-41 from the perspective of an aspect of my own story.

# 55.

## Prelude to the Divine Entry

GOD, WHO LEFT THE NARRATIVE AS AN ACTIVE PARTICIPANT AFTER Job 2, has finally returned. The penultimate section of this great book (Job 38-41) belongs to God. In these chapters God speaks with poetic eloquence and beauty unmatched in the Bible, even though many of the verses God speaks are as unclear as those of any other speaker. The breadth of the vocabulary and literary imagination of the author is stunning. Who can forget the majestic lines in Job 38 that God uttered to the sea, "This far shall you come and no farther, and here shall your proud waves be stayed" (v 11)? Or, to Job, "Have you entered the springs of the sea? Or have you walked in the recesses of the deep?" (v 16). Or, "Has the rain a father? Who has given birth to the drops of dew?" (v 28). If the author wanted to convince us that what we have in Job 38-41 is a powerful and mysterious God, a God who gives and takes away life, a God who makes the most fearsome creatures his playthings, then we are absolutely convinced. There is no God like God. Simple. Amen.

But, as nearly all scholars also have noted, but not all have really addressed, one wonders if this amazing display of divine facility and power, of awesome and breathtaking capacity, is really relevant to the discussion at hand. Even Evangelically-inclined scholars, who almost always fearlessly step into the breach to defend God, have scratched their heads and said, "God's two lengthy recitals (in Job 38-41) are not replies to the questions that have tormented Job and which his friends have failed to answer" (Anderson, *Job*, p 268). If we looked at God's words in Job 38-41 from the perspective of a legal case, we might well ask, 'Would the testimony that God submits here be disallowed because of irrelevance and immateriality?'

Ah, it would not be thrown out if God is *both* witness and judge. And that will be the rub, and the problem, here. The thing that Job most feared is that God would appear and *not* speak to him in the alluring language of love but would simply do whatever God wants and blow him away because God is so powerful (23:15-16). In other words, the divine judge will have the last (and a good deal of the penultimate) words.

A good case can be made that Job 38-41, in trying to present God as an awesome and powerful God who holds the destiny of the world in the divine hands, has come perilously close to arguing that human concerns are of no concern to God. God can do whatever God wants and really isn't beholden to any tortured objections from puny creatures. Not only is God not beholden to the creature, but God is so great that He doesn't even have to deign to answer the creature's question, however reasonable, clear and justified they might be.

Thus, the paean to the divine power and majesty in Job 38-41 has an incredibly powerful shadow side: that God's loftiness may mean that God is unaccountable, i.e., that no human or other force can expect an answer to the question, 'Why, God, this pain?' Hm, is this the kind of God that is really presented here? And, if so, is this the kind of God Job really wants to serve?

What is at stake here in reading these amazing chapters are two questions: 1) Has God answered Job's questions in these speeches? And, a two-part second question: 2) If we think God *has* answered Job's questions, what is that answer? but If we think God *has not* answered Job's questions, what is going on here?

In dealing with the question of whether God has answered Job's questions in these chapters, we generally receive two types of answers: 1) No; and 2) Not explicitly, but... We understand what 1) "No," means. The second approach is that God might not have given Job a point by by rebuttal or answer, but that by speaking of the divine glory and power, Job's questions either are answered or fade into insignificance. It would be like answering the complaint made by a camper without a flashlight at night, 'I lost my backpack somewhere in the darkness,' with the line, 'The sun will be up in the morning.' While not directly answering the backpacker's complaint, it really is an answer to the question. The light of the sun will show you where you left your backpack.

Are the speeches of God in Job 38-41 to be construed that way? It would then be sort of like God's saying, 'I am the sun, and my light lightens the world and dispels all darkness and therefore, by definition, it dispels your darkness, Job. Return to your worship.'

A resolution to the problem of whether we think God is actually addressing Job's concerns might be aided by considering the following personal story.

# 56.

## A Personal Story to Understand the Divine Strategy of Job 38-41

ONE OF THE MOST IMPORTANT QUESTIONS IN UNDERSTANDING JOB 38-41 is why God seemingly ignores the questions Job has raised all along and instead turns His speeches into a kind of catechism that aims to show Job's ignorance and limited experience of the world. This essay gives an insight into the divine strategy through a personal story.

My insight into the divine strategy in Job 38-41 comes from my experience as a litigation attorney. Yet, the specific instance I relate below arose when I was not functioning in my attorney role but as an expert witness for the defense in the re-sentencing of Oregon's most notorious serial killer in November 2015.

I have written extensively on the history and workings of the capital punishment system in Oregon. All one needs to know at this point is that after a defendant has been sentenced to death, he still has several legal venues available to him to question the propriety of the sentence of death as well as the verdict of guilty. When a death penalty defendant's case is remanded by a higher court, it generally is because there was a serious procedural error below, an error that can only be corrected by a new sentencing trial. At the new sentencing trial, the jury will be asked whether the person should, despite the procedural error, be re-sentenced to death.

I was an expert witness in a re-sentencing case not because I had witnessed the crime or had experience as a DNA expert, but because I had compiled the most detailed study of what you might call the procedure of the death penalty in Oregon. I had convincing evidence that it would take at least 30 years from the date of a sentence/re-sentence of death before the actual sentence would be carried out.

I was put on the stand by the defense to show that the defendant, over 60 years of age at the re-sentencing, would be in his 90s before the state would execute him, barring further procedural delays. I showed that it was highly unlikely, therefore, that he would ever be executed. But, I further argued, if the jury re-sentenced him to death, the cost to the state for his future appeals would be huge. The defense argued that a better solution was for the killer to be given life without the possibility of parole and give up all future appeals.

I laid out the case for this approach on the stand. The defense lawyer thought that our case was airtight. A (Re)sentence of less than the death penalty was the defense attorney's goal. I suspected things would turn out differently. When it was the turn of the District Attorney to cross-examine me, he pursued an interesting strategy, a strategy that may have been influential in convincing the jury to re-sentence the man to death.

He looked at me and, in a civil but slightly cynical tone, began to ask me questions. I am quoting from memory and not from the actual transcript of the case—mostly to illustrate the type of questions that were raised:

District Attorney: "Dr Long: Your approach is based on numbers. Are you a mathematician?"

Me: "No."

District Attorney: "Dr Long: Do you have an advanced degree in statistics?"

Me: "No."

District Attorney: "Dr Long: Have you personally calculated how much it will cost the state if he is re-sentenced to death?"

Me: "I have a good estimate."

District Attorney: "That was not my question. Have you personally calculated the costs that you say the state will incur in putting him to death?"

Me: "No.

District Attorney: "Is it possible that what you consider will take 30 years will take considerably less? Is it possible?"

Me: "It is highly unlikely."

District Attorney: "Unresponsive. Please answer the question directly."

Me: "It is possible."

District Attorney: "Dr Long. Do you have a degree in social work?"

Me: "No."

District Attorney: "Do you have considerable experience in counseling those on death row?"

Me: "No."

The questioning continued for some time. Never did the District Attorney ask me a question about my method, about the historical data I advanced, about comparable cases, about the effect of my testimony. All he wanted to know, apparently, was I had expertise in areas that were tangentially, at best, related to my testimony.

I don't think it was his approach to me, necessarily, that led the jury to re-sentence the defendant to death. But I think it was effective from his perspective. The reason it was effective is that he basically *ignored* my testimony and tried to get me to admit ignorance on things. I had come in and was presented as a person of knowledge; the District Attorney's approach was to try to show me as ignorant. I have no problem admitting my ignorance when that label applies. But his approach was to try to have my words, "No" or "I don't know" ringing in the ears of the jury so that they might begin to believe that I really knew very little, perhaps about anything.

Was the District Attorney engaged in a dispassionate search for the truth? Of course not. His job was to make sure that the jury would have ample grounds for re-sentencing the defendant to death. If the defense's "expert" was seemingly ignorant, what need is there, really, to deal with the substance of his testimony?

This experience as an expert witness in such a high-profile case has, perhaps surprisingly, given me insight into God's method or strategy as described in Job 38-41. As mentioned, most scholars are honest enough to admit that God really doesn't answer Job's complaints in the two long speeches in these four chapters. Rather than dealing with the simple question of 'Why has your hand done this/permitted this to happen to me when I have lived a blameless life even by your own reckoning?,' God goes in a different direction. God deliberately asks questions to expose Job's ignorance. God will ask Job whether he has seen things that no human could possibly have seen. God will ask Job if he existed at a time when no human could possibly have existed. God will pose all kinds of questions that seek to undermine Job's credibility.

In a word, God is like the District Attorney in my case. God isn't interested in a dispassionate search for truth in this instance.

I will argue below that if God were truly interested in such a quest, He would have to 'fess up' to Job about what He had done. Even Elihu thinks that God is in the process of luring or enticing Job into a broad place of freedom, but God's approach seems designed to attack Job's credibility by a method of indirection. God never says, 'I know you have a complaint against me. Here is what you have said to me. Let me try to answer as follows...'

Rather, God just pulls rank, diverting attention of the listeners (perhaps the readers might be likened to the 'jury' here) both by magnificent language as well as demonstration of Job's obvious inadequacies in understanding and powerlessness to control the creation. What I will argue in the conclusion to this book is that Job is not 'wowed' by God's questions, just as I was not at all 'wowed' by the District Attorney's method. I saw it as a strategy to win, and it did, but it definitely was not a strategy designed carefully to sift the truth. Job, I argue, also 'sees through' the divine approach and realizes it for what it is: a power play to undermine Job's credibility. But what God doesn't count on is that Job, unlike me as expert witness, will have the last word on this one.

# 57.

## Job 38:1-38, God Enters and Is not Pleased

JOB HAS PRESENTED A MULTI-PRONGED COMPLAINT TO GOD. He would like an answer to the question of why he has suffered so severely in this instance. Elihu has given Job a possible interpretation of his dilemma—that God, as teacher, is luring or coaxing him out of his distress into a broad place of freedom. My point above is that by the end of Chapter 37, Job is very ready to meet a God who will tell him more of this process of allurement, or this broad place of freedom. Elihu has prepared him to meet such a God. God is a mysterious and powerful God, but Elihu has also portrayed God as the teacher.

A serviceable outline of most of Job 38 is as follows:

Job 38:1-3, God Appears and Beckons Job
Job 38:4-11, The Quiz Begins
Job 38:12-18, Where Have You Been When I Was Working So Hard, Job?
Job 38:19-24, Rubbing It in ...
Job 38:25-38, More Divine Wonders

## Job 38:1-3, God Appears and Beckons Job

> 1 Then the Lord answered Job out of the whirlwind:
> 2 "Who is this that darkens counsel by words without knowledge?
> 3 Gird up your loins like a man,
>    I will question you, and you shall declare to me.

What is God's "teaching method," then, in Job 38? The prelude to God's first speech, 38:1-3, gives us some hints. God says, "Who is this that darkens his counsel by words without knowledge?" (v 2). God has used the rather rare verb form of the common noun *hoshek*, or "darkness" in the opening question. As a verb, it is rendered either "to have a dark color" or to "make dark/bring darkness." The latter is obviously intended here. Who is it, God wants to know, who brings darkness to this situation by ignorant words? Rather than bringing light, Job's words bring darkness. That is what God is saying and asking about.

You wonder what Job must have wondered when he heard that question from God. His first reaction no doubt, given his intelligence and determination that we saw in Job 3-31, would be to say, 'Hm...I thought my questions actually were pretty good. In fact, as I refined my arguments through three cycles of speeches, I became really convinced that my questions were good ones. But now I am being called someone who brings darkness, and speaks without knowledge. Interesting teaching strategy, God.'

So, is this teaching through shock therapy? I know teachers who are not averse to shocking their students by their opening lines, perhaps to bring the students out of excessive reliance on their digital worlds, but normally this is done through the presentation of a challenging question about a subject matter rather than a seeming attack on the diligent listeners.

Then, in verse 3, God doesn't ask a question but beckons Job to engage in a discussion. But how does God beckon Job? "Gird up your loins like a male; I'll ask questions and you will bring me knowledge." The last verb is *yada*, the verb form of the noun used at the end of verse 2. In verse 2, God asserted (through a question) that Job has no knowledge. Now God says He will ask Job a series of questions so Job will teach God. The one without knowledge will now teach the one who has all the knowledge. Yuk yuk. We might not be wrong if we think we have just heard the slightest tone of mockery in God's statement in verse 3. 'I'll listen while you teach me knowledge,' is what God is saying. 'You student, go ahead and tell me how the chemical elements interact with each other,' the Nobel Prize winner in Chemistry has just said to an impudent first-year student. That is a little of the tone we get here.

We can't of course hear the tone of God's words, but they certainly aren't the inviting tone of someone who is luring a person into freedom. They sound more like they partake of either mockery or impatience. I have mentioned mockery above. If we also read God's opening words as partaking of impatience, it would be the impatient tone of someone who has been governing the world just fine, thank you, and has been disturbed by an impertinent subject who would like an explanation for something that God has had a hand in making happen. But God is in no mood to lower Himself to consider the questions actually raised. In fact, God will show this pusillanimous creature how little he actually knows. God will show Job that the real question in the world is *not* how to explain his suffering but how to recognize the divine glory aright. In the next several chapters, the divine tone is more like, 'You know so little, Job. If you really knew what it took to run a universe, you wouldn't be raising your petty concerns.'

Can this possibly be a satisfactory answer to Job? Of course not. But it *will* shut him up. Examination of how God's response can both be unsatisfactory and can nevertheless shut Job up will be the focus of my consideration of Job 42. Now that I have tipped my hand, however, in saying that the divine tone in Chapter 38 is one of either mockery or impatience, let's only briefly consider briefly the chapter's contents.

## Job 38:4-11, The Quiz Begins

> 4 "Where were you when I laid the foundation of the earth?
>     Tell me, if you have understanding.
> 5 Who determined its measurements—surely you know!
>     Or who stretched the line upon it?
> 6 On what were its bases sunk,
>     or who laid its cornerstone
> 7 when the morning stars sang together
>     and all the heavenly beings shouted for joy?
> 8 Or who shut in the sea with doors
>     when it burst out from the womb?—
> 9 when I made the clouds its garment,
>     and thick darkness its swaddling band,
> 10 and prescribed bounds for it,
>     and set bars and doors,
> 11 and said, 'Thus far shall you come, and no farther,
>     and here shall your proud waves be stopped'?

While my longer commentary deals with the specifics of the language, I will confine myself to general comments here on the flow of the argument. After what one might consider an inauspicious beginning in verses 2-3, God starts in verse 4 by asking Job questions. We will only look at the first. "Where were you when I laid the foundation of the earth? Tell me, if you have understanding?" (v 4). What *kind* of question is that? Is it a question that is calculated to produce knowledge? Perhaps one might argue it is calculated to produce some *self-knowledge* in Job, because it certainly isn't designed to draw out information to help God answer the actual question of where Job was when the world was made. If Job were a Buddhist, he might say that he was living a prior life, but he doesn't have that option, and that option probably wouldn't have appealed to him even if he knew of it. So, God's question can't be one that is taken literally. The only reason it might be important is if God wants to use it as the opening salvo to make Job realize something else..that Job, indeed, is a small, insignificant part in the scheme of creation. I think God will convince Job of this by halftime of the divine speeches (40:4-5), but the underlying question that a persistent reader ought to ask is whether this satisfies Job's (or our) questions on suffering.

Though I am just skipping over large swaths of text here, one can't help but notice the poetic beauty of verses 8-11, where the contrasting efforts of God's confining the sea and its bursting forth from the womb are emphasized. Finally, in this section, are the majestic words of 38:11, where God places a limit on the movement of the sea. All of this demonstrates the divine power, vastness and eternity—three things that can't really be predicated of Job.

## Job 38:12-38, Where Have You Been When I was Working So Hard, Job?

> 12 "Have you commanded the morning since your days began,
>     and caused the dawn to know its place,
> 13 so that it might take hold of the skirts of the earth,
>     and the wicked be shaken out of it?
> 14 It is changed like clay under the seal,
>     and it is dyed like a garment.
> 15 Light is withheld from the wicked,
>     and their uplifted arm is broken.
> 16 Have you entered into the springs of the sea,
>     or walked in the recesses of the deep?
> 17 Have the gates of death been revealed to you,
>     or have you seen the gates of deep darkness?
> 18 Have you comprehended the expanse of the earth?
>     Declare, if you know all this.
> 19 Where is the way to the dwelling of light,
>     and where is the place of darkness,
> 20 that you may take it to its territory
>     and that you may discern the paths to its home?
> 21 Surely you know, for you were born then,

and the number of your days is great!
22 Have you entered the storehouses of the snow,
    or have you seen the storehouses of the hail,
23 which I have reserved for the time of trouble,
    for the day of battle and war?
24 What is the way to the place where the light is distributed,
    or where the east wind is scattered upon the earth?
25 Who has cut a channel for the torrents of rain,
    and a way for the thunderbolt,
26 to bring rain on a land where no one lives,
    on the desert, which is empty of human life,
27 to satisfy the waste and desolate land,
    and to make the ground put forth grass?
28 Has the rain a father,
    or who has begotten the drops of dew?
29 From whose womb did the ice come forth,
    and who has given birth to the hoarfrost of heaven?
30 The waters become hard like stone,
    and the face of the deep is frozen.
31 Can you bind the chains of the Pleiades,
    or loose the cords of Orion?
32 Can you lead forth the Mazzaroth in their season,
    or can you guide the Bear with its children?
33 Do you know the ordinances of the heavens?
    Can you establish their rule on the earth?
34 Can you lift up your voice to the clouds,
    so that a flood of waters may cover you?
35 Can you send forth lightnings, so that they may go
    and say to you, 'Here we are'?
36 Who has put wisdom in the inward parts,
    or given understanding to the mind?
37 Who has the wisdom to number the clouds?
    Or who can tilt the waterskins of the heavens,
38 when the dust runs into a mass

| and the clods cling together?

I will briefly comment on this entire section, even though in the outline above I broke it down into the following parts:

38:12-18, Where Have You Been When I Was Working So Hard, Job?
38:19-24, Rubbing It in ...
38:25-38, More Divine Wonders

My larger commentary goes through this passage verse by verse. God establishes a pattern of questioning Job here, but there is no need to go through the catalogue of heavenly or meteorological features which God introduces. Suffice it to say that the barrage of questions continues, all of which are designed to show Job's pusillanimity and God's greatness. God seems to get a dig in against Job in verse 21, when God says, "Surely you know (the answer to an impossible-to-answer question), for you were born then, and the number of your days is great!" All those of us who have spent a good portion of our careers in teaching are now scratching our heads. If this is alluring teaching, *we* have missed out on some pretty important lessons... But, if one considers the argument above regarding my being an expert witness, perhaps God's conduct is explicable.

Our chapter concludes with many more questions to Job like this. The questions often are presented in beautifully-wrought poetry, like the most exquisitely carved vase, but the big question will be whether Job, and we, really want the vase...

# 58.

## Job 38:39-39:30, Prelude to a Biblical Natural History

Job 38:39-39:30 consists of a catalogue of wonders and mysteries of the animal kingdom. The list of creatures that God speaks of includes the lion and raven (38:39-41), and then the wild goat (39:1-4), the wild ass (some scholars say "onager"; 39:5-8), the wild ox (some scholars say "aurochs"; 39:9-12), the ostrich (though an article by Arthur Walker-Jones says that a "sand grouse" fits the description better; 39:13-18), then the horse (no dissent here; 39:19-25), the hawk and the vulture (39:26-30). Nine animals are picked out of thousands to show Job his ignorance of nature's ways and also to proclaim God's greatness.

When read together with Job 38, then, we have a breathtaking description of God's glory in the heavenly and earthly realms. Yet, we don't just have beautifully-descriptive poetic language; this description is in service to the larger goal of showing Job the limitedness of his understanding. Such a lesson is salutary for us humans to hear almost any time of our lives. We have a tendency to become so proud in our mastery that we scarcely realize that even those things we are most sure of often are shown in short order to be poorly or partially understood.

Yet, the question keeps coming back in our minds: what *is*

God trying to do here? To be sure, perhaps one of the ways God exercises complete sovereignty over the world is that God also confounds the minds of scholars and makes our questions look foolish, but still we are people who are inclined to raise questions. That is how we are made. The wild ass may scorn the tumult of the city (39:7), but good students are taught to learn subject-area content and ask good questions.

So, I repeat, what *is* God trying to do here? God has already exposed Job's ignorance of the heavenly realms and the creation of the world in Job 38 and, for good measure, has not been above mocking Job's ignorance. There is no other way to read 38:21. While purportedly asking Job about the origins and locations of light and darkness, God then says, "Surely you know because you had been born then, and the number of your days is very big" (38:21). We can't avoid the feeling that God considers Job a rather confused, ignorant and impertinent plaything whom he would rather mock than answer. Job has never made a claim to omniscience; he would just like an answer to the question of why he is suffering so much in this instance when he knows (and God has admitted) that he is upright and blameless.

Maybe Job doesn't deserve an answer. Maybe faith is just about submitting to whatever comes along without question. Maybe life is so complex and even absurd that there often is no explanation for things. Maybe the purpose of God's speeches in Job 38-41 is to drive home these points so powerfully that Job is left in emotional brokenness as well as physical pain as he submits to God. Some psychologists might even argue that one has to get to a "breaking point" or point of total relinquishment before one becomes open to a new way of seeing the world. Also, God may be using this method to divert Job's attention from his pain because diversion from pain may be the first step in forgetting pain. We all know that one of the best ways to get infants out of their self-centered puling rants is to show them something shiny or play "hide the ball." Perhaps God is then doing Job a favor by breaking him down through the magnificent display of divine glory, playing "hide the ball" with Job, and then leading (or forcing) Job to confess his complete inadequacy in Job 42.

But, this explanation just doesn't seem right. It gives the impression that one of the central characteristics defining humans and dividing humans from the rest of creation (the ability to reason, question and come to deeper understanding) is really not a good thing after all. And, all of this doesn't seem to square with God's shocking statement near the end of the book that Job has spoken correctly about God, while the friends (no reference to Elihu) have not (42:7). We will have to look at that statement more closely below, but if Job has been right all along, he certainly is right to question God.

If all this is true, we are starting to face the uncomfortable possibility that God is overreacting here, overplaying the divine hand. An illustration may help. The following scene plays out almost daily in the workplaces of America and around the world. A subordinate sees something wrong and points it out. A defensive executive, rather than addressing the concern actually brought up, flies into a rage and mocks, humiliates and otherwise attacks the questioner. Perhaps the executive even fires the questioner. That is why whistleblower statutes were enacted about a generation ago in America—to protect a worker who has a legitimate beef, in certain specified circumstances, from summary termination by executives who have been exposed.

But rather than singing the glories of the executive, who is often given powers in law and in company position (through the doctrines of at-will employment and protections because of length of service), we look at a situation like this with anger. It just isn't right that a faithful and suffering subordinate should be further humiliated by a more powerful executive, especially if the executive is responsible for the employee's pain in the first place. We just do not like that situation at all.

Why should we tolerate it in the sphere of divine/human

relations? What are Job's real options now? Before answering that question, let's turn briefly to the contents of Job 39.

# 59.

## Job 38:39-39:30, A Biblical Natural History

WITH THE PRECEDING THOUGHTS IN MIND, WE CAN MOVE DIRECTLY to a summary of the contents of Job 38:39-39:30.

Job 38:39-39:8, The Lion, Raven, Mountain Goats and Wild Ass
Job 39:9-18, The Wild Ox and Ostrich

Job 39:19-25, The Majestic and Courageous Ways of the War Horse
Job 39:26-30, The Hawk and the Vulture

### Job 38:39-39:8, The Lion, Raven, Mountain Goats and Wild Ass

> 38:39 "Can you hunt the prey for the lion,
>   or satisfy the appetite of the young lions,
> 40 when they crouch in their dens,
>   or lie in wait in their covert?
> 41 Who provides for the raven its prey,
>   when its young ones cry to God,
>   and wander about for lack of food?
> 39:1 Do you know when the mountain goats give birth?

> Do you observe the calving of the deer?
> 2 Can you number the months that they fulfill,
>   and do you know the time when they give birth,
> 3 when they crouch to give birth to their offspring,
>   and are delivered of their young?
> 4 Their young ones become strong, they grow up in the open;
>   they go forth, and do not return to them.
> 5 Who has let the wild ass go free?
>   Who has loosed the bonds of the swift ass,
> 6 to which I have given the steppe for its home,
>   the salt land for its dwelling place?
> 7 It scorns the tumult of the city;
>   it does not hear the shouts of the driver.
> 8 It ranges the mountains as its pasture,
>   and it searches after every green thing.

Since the purpose of Job 38:39-39:30 is to narrate God's knowledge of and Job's ignorance of the interesting and strange ways of selected animals, let's just indicate a few things from each category that are memorable. We need not go into a detailed examination of each section. One little point by way of introduction that scholars have debated for centuries is whether there seems some organizing principle or reason why these particular animals are presented here. In a few words: no agreement or even a dominant theory.

Job 39 begins by talking about birth. The mystery of birth is one thing that ought to make humans marvel. No human, smart as s/he is, could have come up with a system where a process of biology is wedded so closely with a process of psychology and, often, a desire to nurture that results from the birthing process. We might even argue that our author is so confident of his point that he brings out the interesting fact that the ostrich/sand grouse actually abandons its young (the NRSV has "deals cruelly with" in v 16) early on. But this is because "God has made it forget wisdom" (v 17). The normal process of birth, then, is not simply a biological miracle, but an emotional miracle too. Within two seconds of a child's birth, parents know not only that their lives will never be the same, but they will fight to their death to protect that helpless little thing before them. Marvelous indeed.

The first question of the Job 39, posed by God to Job, is "Do you know…?" Job 38 was about Job's lack of knowledge (38:2-3); that theme will continue here. Though the verb "to know" isn't repeated with subsequent animals, we know that it is assumed. Job doesn't know the birthing process of mountain goats (vv 1-4). He doesn't really understand why the wild ass has such a longing for freedom (vv 5-8), though it is interesting that God points to this characteristic since, in my mind, it is the idea of freedom that has become more and more prominent once Elihu has mentioned it in 36:16. Does freedom lie in service to God? Or elsewhere?

## Job 39:9-18, The Wild Ox and Ostrich

> 9 "Is the wild ox willing to serve you?
>   Will it spend the night at your crib?
> 10 Can you tie it in the furrow with ropes,
>   or will it harrow the valleys after you?
> 11 Will you depend on it because its strength is great,
>   and will you hand over your labor to it?
> 12 Do you have faith in it that it will return,
>   and bring your grain to your threshing floor?
> 13 The ostrich's wings flap wildly,
>   though its pinions lack plumage.
> 14 For it leaves its eggs to the earth,
>   and lets them be warmed on the ground,
> 15 forgetting that a foot may crush them,
>   and that a wild animal may trample them.
> 16 It deals cruelly with its young, as if they were not its own;

> though its labor should be in vain, yet it has no fear;
> 17 because God has made it forget wisdom,
>    and given it no share in understanding.
> 18 When it spreads its plumes aloft,
>    it laughs at the horse and its rider.

The wild ox also explores its freedom by not wanting to spend the night in a crib that humans create (v 9). The author then moves on to the ostrich/sand grouse in verses 13-18, bringing out several specific features of this creature's life that have been the subject of a lot of study. Many biologists and others have entered into the discussion on whether the description here seems accurate to what we know of ostrich behavior. The answer? Mostly, yes. Especially noteworthy are burying eggs deep in sand and not really caring for young much after their birth.

## Job 39:19-25, The Majestic and Courageous Ways of the War Horse

> 19 "Do you give the horse its might?
>    Do you clothe its neck with mane?
> 20 Do you make it leap like the locust?
>    Its majestic snorting is terrible.
> 21 It paws violently, exults mightily;
>    it goes out to meet the weapons.
> 22 It laughs at fear, and is not dismayed;
>    it does not turn back from the sword.
> 23 Upon it rattle the quiver,
>    the flashing spear, and the javelin.
> 24 With fierceness and rage it swallows the ground;
>    it cannot stand still at the sound of the trumpet.
> 25 When the trumpet sounds, it says 'Aha!'
>    From a distance it smells the battle,
>    the thunder of the captains, and the shouting.

Pride of place in the description of animals has to belong to the majestic war horse (vv 19-25). We can almost see and hear its snorting (v 20). The author creatively interprets its neighing as "laughing at fear" (v 22) as it goes out to battle. Homer, in the *Iliad*, drew memorable pictures of humans and gods going into battle with quivers rattling on their shoulders; here our author does the same with the horse: "Upon it rattle the quiver, the flashing spear, and the javelin" (v 23). The trumpet sounds; the horse lets out a sound like "Aha!" (*heach* in Hebrew), an interjection expressing joy or satisfaction in Hebrew grammar, as it joins the battle amid the din and roar of people and trumpets (v 25). I could understand if someone just wanted to swim in the suggestiveness of this picture all day.

## Job 39:26-30, The Hawk and the Vulture

> 26 "Is it by your wisdom that the hawk soars,
>     and spreads its wings toward the south?
> 27 Is it at your command that the eagle mounts up
>     and makes its nest on high?
> 28 It lives on the rock and makes its home
>     in the fastness of the rocky crag.
> 29 From there it spies the prey;
>     its eyes see it from far away.
> 30 Its young ones suck up blood;
>     and where the slain are, there it is."

Then, in the last section of the chapter, God turns to a brief consideration of the hawk and vulture/eagle. "Is it by your wisdom that the hawk soars?" (v 26) We now see the point of the dramatic recital of animal behavior. It is once again to show Job that he is merely a rather small, and ignorant, player in the entire drama of creation. One potentially ghoulish issue is presented in the words of verse 30. Every place where the word *chalalim* refers to "slain" bodies in the Bible, it refers to human corpses. You wonder if God,

before stopping his speech just a few words after uttering "corpses,"

meant to speak to Job in a threatening manner. Job knows next to

nothing—even about corpses. Someone else, aka God, has been

hard at work all these years putting together the natural world. It

is presented in an awe-inspiring fashion, to be sure.

# 60.

## Job 40:1-5, A Brief Pause

For the last two chapters God has been showing Job, in no uncertain terms, how ignorant and small he really is. Job doesn't really have knowledge of celestial (Job 38) or terrestrial (Job 39) phenomena. Job has stayed silent while God has repeatedly pummeled him by questions on these issues. We have asked ourselves more than once what the purpose of this divine catechism is, and Job 40 will finally provide an indirect answer. By giving the dialogue a break in 40:1-5 and allowing Job to speak, we see that God's interest in these chapters (38-41) is to secure Job's submission. That is, God's question in 40:2 and Job's response in 40:4-5 will show that Job is not yet ready to wave the white flag after the divine assault. So, as a result, God goes on the offensive again for two more chapters, until Job is finally ready to submit, in some form, in Job 42.

Make no mistake about it. God has not yet said a word addressing Job's case that has been meticulously prepared over several chapters. We still need to decide whether God's strategy of not directly providing an answer to Job is, in fact, some kind of answer and whether that divine strategy is satisfying to Job or to us. Job 40 will help us make that question more precise.

## Job 40:1-5, Questioning Job

> 1 And the Lord said to Job:
> 2 "Shall a faultfinder contend with the Almighty?
>     Anyone who argues with God must respond."
> 3 Then Job answered the Lord:
> 4 "See, I am of small account; what shall I answer you?
>     I lay my hand on my mouth.
> 5 I have spoken once, and I will not answer;
>     twice, but will proceed no further."

After the stunning literary display by God in surveying the habits of nine terrestrial animals, God takes a break and asks Job how he is doing with all of this. The question in Job 40:2, however, is not the kind of question that a teacher, which Elihu suggested God was as He was leading Job to freedom, normally asks. Normally, in a lecture pause, a teacher might ask, "Do you have any questions?" Or, "Is there something that wasn't clear to you that you would like to explore further?" Instead, God's question in verse 2 is, "Shall the one who argues with the Almighty be the one who finds fault?" Or "Shall one that contends with the Almighty instruct (God)?" The question is made somewhat difficult to translate because the masculine noun *yissor,* translated here as "one who finds fault/instructs" is a *hapax* or one-time-appearing word. Yet, the verb from which it is derived, *yasar,* is a rather common biblical verb for "discipline/chasten/admonish/instruct." Thus, the emphasis in the question is on instruction in the midst of an argument. Can Job really instruct God in this dispute? That is what God wants to know.

God's question in 40:2 is fully consistent with the tone of Job 38-39. God is posing a question He knows Job can't answer. We already know that Job really can't instruct God. That has been made scintillatingly clear in the previous two chapters. Thus, the divine question in 40:2 may just be a peevish query from someone who feels the divine prerogatives have been questioned or usurped. As the argument in Job 40 unfolds, the issue of usurpation or taking over divine prerogatives actually comes front and center. God is more offended than delighted that Job has brought his case, and God certainly isn't going to deign to give it a point-by-point response.

So Job is placed on the defensive by this curious divine teaching strategy. 'You think you can teach me, you puny fellow?' is the tone of God's question. Job will muster a few words of response in 40:4-5. A good translation is, "Lo I am so small; how can I respond? I place my hand on my mouth. I have spoken once, and will not answer again; twice and will add no more." Job has gotten the message. God is big; he is small. God is great; Job is insignificant. That is what Job confesses in 40:4. It wasn't really at issue, but God has made it the issue. And so Job concedes the point to God. 'Yes, I am of little account. I am very small.'

But then Job exerts his power in the midst of his insignificance. His response in verse 5 about not saying another word means that he just will shut up. By shutting up Job will neither retract anything he has previously said nor really submit to to the impressive display of divine power. He just recognizes that he is small, trifling, even insignificant (a few meanings of the verb *qalal*). That is what God has seemingly wanted to teach him in the previous two chapters. So, Job agrees with God on that point. But he still, as it were, clutches his case close to his body so that the papers won't be ripped away in the fury of the divine whirlwind.

Yet Job's response, thought sought by God, apparently isn't enough for God. It is a bit too much to say that Job's continual impertinence enrages God, but it is not incorrect to say that Job's unwillingness to submit now causes God to double down on the issue of getting Job to submit to him. 'Why don't you submit, dammit?!' Or, 'What more do I have to do to you to get you to submit, Job?' That is a bit of the tone as things continue.

To be fair to God in the divine approach here, Job has framed the issue as a lawsuit, which is a fight using words, rather than

sabers, for weapons. God has responded as if it were a lawsuit, a contention. God's response might be construed like the District Attorney's questioning a witness closely or bringing up irrelevant questions, but often a such an attorney is given some latitude in shaping an argument. We just have a hard time seeing the God's theory of the case at this point.

# 61.

## Job 40:6-24, Ruling the World and Introducing Behemoth

The rest of the chapter may be divided as follows:

Job 40:6-14, God's Invitation to Job to Take Over Management of the World
40:15-24, Behold, Behemoth!

Note, the English text of Job 40 ends after verse 24, while the Hebrew text of Job 40 includes eight more verses, which are Job 41:1-8 in the English version. I will follow the English text at this point.

### Job 40:6-14, God's Invitation to Job to Take Over Management of the World

> 6 Then the Lord answered Job out of the whirlwind:
> 7 "Gird up your loins like a man;
>     I will question you, and you declare to me.
> 8 Will you even put me in the wrong?
>     Will you condemn me that you may be justified?
> 9 Have you an arm like God,
>     and can you thunder with a voice like his?
> 10 Deck yourself with majesty and dignity;

> clothe yourself with glory and splendor.
> 11 Pour out the overflowings of your anger,
> and look on all who are proud, and abase them.
> 12 Look on all who are proud, and bring them low;
> tread down the wicked where they stand.
> 13 Hide them all in the dust together;
> bind their faces in the world below.
> 14 Then I will also acknowledge to you
> that your own right hand can give you victory.

God resumes the divine questioning of Job. He repeats his earlier words to Job to gird up his loins and be on his guard (v 7; see 38:3). But then God follows with a question that requires a lot more attention than can be given here: "Will you annul my judgment? And will you declare me evil so that you can be righteous?" (v 8). God is going right at the underlying premise of Job's case—that Job is really questioning the order and management of the universe by God. Not only that, but Job is attacking God's sense of justice with the goal of making Job to be the righteous one. That is what God is saying.

But rather than even pausing on that issue for more than a second, God now urges Job, as it were, to "take over" the management of the world. "Deck yourself now with majesty and excellency; array yourself with glory and beauty" (v 10). Indeed, that is what royalty does. It puts on the garments and then it rules. "Look upon everyone that is proud and bring that person low" (vv 11-12). That is what a just God is trying to do. If Job can tread down the wicked and hide them in the dust (v 13), then God will confess that "your right hand can save you" (v 14).

God is more than a bit upset with Job, and God's point is that Job is in no position to judge the divine acts until he has spent some time on the divine throne. Only when Job is on that throne, judging things aright, will God then acknowledge Job's ability to save himself. But even in this interesting admission by God, there doesn't seem to be much room for human questioning of divine activity. Nor does God actually offer to put Job on that throne...

We can't help but return to our earlier analogy of a worker who believes s/he has been unjustly hurt by an irrational practice of management and who wants to lodge a complaint. In Job 38-39, the response of God was, "You are just so small" or "I can do whatever I want." But in Job 40, the tone has changed. Now it is "Well, why don't you try to manage things for a while?" Yet, we never get the impression that God is truly interested either in answering Job's complaint or in relinquishing control of the world to Job. But we have to admit that these verses present an impressive display of divine eloquence.

## Job 40:15-24, Behold, Behemoth!

> 15 "Look at Behemoth,
>    which I made just as I made you;
>    it eats grass like an ox.
> 16 Its strength is in its loins,
>    and its power in the muscles of its belly.
> 17 It makes its tail stiff like a cedar;
>    the sinews of its thighs are knit together.
> 18 Its bones are tubes of bronze,
>    its limbs like bars of iron.
> 19 It is the first of the great acts of God—
>    only its Maker can approach it with the sword.
> 20 For the mountains yield food for it
>    where all the wild animals play.
> 21 Under the lotus plants it lies,
>    in the covert of the reeds and in the marsh.
> 22 The lotus trees cover it for shade;
>    the willows of the wadi surround it.
> 23 Even if the river is turbulent, it is not frightened;
>    it is confident though Jordan rushes against its mouth.

> 24 Can one take it with hooks
> or pierce its nose with a snare?"

God will conclude his speech here and in Chapter 41 with lengthy discussions of two curious and apparently giant creatures: Behemoth (Job 40) and Leviathan (Job 41). The latter so captured the Western literary mind that Thomas Hobbes could entitle his 1651 classic on the best form of government *Leviathan*. Job 40 introduces us to the Behemoth, but doesn't really tell us what the creature is. Naturally, there has been a long and inconclusive debate among scholars as suggestions such as elephant, rhinoceros, hippopotamus have been made. Perhaps it would be best to say that Job 38 deals with celestial phenomena; Job 39 with terrestrial; and Job 40-41 with mythological phenomena. Whereas Behemoth is probably a mythological land creature, Leviathan is a mythological marine creature, where mythological refers to creatures who existed in a shadowy and prehistoric time. God likewise controls these. Some have even seen Ps 74:13-14 as providing a psalmic echo of these two mythological creatures, though it appears to speak only of marine creatures:

> "You divided the sea by your strength; You smashed the heads of the the dragons of the sea; You crushed the heads of Leviathan..."

At first this Behemoth is nothing special. "He eats grass like an ox" (v 15). But then the description quickly changes. The author describes its "loin strength" in verses 16-17 and then its "bone strength" in verse 18. Then we see Behemoth lounging under the lotus tree, dwelling in reeds and fens (v 21). No doubt this triggered someone's identification of Behemoth with a crocodile-type figure.

Rather than asking whether Job "knows" of any of these things about Leviathan, God asks whether anyone can "take it by the eyes and with a snare pierce its nose?" (v 24). Whereas the

discussion in Job 38-39 primarily centered on Job's *understanding* of the processes or animals of creation (with some emphasis on control), the discussion in Job 40-41 focuses on whether anyone, much less Job, can *control* these creatures. The implication is clear. Job can't control these, but God can. Job can't rule them, but God can. We are to think that if Job can't rule them he certainly would make a pitiful ruler of the world. And as a pitiful ruler of the world, much less an insignificant person, he really isn't entitled to a direct answer from God. Again we are touched by the magnitude and sheer eloquence of the poetry, though Job must be sitting there wondering what this really has to do with his complaint...

# 62.

## An Approach to Job 41

THREE POINTS SHAPE OUR APPROACH TO JOB 41. FIRST, WE MUST KEEP in mind that God's 34 verse-long chapter describing one figure, Leviathan, comes after Job's words in 40:5-6 saying that he would keep quiet. Even though he shuts up, Job doesn't abandon his complaint or say, figuratively, 'I give,' to God. He maintains silence, though he doesn't concede. Admittedly, the tone of defiance has disappeared in 40:5-6, but Job is still unwilling to give up his complaint. Thus, one of the divine purposes in Job 41 is for God to continue to speak in order to get Job to concede, to give up, to abandon his 'case.' That is God's goal. But it hasn't happened so far. We have to assess, or at least keep the question in mind, whether the strategy God chooses in Job 41 is a good one to get Job to submit. My thesis will be twofold: first, that it ultimately has that effect. By Job 42, Job is exhausted and he gives in, he concedes, he yields. But, then, God will win the battle but ultimately will lose the war. I explain that in my treatment of Job 42.

Second, Job 41 presents what I call 'extreme abstraction.' That needs unpacking. Elsewhere I have argued that the central requisite for intelligent theological thinking and writing in our day is to eschew or abandon abstraction. What I mean by that is that the theological endeavor should begin and progress through statements that are understandable and clear, that come from the realm of human experience, or are clearly deducible from unquestioned theological sources (e.g., the Scriptures or the authoritative statements of church bodies). Abstraction is employed whenever a person tries to bring in statements beyond ordinary human experience. Confusion then arises. I use the common Christian expression, "Christ died for your sins" early in that book to explore more deeply the meaning of abstraction.

As it relates to Job 41, 'extreme abstraction' means that God is using an approach unrelated to human understanding and experience to make the point that Job ought to submit. God has already established the divine greatness, intelligence, and creative genius in Job 38-39. Job has not contested that. But the thing that now sticks in the divine craw, if God has a craw, is that Job won't submit. Job 41 is designed to get Job to give up. But God draws from the realm of either a mythological or some unknown prehistoric monster, Leviathan, to try to get his point across. It is "abstraction in spades" because it seems to assume that if God argues that there is a shadowy creature named Leviathan, that this creature is scary, and that God has tamed this creature (though that argument isn't actually made in Job 41, but is made elsewhere—Ps 104, for example), that this will somehow relate to Job's pain and struggle, and will be convincing evidence that God somehow not just understands Job's pain but is sympathetic or able to handle it. And, then, Job will give up his case. But it certainly is a funny way of arguing. If I had taught my law students that the way to win your case at trial or on appeal was to argue as God has done in Job 41, not only would my students have been thrown out of court, but I would have lost my job.

Third, though all the attention is directed to God now, one has to wonder what Job is thinking. Job has been sitting there all along, first listening to Elihu and then listening to God. He is still suffering. If I were Job I would be thinking two things: first, 'Why can't God simply attend to my questions? Does God suffer from a primitive form of ADHD? As I listen to God go on and on about Behemoth and, then, Leviathan, I realize that

it doesn't really attend to my questions.' This doesn't make Job more sympathetic to God; rather the reverse. Perhaps, he thinks, God is afraid, just like the friends. Perhaps this problem that God permitted to happen got out of hand in a way that God hadn't anticipated and now God doesn't know how to get it under control. The argument on Leviathan (and Behemoth, too) is perhaps an elaborate ruse to try to get Job to forget that God is really not dealing with his questions. It is smoke and mirrors, bread and circuses, when Job really would like an answer.

But if I were Job I would also have a second reaction. It would relate to his exhaustion. By this time Job would be getting worn out. That God can speak on seemingly irrelevant details about Behemoth for ten verses and then speak about Leviathan for 34 verses means that God *may* just be getting warmed up. God is now showing Himself the master of the filibuster. God is giving Job just a glimpse that He can go on and on almost interminably. Job realizes that God may indeed do that—perhaps God will next start naming the angels or other ancient creatures. Perhaps God would give 60 verses to snail; 120 to the ant; 240 to the oak tree. Job sees that God can go on forever. But Job can't. He has to give up sometime. God's going on for 34 verses in Job 41 about a creature that has little relation to Job's life shows that God is not above doing whatever it takes to win—to get Job to submit. Job already knows that God has worn him out with the emotional pain of loss of family and the physical pain of bodily ailments (e.g., Job 16:7). After Job 41, Job is utterly convinced that God could wear him out also with the divine words. That is why Job will pull the plug and give in to God in Job 42. Will Job be satisfied, however? Not on your life...

# 63.

## Job 41 Meet Leviathan

AFTER THE PREVIOUS ESSAY, THE ACTUAL ARGUMENT OF JOB 41 SEEMS rather anticlimactic. We have already seen what God is up to in the argument; we even have a reason for its length. The purpose of this essay is to summarize the flow of God's words about Leviathan in Job 41. To be more precise, as said above, the Hebrew text of Job 40 includes what is the first eight verses of Job 41 in English. For simplicity's sake, I will follow the English text here. Thus, I will summarize the argument in the English text of Job 41 here.

The text may be divided as follows:

Job 41:1-11, Job's Inability to Control Leviathan
Job 41:12-25, Describing Leviathan
Job 41:26-34, Leviathan the Terrifying

## Job 41:1-11, Job's Inability to Control Leviathan

> 1 "Can you draw out Leviathan with a fishhook,
>     or press down its tongue with a cord?
> 2 Can you put a rope in its nose,
>     or pierce its jaw with a hook?
> 3 Will it make many supplications to you?

> Will it speak soft words to you?
> 4 Will it make a covenant with you
>    to be taken as your servant forever?
> 5 Will you play with it as with a bird,
>    or will you put it on leash for your girls?
> 6 Will traders bargain over it?
>    Will they divide it up among the merchants?
> 7 Can you fill its skin with harpoons,
>    or its head with fishing spears?
> 8 Lay hands on it;
>    think of the battle; you will not do it again!
> 9 Any hope of capturing it will be disappointed;
>    were not even the gods overwhelmed at the sight of it?
> 10 No one is so fierce as to dare to stir it up.
>    Who can stand before it?
> 11 Who can confront it and be safe?
>    —under the whole heaven, who?

God had seemingly dispensed with the catechism-like questions of Job when Behemoth was introduced in 40:15. But now God returns to the questions. Before looking at a few of them, we note that Leviathan, in contrast to Behemoth, is actually pretty well-known in the Biblical tradition. As with Behemoth, we are never told specifically who Leviathan is. Is it a mythological creature, existing before the creation of humans? Is it the alligator (a popular scholarly approach today). I tend to see it as the former—we then would have God speaking about the cosmic realm (Job 38), the earthly realm (Job 39) and the mythological realm (Job 40-41). Three extra-Job passages speak of Leviathan: Ps 104:26; Is 27:1; Ps 74:13. In addition, as scholars have taught us since the discovery of Ugaritic-language texts after the dramatic textual finds at Ras Shamra (present-day Syria) beginning in 1929, we also need to look to the mythological texts in Ugaritic to enhance our understanding of creatures like Leviathan. For the purposes of this summary, however, my major point is that Ps 104:26 and Ps 74:13 speak of Leviathan as a creature whom God has tamed. Ps 104:26 unforgettably tells us that God actually formed Leviathan as the divine plaything. Is 27:1 speaks of a *future* punishment of Leviathan—a somewhat confusing thought until we realize that in Isaiah's mind Leviathan may represent one of the dominant political powers of his day. Job 41 doesn't specifically make reference to these stories, but God's description of Leviathan is consistent with those passages.

What Job 41 does, however, is introduce more details about this creature Leviathan. After we learn of its fierceness, and seeming impregnable body, we can understand the significance, and maybe difficulty, of the divine victory over it. You wonder for a moment if such amazing details like "Sharpest potsherds are under him/his undersides are like sharp potsherds" (41:30) arose from God's memory of having grappled with this creature. God not only knows all the hairs on our heads but all the sharp edges of Leviathan's undersides.

We can see how much God missed the inquisitorial tone of questions in Job 40 when we realize that each of the first seven verses of Job 41 has at least one question in it. Job already knows his ignorance of and impotence towards celestial and terrestrial phenomena; God can't imagine that it would be any different with this prehistoric or mythical creature. But nevertheless, God's questions continue. They can't be serious questions—that is, they can't be questions that seriously seek an answer other than the answer which Job ultimately gives in Job 42, "I give up!" Yet, the questions are interesting, and may give us a hint into how God actually handled this creature after conquering it. "Can you draw out Leviathan with a fish-hook?" (v 1). We can see God, in our mind's eye, declaring victory over this refractory creature by hauling it in. "Can you put a ring into its nose?" (v 3). We assume that this was before the time of rings as body art; the ring was meant to suggest the total domination of the creature. Again, Job is silent. Job can't play with him like a pet bird (v 9), but God plays with it (Ps 104:26). Nah-nah. Leviathan is as fierce as they come (vv 10-11); no one can stand before it.

## Job 41:12-25, Describing Leviathan

> 12 "I will not keep silence concerning its limbs,
>    or its mighty strength, or its splendid frame.
> 13 Who can strip off its outer garment?
>    Who can penetrate its double coat of mail?
> 14 Who can open the doors of its face?
>    There is terror all around its teeth.
> 15 Its back is made of shields in rows,
>    shut up closely as with a seal.
> 16 One is so near to another
>    that no air can come between them.
> 17 They are joined one to another;
>    they clasp each other and cannot be separated.
> 18 Its sneezes flash forth light,
>    and its eyes are like the eyelids of the dawn.
> 19 From its mouth go flaming torches;
>    sparks of fire leap out.
> 20 Out of its nostrils comes smoke,
>    as from a boiling pot and burning rushes.
> 21 Its breath kindles coals,
>    and a flame comes out of its mouth.
> 22 In its neck abides strength,
>    and terror dances before it.
> 23 The folds of its flesh cling together;
>    it is firmly cast and immovable.
> 24 Its heart is as hard as stone,
>    as hard as the lower millstone.
> 25 When it raises itself up the gods are afraid;
>    at the crashing they are beside themselves.

Now that God has once again established Job's impotence, God launches into a fascinating description of Leviathan. As mentioned above, one wonders if the divine knowledge of Leviathan was gained not so much through creation as through battle. God will speak of its limbs, mighty strength and splendid frame (v 12). We see Leviathan's back made of jutting protuberances, like the jagged back of the stegosaurus (v 15). There is no room for air between them. Perhaps God had tried an assault on the back, only to be unsuccessful. Then, there is Leviathan's mouth (v 19) that flashes forth light. Its nostrils emit smoke (v 20); it breathes fire (v 21). The rest of its body seems to be as impenetrable and impregnable as its back (vv 22-23). To add to all of this, Leviathan's heart is hard as stone (v 24). The rest of the (lesser) gods are terrified when Leviathan raises itself to its full height (v 25). We get the impression that this chapter is not really about Job...but about God, but we still are left a bit breathless by the chilling description of Leviathan's body and movements.

## Job 41:26-34, Leviathan the Terrifying

> 26 "Though the sword reaches it, it does not avail,
>     nor does the spear, the dart, or the javelin.
> 27 It counts iron as straw,
>     and bronze as rotten wood.
> 28 The arrow cannot make it flee;
>     slingstones, for it, are turned to chaff.
> 29 Clubs are counted as chaff;
>     it laughs at the rattle of javelins.
> 30 Its underparts are like sharp potsherds;
>     it spreads itself like a threshing sledge on the mire.
> 31 It makes the deep boil like a pot;
>     it makes the sea like a pot of ointment.
> 32 It leaves a shining wake behind it;
>     one would think the deep to be white-haired.

> 33 On earth it has no equal,
>     a creature without fear.
> 34 It surveys everything that is lofty;
>     it is king over all that are proud."

Though it is never explicitly mentioned that God tamed Leviathan through combat, the description in this section (especially vv 26-30) makes most sense if God got a very close look at Leviathan, probably through combat. The sword attacks Leviathan, but to no avail. Neither dart, spear nor javelin can pierce its outer layer (v 26). The strongest things known to humans at the time, iron and bronze, are like straw or rotten wood to Leviathan (v 27). We can just see the enraged Leviathan snapping iron weapons like toothpicks. Arrows and clubs are likewise worthless (vv 28-29). Whereas we talk about the "weak underbelly" even of the most intimidating and seemingly well-protected creatures, Leviathan has no weak underbelly. Its underparts, as we have seen, are like sharp potsherds (v 30) You kind of wonder how God was able to subdue it.

Not only is its appearance terrifying, but when it moves it churns up the ocean like a boiling teapot (v 31). With unmatched poetic beauty, Job 41:32 says, "It leaves a shining wake behind it; one would think the deep to be white-haired." We see in the mind's eye the deep furrows of white, much deeper than the wake left by the most powerful motored vessel in our day, slicing through the deep to its very center. Leviathan is like that. Terrifying, swift-moving, awesome. In a word, "on earth it has no equal." It simply is fearless (41:33). Then, perhaps closing the divine words with a slight dig at Job—"It (Leviathan) is king over all that are proud" (41:34). Perhaps that is the final divine verdict on Job—he is prideful, and Leviathan is his king.

In any case, the defense (i.e., God) now rests its case. We will now turn to the unexpected resolution of this powerful book.

# 64.

# Reading Job 42, Changing My Mind on the Meaning of The Book of Job

JOB 42 PRESENTS THE RESOLUTION TO THIS CHALLENGING AND alluring book. The somewhat usual or traditional way of reading this ending runs something like the following. Job, being overwhelmed by the glory and grandeur of God, realizes the great gap between God and himself, and then confesses his shortcomings. Before "seeing" God in the marvelous acts of divine self-disclosure in Job 38-41, Job had only "heard" of God (v 5). But now that he catches a glimpse of the marvelous, mystifying and complex world of God's activity, Job recognizes his limited understanding. Thus, he decides to trust God for his future by confessing his sin, repenting and resolving to live differently (v 6). By doing this Job is saying that he really doesn't understand what he has been through. He implies that God is to be trusted in all things. God, he now knows, can "do all things" (v 2).

God, in response, asks Job to pray for the three friends (vv 8-9) and then, graciously enough, restores Job's fortunes as before (vv 10-17). Crucial to the resolution of the Book of Job, in this understanding, is that when Job recognizes his presumptuousness, and confesses that sin, he is restored to right relationship with God and his friends. The restoration of fortunes is a kind of bonus added to restored relationships.

I thought this approach sounded good for many years. It certainly seemed a more thoughtful and refreshing way of resolving this literary classic than, say, Athena's appearance at the end of Book XXIV of the *Odyssey* telling everyone, who has been at each other's throats for several books, figuratively to 'knock it off'—i.e., drop their deep-seated quarrels, and get on with life. Homer can tell a great story, but the ending is far-fetched.

But a number of problems started developing in my mind with the traditional reading of Job 42. One of them was my discomfort with Job's seeming sudden abandonment of his case, a case that he had carefully prepared for many chapters. Had Job's objections really been satisfied by the divine response in Chapters 38-41? I combed those chapters to ask what about them would have "answered" Job's complaint. As we have seen, by the midpoint of God's speeches in 40:4-5, Job still hasn't changed his mind. He has just resolved to shut up. So, what is it in the rest of Chapter 40 and 41 that leads him to change his mind? As I read and re-read these chapters, I said to myself, "Nothing, really." I could find nothing in the text that would lead me to believe that Job would have been convinced to drop his case.

What I mean by that is that God didn't answer Job's complaint directly, but simply pointed to the divine efforts in arranging the world. How, I wondered, was this display of wonderful divine activity at all related to Job's complaint? The only two ways it could have led to Job's dropping his complaint were that Job was either convinced by God's arguments or pressured by God into submission. I didn't want to go down the second road, because I believed that divine pressure into submission isn't the way I understand faith or God's operation in our lives. This left the first alternative: Job was somehow convinced by the divine arguments.

If Job was convinced by God's arguments (i.e, God can do anything), we have to realize that Job had previously been convinced by these arguments. That is, this is nothing new. Throughout the Book of Job, Job confesses God's greatness and power (Job 9; 26). He knows full well that he is a small fry, and of no account (40:4).

Hmm, I thought…that won't work. Perhaps, I thought, it was because he now "sees" God, i.e., he understands God in a new way. We all know that there is a difference between what ancient divines called 'cognition' or a mental assent to something and a heartfelt understanding of God. Perhaps the thing that *really* happened to Job in ch 42 is that he was, as it were, 'converted' to what he already believed.

Hmm, I thought… maybe that is it. Job doesn't have new beliefs; he just has a new *relationship* with God. That was a little squishy for me, but I went with it. But I began to see that whatever this new relationship might have been, it was defined by the next verse—Job 42:6.

Most versions have rendered that verse "I abhor myself and repent in dust and ashes." It is Job's great confession, the linchpin of the argument that Job is repenting. In the last decade scholars have been looking more closely at that verse and realizing that it doesn't say that. In my judgment, a new translation of this crucial verse will be a major development in the study of the Book of Job in the twenty-first century. It will be comparable in scope, or even greater in scope, than the major translation revision of the Book of Job in the twentieth century—the re-rendering of Job 13:15. For centuries after the King James version's rendering of 13:15 as "Though he slay me yet I will trust in him," people took that verse as a sign of Job's dogged faithfulness to God in the midst of terrible trials. Yet we realized in the twentieth century that this isn't a good translation and doesn't fit the context of Job's argument in Chapter 13 well (see my comment on the passage).

A similar change is underway in rendering 42:6. The text really doesn't say "I abhor myself and repent in dust and ashes." I will give my translation in the next essay, but the principal reasons for re-evaluating the translation are that there is no object in Hebrew after the first verb; that the first verb may be translated several ways; and that the second verb is probably better rendered differently than "repent." When read in a more reasonable way, Job 42:6 speaks more to Job's giving up or melting away than of abhorring himself. We will also have to explore what that might mean.

Before getting to that crucial point, I will mention one other thing that made me uneasy with the traditional reading of Job 42. If Job is repenting in verses 4-6, why does God say in the next few verses that Job was "right" when he spoke of God (vv 7, 8)? Commentators who adopt the traditional approach (i.e., that Job was confessing sin or inadequacy in vv 4-6) generally say that when God says Job was "right," God really meant that Job was only "right" in very minor ways—like in giving it the old college try by raising questions—but Job was mostly "right" in confessing. That wasn't convincing to me because God says that the friends spoke wrongly and Job spoke correctly. That implies that God is speaking of the dialogues in Chapters 3-31. How can Job be "right" and then need to confess? It didn't make sense to me.

For all of these reasons, I became open to a new reading of Job 42, which shall be presented in the next essay.

# 65.

## Reading Job 42:1-6, A New Understanding

1 Then Job answered the Lord:
2 "I know that you can do all things,
    and that no purpose of yours can be thwarted.
3 'Who is this that hides counsel without knowledge?'
    Therefore I have uttered what I did not understand,
    things too wonderful for me, which I did not know.
4 'Hear, and I will speak;
    I will question you, and you declare to me.'
5 I had heard of you by the hearing of the ear,
    but now my eye sees you;
6 therefore I despise myself,
    and repent in dust and ashes."

So I was presented with a dilemma in reading Job 42. The traditional reading made little sense to me, but I still didn't have a satisfactory alternative way of reading Job 42. I could have said, "It is all absurd" and spent my weekends watching football, but I wanted to persist in my quest. Nothing better than reading the passage slowly, I thought.

Though there is some disagreement on the issue, most see verses 2-6 as Job alone speaking and not Job and God speaking back and forth. That is, God has previously spoken the thoughts spoken in 42:3a ("Who is this that darkens/hides counsel without knowledge") in 38:2. God has expressed the thought of 42:4 ("I will demand of you and you will declare") in 38:3 and 40:7. Is God repeating Himself here? Most will argue that Job is repeating these words of God in his own mind and then responding to them. This is a rather noncontroversial observation but should be mentioned.

So Job begins in verse 2 with a sentiment he has more than once expressed, that God can do everything. God's power is great; his majesty is incredible. Job had confessed as much in Chapters 9 and 26. Nothing new. Then, in verse 3a, Job quotes God's statement in 38:2, though he changes one word. Rather than the verb "darken" which God had used in 38:2, Job uses "hides" in 40:3. Again, little difference.

Job's response in verse 3b requires some thought. A better translation than the traditional renderings is, "Thus, I have spoken, and I didn't understand. Difficult things for me, and I didn't know." To what does this refer? The most natural way for me to read "Thus, I have spoken and I didn't understand" in verse 3b is to see this as a brief summary of the flow of the book. Job *spoke* by presenting his case (ending in Job 31). He didn't *understand* when God started speaking in Job 38. The second half of the verse emphasizes Job's lack of understanding. He didn't understand when God spoke because the things were too *niphlaoth*. That word can be rendered in many ways, among them "miraculous" or "wonderful" or "difficult." Any of these translations will do. The last part of the verse, then, has Job clarifying what he means when he just said "I didn't understand." He didn't understand what God revealed in Job 38-41. He didn't understand these things because they were too difficult for him or too wonderful for him. They were beyond his scope of understanding. He didn't know them (the final words of v 3).

Thus, verse 3 is Job's summary of the entire flow of the book. He spoke, and then he didn't understand (because God spoke). God's words were just too difficult for him; he didn't understand them. God said that Job really wouldn't understand them and Job is confirming that thought.

So far nothing that dramatic has happened. This certainly isn't a confession of sin so far. Job is confessing only that God is great and that he, Job, doesn't understand everything God does or says. Verse 4 then repeats God's words from the divine speeches, as indicated above. Verse 5 brings us closer to our resolution. Job had "heard" of God; now he "sees" God. The dramatic thing that Job has experienced in Job 38-41 is a different mode of perceiving God.

That results in verse 6. The first verb in verse 6 is derived either from *maas* or *masas*. The verb *maas* means a lot of things, either "despise" or "abhor" or even "fade or melt or waste away," as it is used in Job 7:16. In fact, Job 7:16 may be our closest parallel because there is no object to the verb either here or in 7:16. If our first verb is *masas*, however, as many scholars are coming to realize, it translates also as "melt" or "fade away." What Job is doing in the first verb of verse 6 is "melting away" or "fading" or "dissolving" or "fading out." Job is not confessing; he is what we would say 'checking out.' He is saying, 'I'm finished; I'm done; I'm gone.'

To put it in the language earlier in the book, Job here declares his freedom, the very thing that Elihu said God was leading him into in 36:16. But for Job the freedom is a dramatic one. God's arguments have not addressed his complaint—at all. Job's greatest fear was that when God actually appeared to address him, if God would deign to appear, that God would overwhelm Job with a tempest. That is precisely what has happened. God didn't gently call Job aside to explain anything, as Elihu hinted God would. God decided to answer Job's reasonable questions with a divine clobbering, a divine submission hold that would let go until Job as it were, 'gave up.'

So, in Job 42:6, Job 'gives up,' just as God desired. But Job gets the last laugh. What Job gives up is not necessarily his case, which hasn't been resolved, but his trust in God. Job has suspected that God was behind his great distress, and he is right. Job is convinced he has a good argument to make case that one. He is right. Job would like to approach God but he is afraid that when God appears, that God won't listen to him. He is right. Job knows all these things.

But Job also has own power sources independent of God. He has his Redeemer, separate from God, who will, somehow, save him. He has his freedom, given to him through the argument of Elihu, who said that through this ordeal God is leading Job into a time of freedom where his table will be richly prepared. Now it clicks for Job. He will have to declare his freedom—but his freedom is freedom *from* God.

It is not as if Job *wanted* to leave God but God, really, has given Job little reason to continue in faith. At every turn, Job has been thwarted. He can't get a question answered. He can't even have an 'adult' conversation with God. God seems so concerned with pulling rank, with making Job submit, that Job finally decides, 'I don't really need to put up with this anymore.'

So, what does Job do? That is where the second verb of verse 6 comes in. Rather than "repenting in dust and ashes," he "consoles himself upon the dust and ashes." The verb *nacham* in verse 6 may be taken a few ways, but its strongest meaning in the Bible is of "comforting" or "consoling" someone. Every other appearance of it in the Book of Job (six other times) is best translated "console" or "comfort." Thus, the flow of 42:6 becomes very clear: Job will melt away and find his comfort on the ash heap. That will be his freedom. That will be his satisfaction. He will be finished with God.

The interesting thing is not only that Job realizes that departing from God or leaving faith is a good thing to do, but that God will also try to do whatever He can in the next few verses in a frantic attempt to call Job back. But it will be too late... The next essay begins the discussion of that idea.

# 66.

## Job 42:7-17, Essay One

I ARGUED IN THE PREVIOUS ESSAY THAT THE BEST WAY TO TRANSLATE Job 42:6 is to render it, "So I fade away, and am comforted on/ find my consolation on dust and ashes." By "fading away" Job is giving the strongest statement possible that he not only disagrees with the way God has handled him but that he will exercise his freedom in departing from any further relationship with God. He will learn, hundreds of years before the Apostle Paul said it, "to be content in all circumstances," and in this case to be content in his freedom from God.

When we get over the shock of such an approach to the final part of Job, we recognize that it really is a reasonable thing for Job to do. Job knew that disasters don't just 'happen' in life. God must have had some hand in it (he's right). He knows also that did nothing remotely deserving the kind of devastating experiences he had in Job 1-2. After expressing his pain, anger and grief, he decided to put a case together, calling on God to explain Himself.

But he was also aware that God was a temperamental divinity, disappearing and not appearing, blowing people away with tempests, and so he knew he was treading on dangerous ground by bringing his complaint. Yet, he relied on the merciful character of God that he also knew existed, the fact that his Redeemer lived and the words of Elihu to give him strength to persist.

Did God rise to the occasion to treat Job like a beloved child, with the dignity that his suffering and his character would have merited? No. God not only didn't express one word of sympathy for the racking pains that tore Job's soul and body (pains caused by God's authorization), but not one word of recognition for Job's persistent, reasonable and very specific questions.

Why? Why would God just pull rank, talk about something seemingly irrelevant to Job's insistent and reasonable questions, and keep on pressing Job until he has no option but to submit in exhaustion, to "give up" or "fade away" in 42:6? Surprisingly enough, the Evangelical interpreters give us a hint at an answer, though they would be loath to have their scholarship taken in the following direction.

Many conservative scholars date the Book of Job to the 2nd Millennium BCE, while more liberal scholars see it as a product of monarchical Israel (early-mid first millennium BCE) or even the Exilic period (sixth century BCE). If we go along with the conservative approach for a second, though I ultimately believe Job is a product of the monarchical period, God's response makes perfect sense. It makes perfect sense because God is just getting the hang of running the world and dealing with a chosen people, and will probably be making loads of errors until He fine-tunes the divine understanding of how to sort out issues of mercy and judgment, of power and forgiveness. The divine treatment of Job, then, would be one of these errors.

God had several enormously complex issues on the divine plate when not only setting up the world, which God proudly points to in Job 38-41, but in learning how to govern it well. But everyone, including God, makes mistakes. You learn by doing, since there was no textbook for God to consult.

Seen in this way, God's approach to Job in 38-41 makes sense. God is still trying to calibrate the challenges implicit in the dual powers of strength and sympathy, of mercy and judgment. God is still trying to figure out how best to deal with the issue of human pain, a conundrum that humans haven't had a good time explaining since then, and this may be the first divine chance to deal with it. That God might miscalculate either by speaking too harshly to Job or by abandoning Job in his complaint too long is perfectly understandable.

The two mistakes God made, then, are that he let Job linger too long in his distress and that when He spoke, He spoke too harshly and not to the point. By letting Job linger too long in his distress, he allowed Job to be influenced by the thoughts of his own mind (developing the idea of a Redeemer) and others (in this case Elihu), and then when God sought to get Job's "mind" back, it was too late. By speaking too harshly to Job in 38-41, God showed that He may not have worked out the issue well of how and when to show sympathy with suffering creatures. So, Job does the logical thing—He leaves this God.

In the final eleven verses of the Book of Job, God not only recognizes that He has made a terrible error, but He tries desperately but unsuccessfully to get Job back. The next essay explores God's valiant but fruitless attempt to recall Job from his departure from God.

# 67.

## Job 42:7-17, Essay Two

This essay focuses on Job 42:7-9 and especially on God's commendation of Job in these verses.

### Job 42:7-9, Commending Job

> 7 After the Lord had spoken these words to Job, the Lord said to Eliphaz the Temanite: "My wrath is kindled against you and against your two friends; for you have not spoken of me what is right, as my servant Job has. 8 Now therefore take seven bulls and seven rams, and go to my servant Job, and offer up for yourselves a burnt offering; and my servant Job shall pray for you, for I will accept his prayer not to deal with you according to your folly; for you have not spoken of me what is right, as my servant Job has done." 9 So Eliphaz the Temanite and Bildad the Shuhite and Zophar the Naamathite went and

> did what the Lord had told them; and the Lord accepted Job's prayer.

My contention is that in the last eleven verses of Job (42:7-17), God used three methods to try to win back Job's devotion: commending Job's words, making Job pray and then restoring His fortunes. This essay will just deal with the first.

God commends Job. We really didn't expect God's words in 42:7-8. God is angry at the friends. God says, "You have not spoken of me what is right, as my servant Job has." Note that God is only angry at the three friends, Eliphaz, Bildad and Zophar. Elihu doesn't merit a mention. This usually is explained by the theory of the Elihu speeches being a later addition to the book. When 42:7-8 was written, the author just knew about the three friends. So the argument goes.

Maybe. We really have no idea. But I think it is more interesting theologically to take look at the Book of Job as a literary whole. What others might see as a literary oversight I see as God's deliberate ignoring of Elihu. Why would God do that? Because Elihu has given Job the ticket to his freedom, by hinting at Scriptural concepts captured in that most familiar of Psalms (Ps 23), and God really has nothing to disagree about with Elihu on that point. Maybe, God thinks, we will forget Elihu if he is not mentioned in 42:7. Nope.

But the more interesting issue here is why God is angry at the friends but commends Job, and what the scope of that divine commendation of Job is. If Job is "right" in speaking about God, he not only is a righteous and blameless person in living, but a righteous person as he speaks. That God couples Job with the friends suggests that we have to look at all of Job's words as "right." Thus, he is "right" when he says such things as "God has torn me in his wrath and hated me" (16:9).

Isn't God overreacting here, too, just as He has overreached when He spoke to Job in Job 38-41? Yes, indeed, but God is overreacting in the same way worried parents would overreact when they know they have done something wrong with their child and desperately want the child back. 'Not only can you have the car tonight, but take the credit card, too!' Parents become desperate for their children's affection, too, especially when they realize that they may have made a grave mistake in dealing with their child.

My point is that Job's bold and courageous action in 42:6 has made God look at Himself. When God does so, He realizes that He has committed some mistakes. He has let this thing go on far too long. He has not treated Job with the dignity that he deserves. And so God does what the desperate parent does. He starts to shower gifts on the child in the vain hope of winning back the child's affection.

The first thing that God does, then, is to say to Job, 'You were right all along.' Very few scholars really can stomach the literal meaning of that verse. They all try to qualify in some ways. But we can save God's meaning if we realize that God now is the desperate one, trying to win back the affection of his child. 'You were right all along, Job. Please come back,' then would be the meaning of the divine words.

It is a good try on God's part, but now the power dynamics have changed in the relationship between God and Job. Job, because of his Redeemer and his understanding of freedom, holds all the cards. God has to come to Job as the suppliant, even though God is the ruler of the universe. God's first way of doing this is to say something that is so sweeping, and even incorrect (that is, Job even realizes that some of his words have been rash and ill-chosen—Job 6:3) that we are left a bit stunned. If Job is right all along, then God admits He has done some pretty bad things. Only a desperate parent would make that kind of admission.

God *so* wants Job to return to Him. Does it work? We have no indication that it does. But God still has two more methods to try to win Job's allegiance again.

# 68.

## Job 42:7-17, Essay Three

BEFORE GETTING TO THE SECOND AND THIRD THINGS THAT GOD does in these verses, I would like to reiterate my thesis regarding Job 42. I argued that Job's "confession" in 42:6 is more of a declaration of independence from God than a confession of any sin or wrongdoing on Job's part. There is no reason for Job to "confess sin" since God's words both in Job 1-2 and Job 42:7 indicate he has neither spoken nor done anything needing confession. Job does recognize God's greatness in Job 42, but he has been saying that all along. The only new thing that Job realizes in Job 42 is that he now "sees" God (42:5). He doesn't explain what "see" means, but it must relate to the special words of God in Chapters 38-41, since God has otherwise been silent since the friends started speaking in Job 3. Job now has a new appreciation of what it means for God to be creator and ruler of the universe. In that sense, he now "sees" God.

But upon "seeing" God up close, he decides that it is better if he and God part ways. This 'up close' God really doesn't show any indication of wanting to listen to Job or answer his questions. It might seem presumptuous, to some people, that the creature has any right to ask the creator questions in the first place, but because of the literary form of the book, which specifically placed responsibility for Job's suffering in God's hands, Job *does* have that prerogative. Otherwise one would be arguing that God can visit, through the Satan or any other source, the most horrid and painful sufferings on people and they have absolutely no recourse to the supposedly merciful one that is behind their sufferings. Arguing that Job has no right insistently to ask God for answers would be tantamount to saying that one just has to serve the merciful and loving creator of the universe in the midst of racking pain without a whimper. That approach won't capture the hearts of many.

Yet in Job 38-41 God treats Job as if he is an impertinent meddler rather than a serious quester for answers. God even says that Job brings darkness rather than light. So, God's response is, 'Just shut up and admire my glory.' That really is the tone of Job 38-41. Some may see magnificence both in the poetic language and the ideas expressed, but asking someone to dine on the glory of God when the stomach is growling in pain is often scant comfort to the starving person.

I also argued that once Job declares his independence it dawns on God that something seriously is amiss. God is on the verge of losing Job, if He has not lost him already. But, God doesn't want to lose Job. It would be serious blow for God who has orchestrated all of these things to reach the opposite conclusion.

So, God says exaggerated words in 42:7, words that are meant to try to quell the rising rift between him and Job. God gives a blanket pronouncement on the debate that we have just witnessed that is neither nuanced nor true, but is meant to be a peace offering to Job. God *can't* mean that everything the friends said was not right, since so much of it, especially Eliphaz' first speech, is vintage Biblical advice and sensitive personal counsel.

God *can't* mean that everything Job said is right, because otherwise God would be admitting that He is just an angry God, controlled by that emotion since the beginning of time. So, God overstates his point as a means to regain Job's loyalty.

Parents do this all the time when they are afraid of losing their children. They bend over backwards to make sure that the child will think twice about leaving them. What the parents don't realize is that by leaving the child "alone" for so long, as God left Job "alone" for thirty-five chapters, is they have created the conditions for the child to invent his/her own life independent of the parents. Thus, even though the parents try to get back into the child's life, the child has already so constructed a satisfying alternative world that the child is little inclined to return to the parent.

Finally, God tries other strategies to regain Job's affection and loyalty. The second and third strategies God employs are to require Job to pray (vv 8-9) and then shower him with gifts (vv 10-17). The requirement to pray for the friends is sort of like requiring a child who is on the verge of leaving the family to show up at Thanksgiving dinner. Perhaps by going through the ritual of a good meal, a warm family atmosphere, times with familiar people (and perhaps a special pet), the child will be won back into the family. So, Job prays when God tells him to pray. He is, as it were, "brought back" by God into the family.

We aren't told how or what Job prays. He doesn't object to God, in my theory, because he has just experienced how God can make life pretty uncomfortable for him by speaking ten verses on Behemoth and then 34 on Leviathan. Job knows that he basically has to "show up" and pray, because otherwise he may be listening to 100 verses on snails, and then 200 on butterflies. Better to pray, and keep a semblance of harmony, than object. Better to show up for one last Thanksgiving dinner and not fight with mom. Be civil. It will all be over sooner rather than later.

Job can scarcely wait to return to the heap of dust and ashes, the place of his new freedom. But first, he has to pray. He does so.

# 69.

## Job 42:7-17, Essay Four

THIS FINAL ESSAY WILL FOCUS ON JOB 42:10-17 AND ESPECIALLY THE restoration of Job's fortunes.

## Job 42:10-17, Job's Restoration

> 10 And the Lord restored the fortunes of Job when he had prayed for his friends; and the Lord gave Job twice as much as he had before. 11 Then there came to him all his brothers and sisters and all who had known him before, and they ate bread with him in his house; they showed him sympathy and comforted him for all the evil that the Lord had brought upon him; and each of them gave him a piece of money and a gold ring. 12 The Lord blessed the latter days of Job more than his beginning; and he had fourteen thousand sheep, six thousand camels, a thousand yoke of oxen, and a thousand donkeys. 13 He

> also had seven sons and three daughters. 14 He named the first Jemimah, the second Keziah, and the third Keren-happuch. 15 In all the land there were no women so beautiful as Job's daughters; and their father gave them an inheritance along with their brothers. 16 After this Job lived one hundred and forty years, and saw his children, and his children's children, four generations. 17 And Job died, old and full of days.

God has already tried two strategies to win back Job's affection: overstated words commending Job and the requirement for Job to pray. The first is a strategy of *commendation*; the second of *coaxing*. In the final verses of the book God will use a third strategy: *complete restoration*. Though it is not specifically mentioned, we assume that Job's health is also one of the things restored to Job in 42:10. The language of 42:10 should make us pause. Literally it says, "The Lord returned the returning" or "restored the captivity" of Job. It is the same phrase used powerfully in the prayer of Ps 85:1, "You have restored the captivity of Jacob." It is the same phrase used in the memorable Psalm of Ascent (126:4) where the Psalmist asks for the Lord to "restore the captivity" of the people. Thus, this restoration of Job should be understood in its full glory—it functions on the personal level like a great act of salvation on the national level. It is *that much* of a restoration. And, to add to it, God gives it back *double (mishneh)*. God is really pulling out all the stops now. There may be very few arrows left in the divine quiver after this one.

I see God's doubling of Job's assets as the final, or third, way for God to try to recapture Job's loyalty and affection. It is like the parent who opens the wallet, looks pleadingly at the apparently errant child, and says, 'How much do you want?' But rather than asking Job this question, God just doubles the fortune. Perhaps the reason God doesn't ask Job for what he wants is that Job might just say, 'I am fine, thank you God.' God couldn't endure such an answer.

So, God showers Job with blessings. We even have new characters added to the mix: Job's sisters and brothers and some acquaintances. Like the friends in 2:11, before they had said a word, Job's sisters, brothers and "all who knew him" "sympathize with him (*nud*) and comfort (*nacham*, the same verb as in v 6) him (42:11). Are we to assume that the three friends of Job 3-27 have disappeared, since Job's siblings and acquaintances now take up the *nud/nacham* responsibilities? Well, the friends, too, had enterprises to run and so they probably departed to their places. Job is left, then, with his sympathetic and comforting family and acquaintances.

This is, of course, problematic though realistic. The acquaintances and relatives ditch you in your distress, but once you win the lottery they are back at your doorstep. What makes this passage laughably realistic is that the friends appear with their tokens or gifts to Job—a single silver or gold piece—just at the time when Job doesn't need it. It is like friends showing up with a bottle of wine when you have just opened your own winery.

Job's possessions or fortunes are doubled, though the family size will stay the same: seven sons and three daughters. Perhaps this also induces a smile in the reader, who knows that fourteen sons and six daughters might be a little *too* much of a blessing...

What is worth noting is that the daughters, but not the sons, are given names. The beauty of the daughters is also mentioned (vv 14-15). We are to assume a happy and long life for Job after his restoration. Missing, however, is any reference to God, any reference to Job's goodness, or any reference to Job's religious fidelity. One would have expected that since Job's being upright and blameless were the fundaments or anchors of his pre-distress existence, that they would have been mentioned (or doubled) in this post-distress existence. Of course they don't have to be mentioned, but don't you think that if God had successfully wooed Job back to loyalty, that would have been mentioned?

Job dies old and full of days, happy with his family surrounding him (we assume that his wife is reconciled to him, but she doesn't come in for mention). Part of his happiness is no doubt that he no longer has God in his life. He has gone down that path once, and saw where it led. Who is to say that God might not just try "Experiment # 2" ten years later on Job? God gives Job no "rainbow-sign" to assure that such a disaster will never befall Job again. Best not to deal with such an unpredictable, and seemingly unsympathetic, God.

If a person argues for the correctness of he traditional approach to Job—that Job actually confesses his inadequacy and ignorance, gives up his complaint and then wants a fully restored fellowship with God in 42:1-6—it is pretty bleak news for us. The best we can hope for is holding out for a while and then submitting to the withering questioning of God. God might or might not restore the fortunes and try to make things right, but after you have gone through a series of devastating losses as Job has faced, you realize that even the restoration of fortunes can't give you back your little ones who died. Job doesn't have a concept of resurrection to deal with, and it probably doesn't cross his mind that any kind of revivification of corpses is possible. Replacement children is the next best thing, to be sure, but sometimes in the dark of the night, you just never forget the smile of little Noah or Samuel, and you weep. The traditional approach argues that the Book of Job ties things together neatly with a richly ruffled red ribbon, but it doesn't realize that the bottom of the package is ripped, and the gift has already fallen out.

www.ingramcontent.com/pod-product-compliance
Lightning Source LLC
Chambersburg PA
CBHW031055080526
44587CB00011B/699